NO MATTER WHAT!

You can overcome every obstacle...

NO MATTER WHAT!

9 Steps to Living the
Life You Love

Lisa Nichols

**WELLNESS
CENTRAL**

NEW YORK   BOSTON

Copyright © 2009 by Lisa Nichols
All rights reserved. Except as permitted under the U.S. Copyright Act of 1976, no part of this publication may be reproduced, distributed, or transmitted in any form or by any means, or stored in a database or retrieval system, without the prior written permission of the publisher.

Wellness Central
Hachette Book Group
237 Park Avenue
New York, NY 10017

Visit our Web site at www.HachetteBookGroup.com.

Wellness Central is an imprint of Grand Central Publishing.
The Wellness Central name and logo are trademarks of Hachette Book Group, Inc.

Printed in the United States of America

First Edition: April 2009
10 9 8 7 6 5 4 3 2

Library of Congress Cataloging-in-Publication Data
Nichols, Lisa.
    No matter what! : 9 steps to living the life you love / Lisa Nichols.
—1st ed.
      p. cm.
   ISBN 978-0-446-53846-6
  1. Self-actualization (Psychology) 2. Success. I. Title.
   BF637.S4N523 2009
    158.1—dc22
                                                        2008046696

Book design by Charles Sutherland

I dedicate this book to my grandmother Bernice.
Thank you for being God's example of unconditional
love, His expression of unwavering faith, and my first
model of living in authenticity.
You taught me how to stand and to love—no matter what.
Please continue to watch me from heaven.
I feel your presence.

CONTENTS

NO MATTER WHAT!

FOREWORD

In my thirty-three years as a success coach, I've helped a lot of people make the often challenging journey from where they are in life to where they want to be. So I was thrilled to discover this book, which is pure rocket fuel for that crucial trip. I believe that in these pages, you'll find the wisdom, knowledge, and inspiration to get you on track fast—and take you all the way to your final destination.

My colleague and dear friend Lisa Nichols is a living example of what it takes to overcome the inevitable obstacles in your path and come out the other side strong, graceful, and loving the life you've created for yourself. Her story is a testimony to the fact that anyone, no matter how difficult their circumstances or how challenging their setbacks, can rise above anything. How? By being determined, by developing certain skills, and by adopting useful attitudes—in short, by building what Lisa calls the "muscles" of character, which she outlines in the pages of this life-changing book.

When I first met Lisa, she was working primarily with teens, and I was deeply impressed with her ability to transform their lives through a magical combination of inspiration, profound insights, effective life strategies, and tough love. A few years later, I founded an organization called the Transformational Leadership Council (TLC), consisting of the top leaders in the human potential movement who own training companies. I instantly knew that Lisa had to be one of the people invited to the first meeting, as I felt certain that she would be a great asset to the organization.

My intuition was proven right at our next gathering, which took place at John Gray's ranch in northern California. During the course of the three-day conference, Lisa conducted a two-hour workshop with the group. At the time, Lisa wasn't as well known as she is now; in fact, many in the room had never even heard of her before.

In the workshop, she taught us a technique for dealing with negative self-talk (a technique she has wisely included in this book). There I was, sitting with sixty people from around the world who were titans in the work of personal transformation, and we were all identifying and discussing our negative self-talk. I was shocked by two things: (1) how much negative self-talk we all still had, even though we'd done so much work on ourselves, and (2) that Lisa's simple yet powerful technique truly helped all of us put a stop to it.

By the end of the three days, we all agreed that her session was, by far, the most powerful session at the gathering. Lisa simply blew us all away! She got us out of our heads and into our feelings. Many of the participants said, "This is the most open, vulnerable, and empowered I've felt in ages." It was very clear that Lisa's ability to transform lives wasn't limited to young adults. Lisa is indeed a master teacher, a master facilitator, and a master speaker.

When Rhonda Byrne, the creator of the hit film and book *The Secret*, came to one of our TLC meetings to film some of our members for her movie, she also immediately recognized Lisa's brilliance and invited her to appear in the film. And so Lisa, one of the least well known among us—the one whom I'd often referred to as "the human potential movement's best-kept secret"—became one of the major stars of *The Secret*.

After the film was released, Lisa and I both spoke at a conference in Canada, along with two other teachers from *The Secret*. During a break in which the conference attendees could buy books and have them signed, I wasn't the least bit surprised to see that the line at Lisa's table was twice as long as anyone else's. She connected so easily and naturally with everyone, and she had a gift for moving people beyond the abstract theory of the Law of Attraction and providing practical and grounded steps for them to apply the law in their lives. That's Lisa's talent in a nutshell: she takes universal concepts and shows people how to apply them on a personal level—and she models how to do that by being utterly and totally herself!

Recently, I had the opportunity to experience Lisa's tremendous gifts closer to home. When we discovered that my teenage son was going through a difficult time emotionally, my wife and I signed him up to attend one of Lisa's workshops. Within two days, he achieved a major transformation. It was astounding to see the sudden reemergence of the young adult we knew was there inside—the one with a sense of humor and a willingness to cooperate and be vulnerable, and to share his painful feelings and deal with them in a constructive and healthy way.

So when Lisa told me she was writing a book, I was thrilled that she would be bringing these ideas and techniques, as well as her own inspiring life story, to the general public. But I wondered if she'd be able to transmit the incredible power that I'd experienced in her workshops through the pages of a book. To my amazement, she has definitely succeeded. Lisa's remarkable voice comes through on every page—and with it, her rare ability to combine motivation, humor, and gutsy truth-telling while giving you practical tools for growth and success that you can use every single day.

This means that as you read this phenomenal book, you'll have the same opportunity that I've had, that my family has had, and that millions of others have had to transform yourself and your life. You'll be able to confront your fears, overcome your feelings of victimhood, reclaim your power, and, as Lisa says so often, step into your greatness. Because, as she's shown us, whatever you've been through, that greatness is still there inside you, just waiting for you to claim it. With the help of this book, I'm convinced you'll be able to soar to success—no matter what!

—Jack Canfield

PART ONE

Putting Some Skin In

*Peeling Back the Layers of
Self in Order to Grow*

Be the change you want to see in the world.

—Mahatma Gandhi

PROLOGUE

Thank You for Using This Imperfect Child

Ask for what you want—even at the risk of getting it.

—Anonymous

IT WAS EVERY MOTIVATIONAL SPEAKER'S DREAM. I'D BEEN INVITED to appear on a wildly popular, nationally televised talk show and had accepted eagerly.

In my first phone conference with one of the show's producers, she asked me, "Can you tell me more about your life? How has it changed now that you've had a measure of success in your career?"

I replied, "In order for me to tell you how good my life is now, I have to tell you how much of a mess it was before. It's the only way you could adequately understand the miracle of my journey."

The two of us clicked; she seemed genuinely interested as I revealed the raw truth of my past. She ended the call by asking, "Would you be willing to share these kinds of details about yourself on the show if we asked you to?"

"Yes" jumped out of my mouth before I really thought it through.

Immediately, my mind screamed, *Lisa, what have you done?* Although my spirit was all for it, the rest of me had to catch up. This really hit home when the producer asked me to package up the vision board I'd described to her, a collection of images that spoke to my most personal dreams and goals, and send it to her for the show. Talk about feeling exposed!

For the next two weeks, I wrestled with myself and my qualms. I had enough esteem to tell my story—breakdowns, imperfections, and all—to five thousand other people, ten thousand other people, even fifty thousand other people, as I routinely did in my seminars. But was I ready to let *millions* of people whose faces I would never see know the most intimate details of my life?

The morning of the show, I woke up at 3:00, overcome with anxiety. I wasn't ready for this. I didn't have the formal training to be an "expert." All I knew came from experience. How could I possibly go in front of all those people and let them know how often and how badly I'd screwed up in my life? Eventually, I called my friend and prayer partner, Fluke. He was the only one I knew who wouldn't mind a call at such an hour, and I asked him to help me get through this fear-storm. I was going to do the show, but I wanted to be at peace about it. He heard me out and began to pray with me.

As I sat listening to his voice, still shaking inside, one line of his prayer hit me like a thunderbolt. "God," he said, "thank you for using this imperfect child of yours to help your other imperfect children."

Yes! That was it! I wasn't perfect, but I was being used to help other people like me—people who had gone through hard times, who wanted to be good but who had made mistakes and wanted to bounce back.

Suddenly, I could breathe again; I felt a cloak of calm descend. I'd finally given myself permission to just be me.

Are *you* ready to just be you? Ready to accept that even though you may not be perfect, you have an important place in the world to fill?

Know, right now, that there are things you are here on earth to do, people's lives you are here to touch, and everything—and I mean *everything*—that's happened to you from the moment you were born has been preparing you for that purpose.

Once you accept this truth, all that's left to do is to walk forward with arms open to embrace that purpose, knowing that you can handle whatever lies ahead.

All that's left to do is to develop your bounce-back muscles.

INTRODUCTION

A Confession and a Promise

I HAVE A CONFESSION TO MAKE.

Though I'm featured in the hit film and book *The Secret* and travel around the world speaking about the Law of Attraction, for most of my life, I've been guided by a different law, the one I call the Law of No Matter What. No matter what happened to me, no matter what people said to discourage me, no matter what I looked like or what I weighed, a small voice inside kept reminding me that I had the right to live the life of my dreams. Over and over I told myself, *Keep going for what you want*—no matter what! I was determined to set free my "inner champion," and I stayed focused on that goal.

Today, I've come to see that using the Law of No Matter What is an integral part of the process of having what you want in life—in fact, if you don't use it, you can't expect the Law of Attraction, which simply states that like attracts like, to really work for you. That's because the Law of No Matter What is a commitment to action. You can ask for what you want, you can think about it, focus on it, but when you say "no matter what," you add acceleration to your desires with your unwavering intention. Without it, you remain stuck in "I hope," "I wish," and "maybe."

Apply the Law of No Matter What by making the declaration, "I'll do what I need to do. I'll go where I need to go. I'll build the parts of my character I need to build so that I can

get it done!" The Law of No Matter What moves your goals out
of the realm of optional. Instead of waiting and hoping they'll
happen, you're creating them—on every single level of your
being. You increase your success exponentially when you use
both of these powerful laws.

Unfortunately, there have been times when I simply haven't
had the strength or the courage to apply the Law of No Matter What. Negative thoughts and feelings about myself and my
situation would take over completely, and as a result I made
some very poor choices.

Still, even that had a bright side. Every single setback I
faced strengthened what I call my bounce-back muscles—
my Understanding Muscle, my Faith-in-Myself Muscle, my
Forgiveness Muscle, and so on. These struggles made me
stronger and more capable of moving ahead to create a better life. Today, my well-developed bounce-back muscles
help me quickly turn my setbacks into setups for success,
and when something feels challenging or bigger than I am,
those same muscles give me the ability and the confidence
to "bounce forward" in life!

The book you hold in your hands is my way of sharing
that experience with you wherever you are in the world—to
inspire you to know beyond a shadow of a doubt that you
can create the life you so deeply desire. In these pages, I
take you with me on my journey, showing you what I was at-
tracting to myself, the chaos my choices were creating, the
lessons I learned from them, and the tools I used to turn my
breakdowns into breakthroughs. When you see what I've
made it through, you'll know for sure you can do it, too! And
the advice and steps that I've outlined throughout the book
will show you how.

I believe that the power of this book is that I tell the truth
first. I take a risk by climbing off the podium and leaving the
safety of the stage to uncover my truth and share the unvar-

nished me with you. As my grandmother would say, I put some skin in. And because I put some skin in, I can ask you to put some skin in, too. I'd like to start this process by asking you the following question: How would you benefit from opening up to your own truth? And another: Are you ready to let those benefits into your life?

There are some tough, scary scenes in this book, but the sweetness of love and truth is there, too, as it always is in life. This book is your journey as well as mine. May you embrace it and enjoy it!

What You'll Find in This Book

What you *won't* find in this book are a lot of dry, intellectual concepts or complex theories. The strength of *No Matter What!* is that its message is grounded in real-life situations and experiences. Using the events of my past, I show you how I developed my bounce-back muscles so that you can do the same thing. The program I've created describes each muscle and then outlines the four processes you can use to build that muscle in your own life.

Very often what we need to learn is hidden in situations that are painful or frightening. Many times we ask, "Why? Why? Why?" But there's no power in asking that question; it just keeps us in victim mode. Nobody will ever show up on our doorstep or drop from the sky and say, in booming tones of authority, "Let me tell you why this happened, my child." It's not gonna happen!

Once you read this book, you can stop asking "Why?" when faced with problems and ask instead, "What can I learn from this? What bounce-back muscle am I being asked to build here?" Asking those questions will help you find the lessons in your own stories. And believe me, when that happens, your growth and your happiness will both skyrocket.

To facilitate this process, each chapter includes Inspired Action Steps and I'm Not Alone boxes to check, along with the stories from my life.

Inspired Action Steps

At the end of each chapter, you'll find what I call Inspired Action Steps: actions you can take in your life to put your new understanding to work.

One of the main mistakes I see people make is forgetting to put their thoughts and desires into action. They believe that thinking about something really hard or talking about it a lot will make it happen. Sadly, those things are not enough. Desire, thought, and action *all* have to be present for transformation to occur. Without action, it's just a great "aha!" Action is the most pivotal step—it's the catalyst for change and movement.

The Inspired Action Steps are a vital part of developing your bounce-back muscles. They include:

- journaling
- practicing mirror work
- doing exercises, affirmations, and dialogues
- sharing experiences and breakthroughs with an accountability buddy
- completing self-work assignments to help you push through old limitations

I share with you many of the techniques I give in my workshops and coaching programs—techniques that have changed the lives of hundreds of thousands of people.

I suggest that you start keeping a No Matter What journal as soon as you can. Use it to record all of your written action-step items, as well as your insights, ideas, and the emotional responses that come up for you as you go through this book. It's a wonderful way to track your progress and to become aware of the deeper levels of your mind and heart.

I'm Not Alone

You'll also notice framed sections titled "I'm Not Alone" interspersed throughout the chapters. These provide an opportunity to see that you're not alone in the experiences you've gone through in your life.

Millions of people in our country today—including those we label as successful—feel increasingly disconnected and alone. Unfortunately, though we crave connection, with the widespread use of cell phones, iPods, and laptops, we've become accustomed to being "around" one another but not necessarily "with" each other. We're not talking to each other, hearing each other's stories, and saying to one another, "You know what? That's my truth as well."

To facilitate this essential connection in my seminars, I ask people to raise their hands while I'm talking to signal how much they can relate to what I'm saying.

Their choices are: one hand up if you can relate to what I'm saying, two hands up if you've experienced something similar in your life, or two hands up and stand up if you feel, "Hey, that's really me! I've been there. I've come through that," or, "I'm working on the same thing right now!" I do this to let everyone in the room see how much we all have in common.

In *No Matter What!*, the I'm Not Alone boxes serve the same purpose. They are placed throughout the book, and as you come upon them, check one box if you can relate to what's happening in the story, two boxes if you've experienced something similar in your life, and three boxes if you feel, "Hey, that's really me! I've been there. I've come through that," or, "I'm working on the same thing right now!" My goal is to let you know that you're not alone but in great company with amazing people who are also on this journey called life.

A Promise: What This Book Can Do for You

Though I can't promise that reading this book will solve all your problems, I can promise that if you read the stories, reflect on the lessons in them, do the action steps, and realize you aren't alone, the quality of your life will definitely improve. Strengthening the nine major bounce-back muscles is the key to moving toward the life you want and deserve.

All of us are looking for something wonderful to hold on to in life, but what many people don't realize is that before we can hold on to something new, we have to be willing to let go of something old.

In these pages, you'll learn how to recognize when you're living in the country called "Sad" in the town called "Victim-ville" on the street called "Hurt Lane" so you don't stay there longer than you need to. You'll get the tools and techniques to see past the problem, whatever it is, and into possibility—sooner-quicker-faster. Reading *No Matter What!* will allow you to avoid getting stuck and give you the tools to make sure that the speed bumps that come up in your life don't become stop signs.

Remember, success, joy, and personal peace don't come as a result of magic fairy dust, and by the same token, hurt, shame, and pain aren't simply imposed on us by others; they all come as a result of our thoughts and our choices. It's easy to think clearly and choose wisely when our lives are running smoothly, but I've noticed that people often forget everything they've learned when they run into trouble. It's when things are going wrong, wrong, wrong that you need to apply the Law of No Matter What. It'll help you get back on track and keep you moving toward happiness, success, and the life you truly deserve.

I don't live a perfect life. Things have happened and will continue to happen to me. But I'm not concerned so much about what's coming next because, whatever it is, I believe with all my heart and soul that I've built up my bounce-back muscles enough to get through it.

When you focus on your goals instead of your worries, you can begin to live more in possibility and peace and less in fear of deprivation, scarcity, and lack. Bad things may happen, but they won't determine the outcome and the quality of your life.

———————

I've written this book for the millions of men and women who've questioned their greatness. For those who struggle with weight or self-image issues, who feel they aren't attractive enough or smart enough. For those who love others more than they love themselves and look for validation outside, instead of knowing the magnificence they have within.

This book is for the millions of people who are ready to dance their dance, sing their song, tell their story, and set their own inner champion free. You deserve to be happy. You deserve to be successful. You can choose to learn from your past and love your life. I offer my story to encourage and empower you to make the choice to build your bounce-back muscles and experience happiness in your life today and every day, *no matter what!*

PART TWO

Building Your Bounce-Back Muscles

*Our greatest glory is not in never falling
but in rising every time we fall.*

—Confucius

CHAPTER ONE

Developing Your Understanding Muscle
Some Gifts Come Wrapped in Sandpaper

O*NE HUNDRED NINETY-EIGHT . . . ONE HUNDRED NINETY-NINE . . . TWO hundred!* Once again, my daddy and I completed the wonderful hair-brushing ritual that bonded us through my childhood years. Twice a week, I'd grab the softest brush I could find, a jar of Royal Crown hair dressing, and one of my favorite Dr. Seuss books. Stacking the pillows in front of the couch where my father sat, I'd climb onto the pile, where I fit comfortably between his knees. For the next forty-five minutes, I'd read *Green Eggs and Ham* or *The Cat in the Hat* out loud, working hard to bring the characters to life for him, as section by section, he parted my hair, dipped the brush into a cup of water to help him with the detangling, and then worked the Royal Crown in with his fingers, transforming my short, coarse, unruly curls into a beautiful, shiny mane. With each stroke of the brush, I could feel my daddy's love.

My mother showed her love for my brother and me in a different way. As a child, I was sure that if you looked in *Webster's Dictionary*, you'd find Mom's name listed under *fun, exciting,* and *loving.* She'd have easily won the neighborhood "Mom of

Choice Award," routinely fixing enough chili dogs and French fries for all of our friends on the block, as well as our visiting cousins. And on hot summer days, she was the mother who carted all of us off to the beach, to tae kwon do lessons, or even to Disneyland; Mom was the true Pied Piper of fun. Each year on my birthday, fifteen giggling girls slept over at my house, transforming our home into a weekend circus of adventure. My mom was the ringleader, I was the birthday girl, and together we created memories to last a lifetime.

But my parents' love for my brother and me went beyond tender rituals and fun-filled moments. They taught us to stand up for what we believed, to be good people, and most of all to appreciate and love our family. It was a wonderful way to grow up.

So what went wrong? How did I become such an unhappy teenager and young adult? Why for so many years did I believe I had so little value?

Because I hadn't developed my bounce-back muscles yet and was unprepared for the challenges I encountered. Let's take a closer look at exactly what these bounce-back muscles are.

The Scoop on Bounce-Back Muscles

If I asked you to think of muscles that when fully developed could help you live the life you want, you'd probably think of the physical muscles in your body—your triceps, biceps, six-pack, hamstrings, and so on. But did you know you also have another set of "muscles" that significantly add to the quality of your life as they become strengthened? I'm talking about the muscles of your character, the ones I call your bounce-back muscles.

These muscles are not developed at the gym, while running, or by drinking protein shakes. Your bounce-back muscles are shaped and formed by life experiences—by overcoming challenges and rising to the occasion. The main ones are

1. your **Understanding** Muscle
2. your **Faith-in-Myself** Muscle
3. your **Take-Action** Muscle
4. your **I-Know-Like-I-Know** Muscle
5. your **Honesty** Muscle
6. your **Say-Yes** Muscle
7. your **Determination** Muscle
8. your **Forgiveness** Muscle
9. your **Highest Choice** Muscle

You build these muscles the same way you build your physical muscles: by using them! For example, if you're angry at someone for an injustice they've committed against you, the moment that you choose to release your anger and forgive, you strengthen your Forgiveness Muscle. Or if you reach for the stars by going for a new career, trusting love, or relocating—even if you're unsure what the outcome will be—you develop multiple muscles simultaneously: your Faith-in-Myself Muscle, your Say-Yes Muscle, and your Highest Choice Muscle. Choosing to build one or more of these nine bounce-back muscles is the best way to successfully get through a life-threatening or painful situation and to begin experiencing the peace of mind and joy that you deserve.

In this book, I'm going to share the difficult times and defining moments in my life that required me to build the muscles of my character in order to show you that developing these muscles is the catalyst for living your dreams. Strong bounce-back muscles make you a magnet for all that is great in life and enable you to step into your power and stand in your greatness. As you read the chapters outlining each of the nine muscles, look for yourself in the pages and identify the muscles you've already built, along with the ones that are still weak and require your attention. Use the Inspired Action Steps to help you strengthen your muscles and improve your life.

In this chapter, we'll focus on the first muscle, one of the most important bounce-back muscles of all: your Understanding Muscle. This is the muscle that allows you to see beyond the present moment and your immediate situation. A strong Understanding Muscle enables you to recognize the greater good that will come out of a given set of circumstances—even while you're in the midst of it. When this muscle is weak, you constantly feel like a victim, as though life is out to get you. You experience a lot of sadness, hopelessness, and anger.

The School of Hard Knocks

Looking at my own life, I can see that for many years, my Understanding Muscle was almost nonexistent. Like most people, I took my experiences, both good and bad, at face value. I was on a roller coaster, feeling happy when things were going my way and feeling discouraged and sorry for myself when they weren't. I didn't have a clue how all the events in my life fit into the bigger picture.

On top of that, I hadn't learned to truly believe in my own self-worth or to know who I was—especially at those times when everything around me contradicted the image I had of myself. My parents loved me and told me so repeatedly, but they couldn't build my bounce-back muscles for me. I had to do it myself—in my case, through my own trials, breakdowns, and breakthroughs. And there were many of those to come.

One of the biggest jolts to the feelings of unconditional love I'd grown up with came in elementary school. It was the mid-seventies, and I was one of the first African American students to be a part of the integration process in Los Angeles. I can still remember my mother and father sitting my brother and me down one summer day and explaining the Educational Integration Program that was to be instituted in the fall. The program was designed to take inner-city kids like us and bus us over 40 miles to schools in the traditionally white suburban communities, providing us the opportunity for a better education—something my mother and father told me they'd never had.

On the first day of fifth grade, anxious and hopeful, I boarded the bus, expecting that I would be met at my new school with a warm "Welcome to the Valley." Instead, we were greeted by a group of angry parents, yelling, throwing tomatoes and eggs at our bus, and telling us to go back home. I was overwhelmed by fear and confusion.

I had watched scenes like this on television, water hoses being turned on people marching for equality and Dr. King saying, "one day little black boys and black girls will be able to join hands with little white boys and white girls as sisters and brothers . . . free at last, free at last." Now I realized that *I* was that little black girl he was talking about! Could staying in this scary school be my way of contributing to what Dr. King had died for? I wanted to run back to safety, but if I did, then we weren't "free at last." That night I convinced my parents to let me stay in spite of the initial challenges.

The days that followed were dark even though I lived in sunny California. At school, I seemed to forget that I was my father's beautiful girl and my mother's darling. Every day I was told in subtle and not-so-subtle ways that I was different, that I didn't belong, and that I wasn't good enough. No one recognized Lisa, the girl inside.

One of my classmates, a boy named Brian, made it a point to remind me each and every morning of my value, as he saw it. "Lisa, you know what's wrong with you? God accidentally dropped you in the tar pit," or "He left you in the oven too long, and you burned." My skin was dark because God had made a *mistake*?

Still others taunted me by calling me Kizzy, one of the main characters in *Roots*, the miniseries that came out that year about the ancestral journey of African Americans through slavery. It was a great television show, but the timing was terrible for our district's attempt at integration. The white kids, having almost no other exposure to African Americans, assigned some of the sixty black kids in the school names from the series: Kunta Kinte, Chicken George, Binta, Toby. It was humiliating and just one more wedge keeping us separate, if not in body, then in spirit.

I'M NOT ALONE	Have you ever felt like you just didn't fit in—that you were different and somehow not good enough?

Check one box if you can relate to what I'm saying, two boxes if you've had this experience often, and three boxes if you feel as if this has been the story of your life.

☐ ☐ ☐

Socially, I still tried to find ways to fit in and connect with my new classmates, but all of my attempts were met with coldness or outright ridicule. I found it easier to hang out with the other African American kids, because I didn't have to prove anything to them. Then my big break came. I heard that there was going to be an informal *Bionic Woman* and *Charlie's Angels* competition in the school yard. Everyone loved those television programs and watched them faithfully every week. It may sound silly now, but I thought that by winning the competition, things might change. Though I didn't believe it would make me truly popular, I did think that if I won, at least the teasing would stop.

In the days leading up to the competition, I sharpened every skill to ensure my placement and went over and over the key lines from both the *Angels* and the *Bionic Woman* shows.

On the big day, more than forty hopeful little girls and about seventy-five curious onlookers assembled on the playground. The judges were five very popular girls and a boy who I guessed represented Charlie. Though I was the only African American girl competing, I was calm and assured.

"Ready. Set. Go!"

I was out in front instantly! As I finished the 100-yard dash, many of the girls were just approaching the 75-yard mark. There was no question that I'd won the first round!

Only the first six of us who placed in the race advanced to the "Roll, Stop, and Freeze" event. I waited to go last, and my competitors did just as I'd expected—they giggled, fumbled, and flubbed the freeze. When it was my turn, I took a deep breath and launched myself into the roll, freezing right on the mark—hot asphalt and all. I beamed as I heard the audience gasp in a collective "*Wow!*"

Finally, it was time to pick the winners. I stood there as the judges huddled, periodically looking over their shoulders to get one last look at us before their final selection. Of the six girls left, three would be the Angels, one would be the Bionic Woman, and there would be one alternate. This would leave only one person who would not be selected at all.

I looked around, wondering who that would be. Maybe Cindy—she came in last in the race, or Kim—she hadn't been coordinated enough to roll and freeze. Maybe it would be Michelle, who had a habit of calling everyone ugly names and just didn't come across as an Angel. I felt sorry for whoever was not going to be chosen.

"Our decision is made!" exclaimed the one boy on the panel. "The official Charlie's Angels will be Diane, Tiffany . . . and Cindy."

My mind raced, partly in disbelief and partly in hopefulness. *I still have one more chance. I know I'll be chosen for this.*

The young judge went on, "The official Bionic Woman . . ."

I could feel my palms sweating and my chest getting tight.

". . . will be Michelle! And Kim is our alternate."

My whole body sagged. Amid the cheers, I heard some boos, and a few kids even came over to me, telling me it wasn't fair, but all I could see was a blur of tears. I'd been cheated and I didn't know why. Frozen in place, I replayed the entire chain of events in my head to see what I could have done better. After two or three long minutes of scanning my brain, I finally concluded that I couldn't have produced better results—I had clearly outperformed every other girl.

I felt I deserved an answer, so I walked directly over to the judges and asked, "Why wasn't I selected? You know as well as I do that I won every competition."

Suddenly, everyone on the playground fell silent, waiting to hear the reply to my question. Then, as if it were the most obvious thing in the world, one of the girls answered, "Lisa, what hero have you ever seen who was *black*?" Those words would haunt me for years to come.

I stood for a moment, shocked and humiliated. Then, not knowing what else to do, I walked away, the tears streaming down my face. One of the other judges called after me, "We didn't choose you because you don't look like a Charlie's Angel or the Bionic Woman—but you can try again next year if you happen to look more like them then." The crowd burst into laughter.

That was the day that my "sad story" got locked in place. You know that story, the one you always tell when you're revealing your inner self to someone you're getting to know better. It's the story of a painful event or relationship in your past—from your childhood, teen years, or beyond—that explains why you are the way you are: why you choose to no longer trust, why you can depend only on yourself, or why no one truly understands you.

We all know how cruel kids can be on the playground. Being different in any way can make you a target for this type of behavior. For me, the story was about my race, but your story could have been about anything: your weight, the way you looked, the clothes you wore, or that you qualified for the free lunch program.

Think about your own life. What's the first story you locked into place? When did you begin to feel that life hurt or that you just weren't good enough? When did you first ask the question "Why me?" Your personal victim story may have been prompted by an encounter with a family member, a friend, a teacher, a girlfriend or boyfriend. For me it was in the fifth grade, but for you it may have been later or earlier. I ask you to reflect in this way not to dwell on your old pain but to begin to be aware of how these stories stay with us through life, becoming the backdrop to all of our experiences and influencing our decisions.

After that day on the playground, I began to experience depression. Though I had been sad before, like the times when my brother and I fought, I always popped out of it as soon as I was distracted from our clash. This sadness was different; it was more long term and pervasive. I woke up every morning with a weight in my chest that lasted until I went to bed.

Because my Understanding Muscle was weak, I'd made decisions about myself based on others' opinions and actions. I hadn't yet learned how to take a bad situation and find the good in it or to see the bright opportunity in the midst of a dark experience. I couldn't see past the current moment and into a greater future.

Though I smiled all the time to hide the pain, it wasn't long before my parents realized that the integration system had huge flaws in it and that my brother and I were paying the price. Both of us had begun to fight frequently in school, and our grades had suffered dramatically. They decided we should return to the inner-city schools where, even though we had to photocopy our books and squeeze into undersized classrooms, my brother and I were accepted.

But life didn't get any easier when I started going to a local junior high, where I had to face the challenges of my own South Central Los Angeles neighborhood. Living between two gangs, the Harlem Crip 30s and the Rollin' 60 Crips, was an adventure I could happily have done without. Walking home from school, I had to fight my way through the gangs two or three times a week. During that period, when anyone asked me what I wanted to be when I grew up, I told them, "Alive."

Every day when the last bell rang, I'd start praying, asking God to arrange for the local thugs to be busy elsewhere. Some days my prayers were answered, and my walk home was pleasant and uneventful. But on the other days, when I could see from a distance that the Crips were around, I'd make sure that my shoes were tied tight, my backpack was properly closed, and that all my jewelry was off and safely tucked away in a back pocket. Bracing myself, I'd look straight ahead as I neared the group of tough-looking characters sitting on a porch or standing in someone's yard.

One of the lead gang members, a guy named Car Wash, would always make it a point to approach me and ask, "What's up, girl? You ready to become a Harlem and roll with the best, or what?"

Becoming a Harlem Crip girl was unthinkable, but saying no to Car Wash meant that I would have to fight my way through the crowd. Within minutes, fists would be flying. Each time I finally broke away and ran, I left at least three Harlem girls laid out on the cement. That was why Car Wash kept trying to recruit me!

But these were hollow victories. There's no true win in a fight you never wanted to have, and with each battle I felt more of my spirit beaten out of me. I seemed to shrink inside, getting further and further away from that joyful and loving girl I'd once been.

I didn't bother to tell my parents about these encounters, since I knew there was probably nothing they could do anyway. They both worked until 6:00 p.m., and I had to be off the school's campus by 4:00 p.m. And alternate routes only took me through other neighborhoods with their own sets of gangs—ones that were even more frightening than Car Wash and his band of deadbeats. In the end, leaving the Valley had not been the answer. I had simply traded one set of discomforts for another.

Today I've come to realize that it wasn't just my circumstances that affected my spirits but how I chose to respond to them that truly stole my joy. I drew conclusions about myself; I allowed other people's judgments of me to become my reality; I took their words to heart. I didn't see how there could be any positive side to my painful experiences. They were nothing but a source of misery and added to my sense of being wounded by life. What I desperately needed was a deeper understanding to turn them to my advantage.

Unpacking Your Victim Bags

When our Understanding Muscle is weak and we haven't created the space to see the benefit in everything that's happened to us, we become a victim of our perceived injustices. We pack our Gucci bags full of coulda, shoulda, woulda, and why—"Why did this happen?"—and unconsciously begin to drag them around with us. Then with every new situation, every new relationship, on the job and in our personal lives, we open up those bags and allow all of those old issues and past experiences to interrupt our current flow. We use them as reasons to avoid taking new risks. They become our permission slips to play it safe, which can really mean to stay stuck.

A crucial step in developing your Understanding Muscle is to realize that the events in your past can't be changed. They've already happened; you can't wish them away, cry them away, ignore them away, or even pray them away. The only thing you can change is your understanding of them. Strengthening your Understanding Muscle allows you to begin not only to accept the past but even to see that all that you've gone through, all that you've endured, had to happen *exactly the way it did* for you to become the person you are today.

I'M NOT ALONE

Have you ever looked around at your life and realized that you've been playing small and avoiding risks because of something that happened to you way back when? Are you holding on to your anger, hurt, and sadness, dragging them with you wherever you go, without even consciously knowing that you're doing it?

Check one box if this sounds familiar. Check two boxes if you've experienced this often. Check three boxes if you go through this all the time.

Now, it's possible that you may not be exactly where you want to be. You may have some hurt; you may be tired and exhausted from your hard experiences in the past. But you can turn that around by flexing your Understanding Muscle. Viewed with understanding, you can see that those same life experiences have made you more resilient and more compassionate; you know how to treat people—because you know how *you* want to be treated. No matter how much of your mountain you still have to climb, look at how far you've come. And know that you're a stronger person for having gone through those hard times.

I was in my thirties before my Understanding Muscle was strong enough for me to be able to put my childhood stories into perspective and see that those painful experiences were my diamonds—my prize. Being asked the question, "Lisa, what hero do you know who's black?" and having no clear answer was one of the most excruciating moments of my life, but it planted the seed in my heart to become a hero myself. It motivated me to strive for excellence and to make a difference, which ultimately led me to become a motivational speaker.

My past also prepared me perfectly for my transformational work with teenagers. In my empowerment workshops, I'm able to meet my teens wherever they are. My heart smiles when I work with kids who remind me of Brian, one of my elementary-school tormenters. I can see beyond their hatred and fear and just keep loving on them until all of their walls are broken down and a bridge has been built between us.

I can also give a deep, unconditional love to the ones I call my "little Car Wash teens," rough and tough gangbangers who come in mad at the world and ready to fight anyone, anywhere. When they allow that love in, they become the best huggers in the entire workshop. My own well-developed Understanding Muscle allows me to help these young adults stretch their Understanding Muscles.

Today, I know that my past is *not* who I am; it's only helped me to *become* who I am.

Gifts Wrapped in Sandpaper

The key to developing your Understanding Muscle is to recognize that some gifts come wrapped in sandpaper! A situation that may initially hurt and be uncomfortable can often turn out to be a blessing.

When your Understanding Muscle is developed, you find the benefit in every situation and stop suffering sooner-quicker-faster! You shift from asking "Why me?" to more empowering questions that place you in a position of influence over your outcomes, like "What is my lesson in this moment? How can I grow from this and be better and stronger on the other side because of this experience?" If it's not the first time you've found yourself in a certain situation, a strong Understanding Muscle will prompt you to ask, "What am I repeatedly doing or thinking that keeps bringing me to this place? How can I be proactive in the future to avoid this circumstance?"

To strengthen your Understanding Muscle, start stretching

it every day. When something sets you off and you find your-self slipping into "Why me?" or frustration mode, learn to ask yourself *immediately* how what you're going through will make you a better person. Will it make you more patient? Less controlling and more accepting? Will it exercise your ability to forgive and let go? Or to set clear and definitive boundaries in your life? Commit to finding your gifts—even when you still feel the discomfort of the sandpaper they're wrapped in.

Understanding Also Means Compassion

Until you deal with your past hurts in relationships with your siblings, parents, children, friends, or intimate partners, your spirit will always be searching for peace in relation to those painful experiences. Those past hurts will follow you through your life and affect your present interactions with oth-ers. A well-developed Understanding Muscle helps you to be more understanding of the people around you.

When I went to college, I had a roommate, Suzie, who was white and had never seen an African American person except on television programs like *Sanford and Son*, *The Jeffersons*, and *Good Times*. I could tell that she was shocked by her new roommate. She seemed extremely nervous around me and kept her belongings carefully put away. I think she was afraid I might steal something.

I decided to put my own personal items away the afternoon I walked in after class to find Suzie and a couple of her friends looking through my toiletries and exclaiming, "Wow, she uses moisturizer! She has a brush just like mine," and so on. They shut up as soon as they saw me and I pretended not to notice, but the damage had been done. What kind of freak did they think I was?

Still, the worst part was the staring. I'd look up from read-ing, and she'd be watching me. I'd wake up from sleep and invariably find her eyes fixed on me. These incidents served as triggers for my victim stories. All my hurt and humiliation came flooding back as I remembered my elementary-school experiences—the people in my past who had treated me as different, as an outcast, and whose words and actions had left me feeling unimportant and inadequate. I didn't want any trouble, so I kept my mouth shut, but my anger continued to build inside.

Then one day, as Suzie sat on her bed staring at me, I said to myself, *Enough is enough!* I'd been standing at the mirror, putting on a pair of earrings. Now I spun around and screamed at her, "What the hell are you looking at? I don't have a tail! I eat the same damn foods you eat. I put my pants on one leg at a time, the same way you do. That makes me a human being, just like you! So *pleeease* quit staring at me as if you lost something in my face!"

To my surprise, her beautiful blue eyes immediately filled with tears and she began to sob, "I'm sorry. I'm sorry. I don't mean to stare. I just don't know what to do. I just don't know. I don't know . . ." I could hardly understand her, she was crying so hard. "I am not looking at you to judge you; I just want to know more about you."

Suddenly, my Understanding Muscle creaked to life, stretching and flexing as compassion flooded my heart. I felt Suzie's hurt and bewilderment. There had been so many times when I'd felt that way: I hadn't known why they called me Kizzy, or why some of my teachers were so mean, or why the gang members wanted to fight me. I saw that Suzie wasn't being intentionally cruel; she simply had no idea how to act around me.

In that moment, I looked at the stories I'd been carrying around since fifth grade and for the first time I had the thought: *Those people at school were ignorant, too. Brian knew as much about me as I knew about him. The rest of those kids were probably just parroting their parents.*

It was a turning point for me. Though I was not ready to give up my victim bags completely, I could at least stash them in the corner from time to time instead of constantly carrying them around with me. More and more often, I was able to step out of my own shoes, those painful, pinching pairs of hurt, shame, and blame footwear, and start stepping into someone else's shoes to see what they might be going through. I began to see that everyone had a journey, not just Lisa, and that I needed to honor their journeys, just like I wanted them to honor mine.

When someone "pushes your buttons," it's usually because they've reactivated an old experience of hurt or anger in you—perhaps a time when you felt taken advantage of, unfairly accused, or simply treated badly. The next time you find yourself getting upset in reaction to someone's words, actions, or choices, instead of lashing out or shutting down, take a minute to reflect on which of your personal victim stories their behavior is triggering in you. This awareness helps you look beyond your own story and see what's going on with the person in front of you. When you find compassion inside for that person, your Understanding Muscle grows stronger and helps you heal both the past and present.

You Can't Supersize People!

The feeling of being victimized by others is a common one. In my workshops, people often tell me stories about someone in their lives who's hurt them, who didn't love them enough—a mother, father, spouse, or sibling who may have caused more harm than good. My answer is always the same. "All the people in your life are truly doing the best they can with what they have. **People can only love you to the capacity that they are able to love themselves. They can only forgive and embrace you to the capacity that they are able to forgive and embrace themselves. They can only give you what they have the capacity to give.** You may think that you deserve more, and you may be correct. But that means nothing if a person simply doesn't have the ability to give it to you.

I often illustrate this idea with the following example: If

you have an empty 64-ounce cup and you pour the water from a full 24-ounce cup into it, you don't expect it to fill the bigger cup. You accept that that's all the water the 24-ounce cup can hold.

But we forget this when it comes to people. Each time you expect someone in your life with a "24-ounce capacity" for love, forgiveness, or communication to give you the 64 ounces that you want, you're setting *that* person up for failure and yourself up for constant disappointment.

Ultimately, people can increase their capacity for love as much as they want, but if they're at 24 ounces right now, that's all you can expect of them. As much as they may want to have more to give, they don't have it in them at this time. They're still developing their own muscles.

When your mother, father, spouse, siblings, children, or friends reach the limit of their present capacity for giving love, understanding, communication, or forgiveness, they have a choice—they can either stretch themselves or accept that they've gone as far as they can go. They get to make whatever choice they're comfortable with. It's not your responsibility to grow other people. Your responsibility is to love them right where they are. Accepting this is one of the most powerful ways to build your Understanding Muscle.

Once your Understanding Muscle is strong, you experience less resistance in relationships. Instead of reacting with hurt and anger to the negative things people say or do, you give them a break. You can see that they're just dealing with their own victim baggage, their own junk in their trunk. You stop forcing people to be who you think they should be and begin loving, accepting, and celebrating them for who they are.

Remember, you develop your Understanding Muscle by using it. Work this bounce-back muscle every day by:

1. Searching for the gift in each circumstance

2. Looking outside your immediate situation to the bigger
   picture
3. Going into your heart to find compassion
4. Putting yourself in the other person's shoes

Understanding is an inner shift that brings about huge returns in the external world. It frees you from anger and pain and allows you to move through life with more energy, purpose, and joy—*no matter what*!

Here are some Inspired Action Steps to help you make the shift and build a strong Understanding Muscle.

INSPIRED ACTION STEPS

Joan Baez once said, "Action is the antidote to despair," to which I would add, "and the prescription for success." If you want to move forward in your life, you have to take action. You can't just read and think about all these powerful new ideas; you need to apply what you've learned. You've got to do something today that you didn't do yesterday.

What follows are some action steps I'd like to recommend, based on my work with thousands and thousands of people, to help you strengthen your understanding of yourself and others. Feel free to do as many or as few of them as you want. Everyone is different and moves at a different pace. Do the ones that call to you. (To maximize your progress, don't skip the ones that sound the most difficult. If you have resistance to any of these exercises, it usually means that particular exercise will bring you the greatest benefit.) You'll feel a huge shift in your energy when you put down your victim bags, own every part of your journey, and accept everyone in your life just as they are.

1. **Finding Answers, Finding Peace:** All of your experiences, both positive and negative, have helped you to become who you are today: someone who continues to learn, grow, and move forward. The process of reexamining old experiences and changing your relationship with them so that they no longer have a negative impact on you is called reframing. When you reframe your relationship with your past stories, you'll find you have more power in the present.

   - To start this process, take a piece of paper and write down two to four experiences from your past that have caused you a great deal of pain and that still cause you to wonder why they happened to you.
   - When you keep asking the question "Why?" and don't find the answer, you remain a captive to the experi-

ence and a victim to it. You'll find peace of mind when you have answered all of your own "whys." So after each experience, write down the question "Why?" in big letters.

- Now answer each "Why?" question that you have asked with honesty and compassion and in a way that honors the truth *and* honors you. This is an opportunity to claim your power. **You can be a victim or a victor—the choice is yours.** Refrain from making anyone wrong in your answers. Don't beat yourself or anyone else up. Allow every person involved to be growing and evolving just like you. Though you may not like all of the answers, this action step is about completion so that you don't continue to carry the story forward in a disempowering way.

2. **Move it Up to the Present:** Think of something in your life that you are dealing with right now that has you a bit unsettled or perhaps even completely unraveled. In this action step, you're going to find one to three reasons that this situation may actually be a gift wrapped in sandpaper. To do this, stand in front of a mirror and, looking yourself in the eyes, ask and answer the following questions:

   ○ What am I learning?
   ○ How is my Understanding Muscle being built through this situation?
   ○ How will I be a better person on the other side of this opportunity for me to grow?

   Be patient with yourself. Let the words flow without censoring them.

   (For the accelerated learner: commit to do this action step every day for twenty-one consecutive days to make a habit of seeing the blessing in each situation.)

3. **It's Never Too Late to Change Your Response:** The people in our lives are going to say what they say and do what they do. Often we forget that our joy and peace of mind are not determined by others' words and actions but by how we choose to *respond* to them. In a challenging or hurtful situation, it's common to react in a way that leaves us feeling damaged, bad, wrong, or guilty. Our power lies in recognizing that in each new moment, we have the opportunity to make a new choice—a choice that will inspire us and leave us feeling powerful instead of powerless.

   - Think of a situation in your life where you can now see that if you had responded differently, things would have turned out a great deal better for you. Keep this situation in your mind.
   - Now imagine the other person acting and speaking in the same way he or she did in the real scenario, but envision yourself choosing another response—one that would have shifted the entire experience. For example, could you have taken several deep breaths, thought through your next words, and showed more responsibility for what came out of your mouth? Could you have seen past a moment of anger inside and found more compassion for how hurt the other person was or how misdirected his or her actions were? Can you see a different outcome based on your choice to respond in a new way? This sets you up for a more powerful response in future situations.

4. **Don't Try to Supersize Another Person:** You can't control others' capacities to give, to love, or to understand. Accept that they are doing the best they can and honor what they are able to do rather than complain about what they're not doing. To transform a relationship, transform yourself. The following exercise will help you dramatically increase the

love and gratitude you feel for the people in your life: your parents, siblings, children, friends, and intimate partners.

- On a blank sheet of paper, at the top of the page, write down the name of a person in your life (one person per page). Now below the name, draw two perpendicular lines that cross in the middle, creating four separate quadrants on the page.
- In the upper left-hand quadrant, write the heading "What I love about you." Underneath this heading, list all of the things that you love about the person whose name is at the top of the page: characteristics as well as particular things the person says or does. Start each sentence with "I love that you . . ." For example, "I love that you are funny. I love that you cook really well. I love that you protected me as a child." Write down anything that comes to mind that fits in this section.
- In the upper right-hand quadrant, write, "What I choose to embrace about you." In this section, list all of the things about this person that may be challenging for you that you would like to accept and love. Begin each sentence with "I choose to embrace . . ." For example, "I choose to embrace that you don't say 'I love you' as often as I would like you to. I choose to embrace that you work long hours. I choose to embrace that you express yourself differently than I do." Write down anything that you've previously resisted and wished (silently or out loud) that you could change about this person.
- In the lower left-hand quadrant, write, "What I would miss about you." In this section, list all of the specific experiences that you would miss if this person were not in your life. Begin each sentence with "I would miss . . ." For example, "I would miss the games we played as a child. I would miss the way we laugh for hours. I would miss the way you make me feel so special." Some of

these may be the same as the things you love about the person; that's all right.

- In the lower right-hand quadrant, write, "What I want you to remember about our relationship." I consider this final quadrant the most important one of all. Here, you will "begin with the end in mind" by writing down your vision for the relationship as you go forward together in time. Start each sentence with "What I want you to remember about me (or us) is . . ." Example: "What I want you to remember about me is that I loved you unconditionally. What I want you to remember about us is that we could talk about *anything*. What I want you to remember about me is that I said 'I'm sorry' when I needed to." Remember, you are not just reaching back in this section and mentioning the things you've already done, but you are also stretching forward and declaring the relationship that you are creating as well. (I especially encourage you to do this for anyone who may have passed on before you were able to come to peace about your relationship with him or her. Just modify the sentences accordingly. For example, "What I choose to remember about our relationship is . . .") (See the sample diagram on page 40.)

- Now review the entire sheet. Look at what you love about this person, what you are willing to embrace that comes with the person, what you would miss if the person were gone, and what you want this person to remember about you and your relationship.

  This exercise helps you to more fully accept the people in your life by giving you a valuable sense of purpose, enabling you to move past the small challenges that you once considered huge.

- Make a separate sheet for each person in your life.

Don't Try to Supersize Another Person

_____

(Name of Person)

What I love about you.	*What I choose to embrace about you.*
What I would miss about you.	*What I want you to remember about our relationship.*

CHAPTER TWO

Developing Your Faith-in-Myself Muscle
Pressing the Stop Button on Your Mind's Negative Chatter

WHEN A STORM ROARS THROUGH THE FOREST, BLASTING EVERYTHING in its path, it's the tree that's deeply rooted in the earth that doesn't fall over. For people, it's the bounce-back muscle I call our Faith-in-Myself Muscle that grounds us and gives us the strength to stay standing when the winds of fear, anger, or despair threaten to knock us down.

When your Faith-in-Myself Muscle is strong, your self-esteem is high. You believe in yourself. You're kind to yourself. Your self-talk—the conversation in your head—supports you and helps you to achieve your goals. A well-developed Faith-in-Myself Muscle allows you to keep moving forward even when you face obstacles and challenges.

When you don't have faith in yourself, it's almost impossible to succeed—or to be happy. Even when things are going well, you don't feel you deserve your good fortune. You get hijacked by the negative chatter in your mind, and it eventually pulls you down. I know all about this phenomenon. When I was in high school, building my Faith-in-Myself Muscle actually became a matter of life or death.

Leading a Double Life

On the one hand, I had it going on. I was a member of the swim team, head cheerleader, and enjoyed being captain of the track team—especially since we had earned bragging rights by becoming the state champions the previous year. On top of that, I worked on the yearbook and was on the senior-class student council. What most people didn't know was that I was struggling academically. When my friends received a C on their report card or on a test, they'd get upset, but when I received a C, I did the happy dance. I was just grateful for the passing grade.

On the outside, I always had a smile to give or a joke to share, but on the inside I was riddled with self-doubt and sometimes even self-hatred. Besides being down on myself for not being a better student, I'd taken in other people's negative comments and beliefs about me from the past and made them my own. Beneath the mask I wore of social butterfly and free spirit, I felt like a caged caterpillar.

I'M NOT ALONE

We've all had times in our lives when the person we showed the world did not match the person we were in private. It can sometimes even feel like we're living a double life, as though no one really knows us because we let our smile and productivity hide our personal pain.

Check one box if you can relate to this feeling; check two boxes if you have experienced this many times in your life; check three boxes if this describes you exactly.

☐ ☐ ☐

It was my own negative self-talk that did the most damage. On some days it felt as if I had a personal consultant in my head, advising me of my faults and reminding me how unattractive I was. On other days it was more like a small committee pointing out that everyone was secretly laughing at me. On my worst days, I actually felt like I had the entire Verizon network between my ears, persuading me to just give up and quit. The negative chatter in my mind told me that I might fool everyone else, but I couldn't fool myself. Though my popularity and strong school spirit hid my pain, it couldn't eliminate my inner turmoil.

Becoming Aware of Your Own Self-Talk

Whether you're aware of it or not, you too have a conversation going on in your head. Without ever moving your lips, you tell yourself that you look beautiful today, that you don't look beautiful today, that you're awesome, or that you made some mistakes. If you're thinking *I do* not *have a conversation in my head; I don't know what she's talking about*, that's exactly what I mean by a conversation! We all talk to ourselves—and are deeply affected by what we say. We can talk ourselves into doing some pretty dumb things and out of doing great things, as I'm sure you've experienced. The truth is our lives are just a living, breathing manifestation of the conversations going on inside our heads.

To build your Faith-in-Myself Muscle, you have to first become aware of your inner conversations. Do you talk to yourself the way a loving friend would? Or are you hard on yourself—critical, impatient, even verbally abusive? Without awareness, you can't change. Once you're conscious of your self-talk, you can then learn how to stop the negative chatter whenever it rears its destructive head.

You stretch your Faith-in-Myself Muscle by getting out of your own way. Instead of beating yourself up, you love yourself up! At the end of this chapter, I've included action steps that will first help you identify your negative self-talk and then come up with turnarounds that you can use to replace the damaging and discouraging messages that may be dragging you down.

Winners Never Quit

At fifteen, a big source of unhappiness in my life was my performance on the swim team. I loved to swim and had been swimming competitively for about three years, but I was ready to quit—not because I'd satisfied my desire to swim but because I was horrible at it. My favorite event was the 100-yard free-style, but I always seemed to come in dead last. I had a shelf full of honorable mention ribbons, those awards that mean "Thank you for showing up. We don't want you to leave empty-handed, so here's something for you to take home to your mother." And that's what I'd do. I'd take home my honorable mention rib-bon, and my mother would put it on the shelf. Bless my mom's heart, she had no idea it meant I'd come in last. She thought I'd actually done something honorable. That shelf was my official losers shrine, and I was fed up with it.

One afternoon, the day before a big meet, I decided to break the news that I was quitting the swim team to Grandma Bernice. Now you have to understand that though she had to stand on tiptoe to measure five feet two and weighed ninety-five pounds soaking wet, my grandmother was a force to be reckoned with. She ran her house and our family without ever leaving her sofa or raising her voice. I wasn't sure how she'd take my decision to quit. I was the only athlete in the family, but since my family was rarely able to come see me compete, I figured it wouldn't be a major issue.

That day, I took my usual position, laying my big head on my grandma's tiny lap so that she could rub my head. She'd done this for all eighteen of her grandchildren for as long as I could remember. When I told her I wanted to quit swimming, she abruptly pushed my head off her lap, sat me straight up, facing her, and in her fiercest voice said, "Baby, remember these words: A quitter *never* wins and a winner *never* quits."

I was surprised by this. My grandmother rarely used absolutes like "never" or "always." I said, "Grandma, are you saying *never?*"

She said, "I'm saying *never*, baby."

Then she laid my head back down on her lap and began rubbing my head again. She told me about the endurance and strength of my ancestors and reminded me that I was descended from greatness. I remember little tears leaking from the corners of my eyes as she said more softly, "Sweetheart, you're entitled to get tired; you're entitled to get exhausted. You may have to rest, to go hibernate and restore . . . but you always have to come back out and keep going."

In the next instant, her tone changed. I could feel the steel in her as she said, "Lisa, your grandmother didn't raise no losers or quitters. You go to that swim meet tomorrow and you swim like you are a grandchild of mine, you hear?"

I knew better than to say anything but "Yes, ma'am."

The next day, our team arrived at the swim meet late, missing my event, the 100-yard freestyle for girls fifteen to sixteen years old. My coach insisted that I be allowed to swim with the next group, which happened to be the seventeen- to eighteen-year-olds. I wanted to slip out of the gym and run away. I knew she was just including me in the race so our long drive wouldn't be wasted. She had no expectations that I would come in anything but eighth—and that was only because there weren't nine lanes.

As I mounted the board, I looked around at the other swimmers. These girls in their skintight caps, goggles, and Speedo suits were here to do one thing—kick my butt! My shoulders slumped. I knew I was going come in last. *Why even bother?*

Suddenly, my grandma's words began to ring in my head:

Quitters never win and winners never quit; quitters never win and winners never quit.

The gun went off.

SPLASH!

Quitters never win and winners never quit; quitters never win and winners never quit.

I swam hard, harder than I'd ever swum before. Halfway through the first length, as I drew my right arm back, I noticed that I was tied with one person. I assumed we were battling for eighth place. Deciding that the other girl was going to be the one to finish dead last today, I threw my entire body into my strokes. At the end of the length, I turned around in a burst of energy and added more kick as I traveled the last 50 yards.

Quitters never win and winners never quit; quitters never win and winners never quit.

At the finish, I hit the wall and looked to the left and then to the right for the swimmers who had beaten me, but no one was there. I was alone. *Man!* I thought. *I'm so slow, they must have gotten out of the water already.*

I raised my head to see my coach screaming hysterically. My eyes followed her pointing finger, and I couldn't believe my eyes. The other swimmers had just reached the halfway point of the pool! I turned back to the coach and said, "Coach, what happened? Was I supposed to swim more laps? *What happened?*"

She said, "*You* tell *me* what happened, Lisa. You're only fifteen, and you just broke the seventeen- to eighteen-year-old 100-yard freestyle national record!"

At first, dazed by my unexpected victory, I couldn't think how I'd done it. Then I knew: I'd changed the conversation in my head. Instead of thinking, *I don't want to lose, I don't want to lose, I don't want to lose*, like I usually did, I'd told myself, *Quitters never win and winners never quit*. I'd concentrated on winning rather than on not losing!

Think about your own life. Do you focus on what you *don't want*, rather than on what you *do want*? Too often we use our energy to avoid bad outcomes instead of using it to create great results. We say things like, "I don't want to get hurt in another relationship" rather than "I want a healthy and fulfilling relationship," or "I'm afraid that I'll fail" rather than "I'll do what it takes to succeed." Remember, the Law of Attraction states that like attracts like. When we keep our attention on what we don't want, that's what we attract. This is why it's so important to keep our self-talk positive and to stay focused on our goals. You can use your energy to help yourself or hinder yourself. It's really up to you.

Changing the Conversation

No one wakes up in the morning and thinks, *Oh boy, how can I sabotage myself today*? Yet day after day, we're beaten down by the discouraging self-talk in our minds. It's as though we have a CD player in our heads and just can't press the stop button when the negative chatter gets out of hand.

So what can we do to change this damaging conversation and empower ourselves instead? Though this process has many facets, one important key is to develop a plan of action ahead of time, one that includes a physical reminder of your intention.

The following technique is one that I—and thousands of people I've shared it with in my workshops over the last ten years—have found useful for making the switch from negative self-talk to positive. I call it my secret weapon, because it works every time.

To start, imagine that CD player in your head. Now make sure to picture a dual one: the negative CD is on the left and the positive CD is on the right. The next time you recognize that you're listening to your negative self-talk, actually take your index finger and press the left side of your forehead, as if to stop the negative CD from playing, and then press the right side of your forehead to start playing the powerful one.

Hey, I know what you're thinking, *She must be kidding,*

asking me to poke my head to manage my internal conversation! Okay, call me crazy, you won't be the first. But it has worked for me and the thousands of others who have applied it in their lives. Wendy, a young woman who took my workshop several years ago, told me the following story about her experience using this technique:

I'd been selected to speak at my college graduation, but on my way to the stage, my negative self-talk began to kick in, telling me that I was going to "screw up really bad." My old tapes of failure and fear continued to play as I placed my papers on the podium with shaking hands. Looking out at the audience, I felt my mouth go dry. Panicked, I remembered the secret weapon you had shown us. Although there were eight thousand people watching me, I reached up to my forehead and quickly pressed first the left side, and then the right. I felt an instant shift, and a powerful boost of confidence shot through me. Squaring my shoulders, I took a deep breath, opened my mouth, and gave it everything I had. When I finished, to my surprise and delight, the whole auditorium stood in a roaring ovation.

As I left the stage, a woman approached me. She complimented me on my speech and then asked, "I was wondering why you pressed the left side of your head and then the right side before you began to speak."

I smiled at her and said, "I was pressing the stop button on my negative self-talk and the play button on my powerful self-talk so that I could give you my best."

The woman stood staring at me and then began to cry. After a minute, she said, "Thank you. I came here to watch my son graduate, which makes me so proud. Now I know that I also came to meet you. I've been waiting my whole life to hear what you just said to me. Maybe now I can begin to manage my own negative thoughts."

Pressing these spots on the forehead creates a physical cue for you to change your state of mind. This technique is based on Neuro-Linguistic Programming (NLP), the study of people's thinking, language, and behavior patterns. In NLP, using a physical action to trigger a specific state or behavior is called anchoring. If you're in a meeting, on a date, or somewhere else where you need to be a bit more discreet, you can press the center of your left palm and then your right palm. Either way, this anchoring technique serves as a physical reminder of your new commitment to listen only to the thoughts that serve you and move you forward in life.

Hitting Bottom

That day at the swim meet, I experienced the powerful impact my internal conversations had on my life. After that, I tried hard to keep my mind on the right track. But unfortunately, at that point in my life, I couldn't make a permanent shift. There were still many times when I was overwhelmed by negative chatter. That chatter went off the charts a few months later when, out of the blue, my whole world fell apart.

My family had always been a safe haven for me. Family vacations, movie nights, and eating dinner together every evening were the highlights of my life. So when my parents sat my brother and me down and told us they were getting a divorce, it seemed as though my heart was being ripped apart. *Why are they doing this?* I thought. I'd heard them disagree, but I couldn't remember them ever having a real fight.

Almost immediately, my father moved out of the house, and my personal hell seemed to skyrocket. My mother was wonderful, but my daddy was my protector—my knight in shining armor—and my closest friend. I missed him more than I thought possible.

My negative chatter and my struggles in school had been bad enough. Now with the changes in my family, I was in real trouble. By the time I was a senior, I'd become more unhappy and tormented by my own thoughts than ever. While my friends were contemplating which college to attend, I was contemplating suicide. Although my family would have been there for me if I'd asked, I didn't know how to reach out. I didn't actually want to die—I just wanted the pain to stop.

I'M NOT ALONE

Have you ever been in so much pain that you were willing to do anything to make it stop? When you're in a place of deep anguish and loneliness, ending your life can seem like a solution.

Check one box if you've *ever* felt this way. Check two boxes if it's happened more than once. Check three boxes if you've often struggled, or are still struggling, with these feelings. ☐ ☐ ☐

Home alone one Saturday evening, I lay on my bed, planning my death and envisioning my funeral. Everyone would tell each other they had no idea I was so depressed and unhappy. My mother and father would sit together crying, united in their grief.

Picturing this, I began to cry myself. I thought of all the things that I would miss: Christmas, my graduation, all the birthdays and holidays to come that would prompt huge family reunions. But the pain I felt in my heart was unbearable, far greater than my regret about a future I wouldn't be around to see.

I sat up, preparing myself to die. Then, walking to the bathroom medicine cabinet, I looked inside. I wanted to take something that would end my life quickly and painlessly, but all I could find was an almost empty bottle of Tylenol PM. I counted out eight blue pills and hesitated, afraid that amount would make me very ill but wouldn't kill me. Sighing, I tipped the pills back into the container and set it on the shelf where I'd found it.

I closed the cabinet and leaned toward the mirror, looking hard into my own eyes. I imagined my grandmother holding my face between the palms of her soft yet strong hands. Suddenly, I heard her voice speaking to me: "Lisa, a quitter *never* wins and a winner *never* quits."

I burst into tears, knowing how close I had come to quitting. This was not who I had been raised to be. I forced myself to keep looking in the mirror. Though I couldn't see that I was a winner right now, I *could* trust my grandmother—who unfailingly told me I was a winner. In that moment, I decided to believe that what she saw in me was true.

Borrowing Faith

Like me, you may need to lean on friends and family as you develop your Faith-in-Myself Muscle. With even a little more faith in yourself, you start to recognize your own importance—not in an egotistical, braggadocious way but in a healthy way—and you're more willing to ask for help. It's paradoxical, but the more faith you have in yourself, the less you let your ego get in the way of accepting support from other people and allowing them into your intimate space. You see that true strength and humility is about reaching out to others and allowing others to reach out to you.

Later that night, when my dad, whom I was staying with at the time, came home, we sat together talking. I wanted desperately to tell him how close I had been to committing suicide, but I knew that it would upset him deeply. At one point during our heart-to-heart, he must have realized that I was searching for something to hold on to because he looked into my eyes and said, "Lisa, you make me so proud to be your father." He continued, "When you were born, you gave me a new purpose for living." I felt his love pouring into me. It was as though I'd been a plant struggling to survive in the parched ground, and the rain had finally come. He had no idea what he had done for me in that moment. Later, as I lay in bed, I reminded myself again that I was a winner and this time I added that I also gave my dad a purpose for living. I was collecting new thoughts to replace my negative chatter.

A few days later, I went to lunch with my mother. During our conversation, my mom turned to me and said, "Lisa, you've always been a fighter, and I really admire you for that." My heart leaped with joy at the very thought that my mom actually admired *me*. Again, it was the very thing I needed to hear.

I began to see myself through the eyes of my family and friends. Each day, when I ran around the track during training, I would chant to myself, *Quitters never win and winners never quit. I make my father proud. My mother admires my strength. I am a fighter!* Instead of believing my own distorted self-image, I believed that I possessed the strength, love, and goodness that they saw in me. I borrowed their faith when I lacked faith in myself.

Over time, the negative messages inside my head from the personal consultant, the small committee, and the Verizon network began to fade, and I began to feel a genuine affection for myself—this not perfect but unique individual named Lisa.

Reaching Out

Take a minute to think of the people in your life who love you, who encourage you, and who celebrate you. These are what I call your Rocket Booster friends. They are the core of your safe-space community. On those days when you don't see your greatness, when you can't see who you are or who you're becoming, strengthen your Faith-in-Myself Muscle by going to your Rocket Booster friends and saying something like this: "Right now I'm having a difficult time seeing all of the good things I possess. I trust you and value your opinion of me. Please, tell me the good qualities that you see in me." Allow them to paint an empowering picture of you that you can look at until you can paint a similar one for yourself.

I often tell the participants in my workshops, "When you can't use your own legs, borrow someone else's strength. When you don't have the vision yourself, borrow someone else's clarity. When your heart is hurting, borrow someone else's love. When you can't see the light at the end of the tunnel, borrow someone else's faith."

Don't hesitate for a minute to do this. The people who love you are just waiting to be there for you. Sharing in this way creates a sacred, safe space for both of you, opening the door in the future for the other person to come to you for the same purpose.

Haven't you experienced a situation when others say negative things about you, and though you struggle not to believe them, those things somehow stay in your mind? Well, when others pour their love and validation into you, that same power and influence can work in your favor! Just try it and see. I know you'll find that it's a powerful and inspiring process.

The Outer Reflects the Inner

As I developed my Faith-in-Myself Muscle, things began shifting on the outside as well as on the inside. As I began to feel better about myself, new opportunities began to come my way. In the summer of 1984, the Olympic Games were held in Los Angeles. That spring, it was announced that out of the more than 2,500 young female runners in Los Angeles County, fifty female teen track athletes would be invited to work directly with the Olympic runners during the games. For the entire summer, these girls would rub elbows with the top track stars, serve as assistants, and provide support to athletes from all over the world—athletes who would become bronze, silver, and gold medalists and even new world-record holders.

Hundreds of girls much faster than me (and with far better grades) applied to serve on this elite team, so I was grateful even to be nominated by my coaches for my efforts. When I came home one day from school to find a letter from the Olympic Committee inviting me to serve, I was ecstatic! I floated around my house imagining myself hobnobbing with Florence Griffith Joyner, Carl Lewis, and Mary Decker. I could hardly eat or sleep or concentrate on anything else for weeks.

My excitement about the Olympics almost numbed the disappointment that I felt when, by June, I hadn't received an acceptance letter from any of the colleges I'd applied to. All through my dark days and months, I'd put off applying because I hadn't thought I'd even be alive to attend. Once I'd realized that I did have a future, I'd had to play catch-up and submit some applications. Though I was afraid I was too late for the next school year, I kept the conversation in my head as positive as I could—and tried not to think too far beyond the summer.

One evening, just three days before the Olympics were to begin, my father called me into the kitchen. With a very stern look, he said, "Lisa, what do you plan to do after the Olympics are over?"

His question was like a bucket of ice-cold water being poured on me. Forced to face the reality beyond the summer, I answered rather shortly, "I don't know, Dad. I guess I'll just have to get a job since I didn't get into any of the schools I wanted to go to."

"Well," he said, "you might not want to start filling out any job applications too soon."

When I gave him a confused look, he smiled broadly. "Lisa, after you go to the Olympics—you're going to college!" Then he handed me a letter that stated that I had been accepted and was receiving financial grants to go to a four-year university!

I screamed and jumped up and down. My father gave me a huge hug and we danced around the kitchen together, singing joyfully, "Go, Li-sa!! Go, Li-sa!!"

Later, when I had time to reflect on all the good things that had been happening to me, I realized that by building my Faith-in-Myself Muscle, I had also built other people's faith in me. For the first time, I saw that, mostly, *the world sees you the way you see yourself.*

You hold the key to your own success or failure. Everywhere you go, people are just holding up a mirror to you. If someone doesn't seem to believe in you, you may not be believing in yourself enough at that moment. If people are disrespecting and not honoring you, perhaps it's because you're not really expecting to be respected or honored by anyone. Though you may want to be treated with dignity, the way you treat yourself and the way you allow others to treat you may not demonstrate this desire. **Remember, it's up to *you* to show the world how to treat you.**

This was a thrilling discovery for me because it gave me tremendous power. I realized I could create my experience in life by managing my own thoughts and beliefs about myself. Now that's not always an easy thing to do, but I knew it was possible. This was another key breakthrough toward creating the life I wanted.

Standing in Your Greatness

One of the main benefits of recognizing your negative self-talk, questioning it, and turning it around is that you stop letting your fear of failure take charge. When you have faith in yourself, you—the you who knows your own greatness—stands up to the doubts. You don't see them as the truth, but as the opinions that they truly are—opinions you can simply disregard.

Before I developed my Faith-in-Myself Muscle, whenever my self-doubt came up, I took it as gospel. For years, I wanted to become a motivational speaker, and yet every time I got ready to do it, my negative self-talk would stop me: *Lisa, you got a D in speech and failed English. Who's going to listen to someone with that kind of track record?* Or, *How many African American speakers do you see out there? Forget about it—you'll fall on your face!* Even, *How can you empower people to take control of their lives when you have a weight problem?* Hearing all this, I'd scurry back into my safe little box, living a small life, working at a job that paid the bills but not going for my dreams.

Finally, I saw my inner negative chatter for what it was—just a bunch of hot air—and I stopped listening. Today, my work as a speaker has impacted and touched the lives, directly or indirectly, of millions of people throughout the world and has prevented more than three thousand teen suicides.

I often ask myself, *How many more people could I have helped if I had refused to listen to my negative self-talk and had started speaking all those years earlier?* I want you to ask yourself a similar question. What could you do in your life if you pressed the stop button on your negative chatter and pressed play on your powerful self-talk instead?

The people I know who've made that switch choose to play bigger than they've ever played before. They draw clearer boundaries so that others honor and respect who they are. They don't waste time and energy worrying about what might go wrong; they go out and make their dreams come true.

Are you ready to make a quantum leap in your life? Whether you go from hurting to healed, from good to great, or from great to fabulous, *you* are the catalyst, the one who can make it happen. People around you can and will tell you things about yourself, but in the end it's what *you* choose to believe that makes the difference. If you believe that you'll experience a joyful, love-filled life, you're right. And if you think you'll have a drama-filled life full of chaos, debt, and frustration, you're also right. You have the power to choose your quality of life by the conversation you choose to entertain in your head. If you want to uplift your life, begin by uplifting your internal dialogue. The minute you truly believe (and the key word here is *truly*) that you are ready for something new and better in the area of your health, relationships, finances, or your spiritual journey, you give yourself permission to achieve a greater level of success and happiness than you've ever experienced before.

As you know by now, you develop your bounce-back muscles by using them. Give your Faith-in-Myself Muscle a workout by:

1. Turning off the negative CD in your head
2. Treating yourself with respect and kindness
3. Borrowing faith from others when yours runs low
4. Surrounding yourself with people who love, celebrate, and encourage you

When you have faith in yourself, you no longer allow your external situations to shape how you feel about yourself. Even if there's a hurricane around you, you're able to go to the center, to the eye of the storm, where you find that grounded, positive place inside that you carry with you everywhere you go.

Here are some Inspired Action Steps to help you build a strong Faith-in-Myself Muscle—and become your own best cheerleader.

INSPIRED ACTION STEPS

1. **Exposing the Lies and Finding the Truth:** Remember that big boom box with a dual CD player inside your head? For most of us, the negative self-talk CD is full, and the positive CD is almost blank. That's why this action step has two parts: erasing the negative CD and writing the script for your positive one.

   We'll start by identifying what's playing on the negative CD. This will allow you to visually see the junk that you have been feeding yourself and the thoughts that have been shaping your reality.

   - Take out a piece of paper and a pencil. (Don't use a pen; be sure to use a pencil that can be erased.) Now take some time to reflect. When your negative CD begins to play, what are some of the things you tell yourself? *I'm not good enough; I am not smart enough; it's my fault that . . .* These thoughts, or lies, as I like to call them, are the ones that move you to a place of fear, frustration, or personal disappointment about a situation or a person. Without editing, write down each of these thoughts, skipping three to four lines in between each statement. Treat this piece of paper like a toxic dumping zone and just throw everything on the pile. Use as many sheets of paper as you need—some of the participants in my workshops have used as many as sixteen! And I say, "Congratulations!" The more lies you expose, the more conscious you become—and the less likely you'll be to allow that negative chatter to continue.

     Don't be discouraged by the amount of negative self-talk you may find you have. If you judge yourself, you'll only be adding to it! Remember, you're identifying the negative chatter in your head so that you can turn it around.

- Now, one by one, go through each of the negative thoughts you've written down—the lies that you have told yourself over the years—and in the space underneath each thought, *in red ink*, write down what you know to be the truth. Sit quietly and listen to what your intuition (not your head) says to you, and write down a positive statement about yourself. Go deep into your soul, and whether or not you believe it fully right now, remind yourself of this truth.

  For example, if you wrote, "I'm unattractive," you might write something like, "God created me with my own unique beauty. I don't have to look like anyone else because I am me and I am enough." Or if you wrote, "I'll never find true love," you might write something along the lines of "I choose to love myself completely *first* so that others will know how to treat me. I'll make a list of the qualities I want my partner to possess, then choose to cultivate those same qualities in myself *first*. This will attract the perfect person for me into my life." As you can see, these positive statements are not fluffy or superficial. They come from a place deep inside you and are the foundation of the new positive self-talk CD that you'll be creating next.

- Finally, erase the negative sentences written in pencil. The sentences in red that remain are the script for your new CD.

2. **Laying Down New Tracks:** It's time to recondition your mind and replace your old disempowering thoughts with a new, inspiring conversation. It may feel awkward and unnatural at first because you're used to the old toxic lies on your negative CD. As damaging as those thoughts are,

they've become comfortable for you. Here are two ways to accelerate owning your new positive self-talk.

- *Visual Cues*: You'll need visual reminders of your new conversation until you can remember it by heart. When performers like Harry Connick, Jr., Patti LaBelle, or Beyoncé are learning a song, they constantly keep the words in front of them and sing them over and over again until they have them committed to memory. You must do the same. Your positive truths are like a new song that, when sung, will begin to transform your life.

   Each week, write at least one of the positive statements from your script on a fluorescent-colored index card or Post-it Note, and put it someplace where you will see it often. I always start by placing my affirmations on my bathroom mirror because it's where I get ready to meet the world. I also place them on the back of my front door so that I can see them just before I step out into the world. I don't put them on my refrigerator because they tend to get lost in all the other family photos, lists, and artwork. Place them where you'll be sure to take notice, and after thirty days, change the location of each affirmation so that you'll begin to notice them again.

- *Physical Anchoring and Mental Prompts*: Make a commitment to use the "secret weapon" I described in this chapter—pressing the left side of your forehead and then the right—the next time you start feeling overwhelmed by your own negative thoughts. Or develop your own physical anchor, one that feels good to you.

   For some people, mental prompts work best. When a friend of mine realizes her negative chatter is starting to spike, she thinks the word *cancel* to interrupt her train of thought, and then *redo* to make a new choice about how she wants to talk to herself. It doesn't matter what you use, as long as it works for you. Having a plan of action mapped out ahead of time will give you an edge in this process of inner transformation.

3. **Write Yourself a Love Letter:** When I was in high school, one of the most powerful ways I discovered to build my Faith-in-Myself Muscle was by writing a love letter—filled with acknowledgment and encouragement—to *myself*! A teacher, whom I'd confided in about my unhappiness, suggested I try it. Here's what I wrote.

> *Dear Lisa,*
>
> *I just wanted you to know how much I love and appreciate you. I know that you've had it pretty hard lately and you've felt alone, but please remember that I am here with you and that I will always be here with you. I am so happy that you chose to live. I know that your family and friends love you so much and would be devastated if you were gone. I am thankful that you reached out for help and are making a commitment to find the good in yourself. I love you, Lisa, and will be here for you every step of the way. I promise.*

Now it's your turn. Start by asking yourself, *What would I write to my closest friend to show my love and appreciation for him or her?* And then become your own closest friend and begin writing. When you're finished, read the letter back to yourself. You'll be amazed at the surge of strength it brings. Do this on a regular basis, say once a week or once a month.

4. **Identify Your Safe-Space Community:** First, make a list of all the people you communicate with regularly: your friends, coworkers, family members, and so on. Now, on a scale of 1 to 10, rate how comfortable you feel with each

one of them. A 10 means that you can talk to this person anytime, anywhere, about anything, and know he or she will be supportive and loving. A 1 means you don't feel safe enough to share anything personal with this person, ever.

- To rate them, place your finger on each name, hold it there for a minute or two, and write down the first number that comes up for you, based on your experience of the person. (Be fair and truthful; just because someone is your parent doesn't mean he or she automatically gets a 9 or 10.) You use your finger in this process for two reasons. First, it focuses your attention on that particular person and only that person. Instead of seeing what numbers you gave the other people on the list and adjusting your rating in relation to them, you concentrate on your inner feeling about just that person. And second, the sense of touch is intimately connected to your emotions. We use the same word, *feeling*, to describe both the inner and outer activity. I've found that touching the name with my finger helps me access my true feelings about the person I'm rating.

- Review your scores. The 10s on your list are your Rocket Booster friends. These are the people you can reach out to as you strengthen your Faith-in-Myself Muscle.

- Remember, everyone else on your list has an important place in your life, and you can always work to elevate those relationships until they reach a 10. But for now, your Rocket Booster friends are the ones to go to as a safe space to do your inner work.

CHAPTER THREE

Developing Your Take-Action Muscle
Stop Lying on the Nail

LET'S FACE IT: THINGS DON'T ALWAYS GO THE WAY WE WANT THEM TO. Jobs may come and go, relationships can disappoint us, children sometimes have problems—stuff happens! Having strong bounce-back muscles allows you to more easily get through the crises that can and will come up in your life.

You see, developing your bounce-back muscles has as much to do with where you're going as where you're coming from. Being able to bounce back consistently is the foundation of "bouncing forward" in life successfully.

Winston Churchill once said, "If you're going through hell, *keep going.*" This is why I call the specific bounce-back muscle we'll learn about in this chapter your Take-Action Muscle. It's the Take-Action Muscle that allows you to keep going, to continue moving forward in the face of obstacles. Without a strong Take-Action Muscle, it's easy to stay stuck, mourning the failure of your Plan A and missing the other opportunities to grow and succeed that are all around you.

To strengthen your Take-Action Muscle, you must learn to

chart a course for the future based on flexibility and keeping your eye on your higher goals.

Unfortunately for me, when my Plan A went south, I spent four long years—from the time I was nineteen to twenty-three—stuck, stuck, stuck! My weak Take-Action Muscle left me paralyzed, staring brokenhearted at a door that had slammed in my face.

The End of a Dream

After high school, I headed for college. I had received not one but four financial grants to attend a four-year university in a small town in Oregon: one grant based on my family's Baptist background, another for track, a third based on financial need, and the last for being an African American student. Going to college was a big deal for two reasons. First, I was the first person in my family to attend a four-year university, and second, it was the first step toward fulfilling my dream of being a successful businesswoman. I wanted to get a degree in business and communications and then someday run my own public relations company.

It took some adjustment to get used to living in a small, rural, mostly white town after growing up in the center of South Central, but as the days and weeks passed, I found myself enjoying the different experiences it offered me: meeting people from a wide variety of backgrounds, seeing more trees than I had ever seen before, and of course, living with rain—lots and lots of rain.

Being away from my family and on my own taught me a lot about myself. I discovered my own morals and standards. When I decided not to drink at the many parties where alcohol was available, it wasn't because I was afraid my dad would find out; it was because *I* didn't want to. I soon became accustomed to making decisions on my own.

What I couldn't get used to were the demands of the track program.

All through elementary school, junior high, and high school, I'd loved to run. It gave me a huge sense of accomplishment to push myself to new levels of achievement and to have my individual successes serve the team as well.

That first year at college, I was running six events every week in our track meets, which I later discovered was excessive by any standard. All I knew at the time was that my body was suffering under the strain, and I couldn't keep it up indefinitely. I complained to the coach, but since we were enjoying an undefeated season (after not having won a single track meet in the past two years), he wasn't willing to reduce my number of events. I began to feel used and frustrated.

Things didn't improve my sophomore year. In the middle of the first semester, after the coach insisted I run in spite of a torn tendon and shin splints, I reached the breaking point. I announced that I couldn't and wouldn't run track for the school any longer. After many "closed-door" meetings (with me on the other side of the door), I was given an ultimatum: continue to run, or pack your bags and head home. When I protested that only one of my grants was related to track and that my grades were good enough for me to remain, I was quickly reminded that all of my financial grants could be "ungranted" or made unavailable at the discretion of the school. I felt helpless and infuriated; what they were doing simply wasn't fair. Perhaps I could have found a way to negotiate a compromise, but I was young, impulsive, and angry. I refused to run. In response, they revoked all of my grants, effective immediately.

During the whole ordeal, I hadn't contacted my parents because I didn't want to upset them. They were so proud of me, I was afraid they'd be disappointed by my decision. Now, knowing my family would be unable to pay my tuition without financial assistance, I packed all of my belongings and asked a friend to give me a ride to the airport to fly home.

On the flight, I gazed unseeingly out the window, reviewing the situation over and over in my head. I felt both despair and shock. *How could I be hailed and adored one minute and in the next minute be abandoned and betrayed by the very same people?*

I'M NOT ALONE

Have you noticed that sometimes the wind shifts direction without you even being aware of it? One minute you know what's happening, and the next minute you're lost—surprised and confused by what's going on. You may even feel as though other influences around you have more control over your life than you do.

Check one box if you've ever experienced this. Check two boxes if it's happened more frequently. Check three boxes if you feel like this happens all the time.   ☐   ☐   ☐

When I reached the Los Angeles airport, I called my dad, but no one was home. He had begun to travel more with his company since I'd been away at school, so I took a taxi home, then using the spare key, I unlocked the front door. After putting my suitcases in my room, I lay down on the bed, overcome by the feeling that the situation wasn't real. I wasn't supposed to be there. I should have been at school, studying for upcoming exams. I stared at the ceiling, numb and confused, until I fell asleep.

The next morning, still reluctant to upset my mom, I finally called and broke the news to her. She could tell by the tone of my voice how devastated I truly was. "Sweetheart," she said, "you're strong and resourceful. You *will* get through this. Remember, one experience doesn't determine your whole life story." I knew that these were words to live by, but I couldn't find any consolation in them at that moment.

Three days later, my dad returned from his business trip to find me at home, studying. I could tell by the look on his face that he was both surprised and alarmed by my presence. When I explained what had happened, I felt a huge sense of relief. *My dad's going to call the administrator and clear this mess up,* I told myself. *Then I can go back to school, take my exams, and move on as if this whole thing was just a bad dream.*

Sure enough, Dad picked up the phone and dialed the school. I could hear him speaking in the other room: "What do you mean she has no choice? . . . I'm aware of the $10,992 annual tuition . . . No, I'm not able to pay that myself . . . No, I'm not going to *make* her run . . . What about her other grants? Isn't there anything that can be done? . . . I see. Well, thank you. Good-bye."

As he walked into the room, I prepared myself for the inevitable. Dad sighed heavily and said to me, "I'm sorry, baby girl, but I don't think you'll be able to return to school. We just can't afford it."

I don't know which was more painful: knowing that I was really not going back to college or seeing the pain in my dad's eyes. It took a few more days for me to fully realize that there was nothing to study for, nowhere I had to be, and no one checking my name off on any roster or attendance log. I went into a tailspin. I'd break into tears for no apparent reason and seldom smiled. Embarrassed that I was no longer in school, I refused the invitations I received to join my friends for their college events or other celebrations. My dreams of a bigger, better future seemed to be evaporating into thin air, slipping from my grasp. Plan A was gone, and I had no idea what to do next.

From Bad to Worse

Think of a time in your own life when you thought something should have happened but it didn't. How did you feel? What did you do? For most of us, the reaction is usually colored by the circumstances of our particular disaster. If our Plan A failed because we screwed up in some way, we may focus on berating ourselves and imagining how we could have done things differently. If we were let down by someone else, we'll probably be absorbed in blaming that person and feeling outraged that his or her mistakes or betrayals could ruin our life. If Plan A failed through no one's fault, we might just get stuck in the details of the situation, trying to understand what happened and telling and retelling our story to anyone who'll listen, but especially to ourselves.

The sad thing is, not only does none of this move us forward, it actually takes us further from where we were headed in the first place. It's like falling into a hole and then using our energy to keep digging. We just sink deeper and deeper into the pit of blaming, complaining, and feeling ashamed until we can't even see the path anymore.

Because I didn't have a strong Take-Action Muscle, I focused all my attention on the circumstances of my leaving college rather than on my original goal of becoming a business-woman, which is why I went to college in the first place. This focus on the past produced an overload of negative emotions—envy, bitterness, self-loathing—that did absolutely nothing for my productivity as a person. Instead of continuing toward my dreams, I spun out and spiraled down.

One of the keys to building your Take-Action Muscle is to step back from the specifics of your situation and remember where you're ultimately headed. Staying focused on the larger outcome you desire will keep you moving and on the right track—no matter how many detours you may have to follow. To take action again, you may need to modify your plan, take a new direction, or even change partners. All of this is just fine. The sooner you can rededicate yourself to your original, greater goal, the less time you'll need to spend recovering from your disappointments.

This principle is useful for breakdowns both large and small. The next time you feel that things aren't going the way you want them to—whether it's a social event that isn't proceeding as scheduled, a vacation ruined by bad weather, or an important business deal falling through—stop for a moment and remember your original intent, the bigger plan. The real purpose of the social event was to have fun with your friends and family; the vacation was to help you relax; the business deal was to bring you closer to financial freedom. Even in the midst of a breakdown, can you remember the bigger goal and find a way to fulfill it anyway? This level of flexibility isn't always easy, but with practice, I promise you it's possible.

Plan A or Nothing

As the days crawled by, I continued to hang around the house, feeling lost. I had no idea what I wanted to be; I only knew what I *didn't* want to be, based on what I'd seen in my community: I didn't want to be on welfare, a drug dealer's girlfriend, or working at a minimum-wage job. But most of all, I didn't want to be here, at home; I wanted to be in college, moving toward the goals I'd set myself.

Worried about the slump I was in, both my mother and father begged me to do *something*. For lack of a better plan, I enrolled in a local vocational business school. This felt like a huge step backward, since it was where the kids in my high school who had low GPAs, skipped school, and got high behind the building ended up. I knew right away that I didn't belong in this place, but I tucked my head down and rolled up my sleeves, determined to complete the accounting certification program I'd signed up for as soon as possible.

I can see now that business school was just a big Band-Aid for me. I didn't really want to be there; I only went because what I truly wanted was unavailable. In my mind, it was college or nothing! So like a sulky child, I grudgingly did what I had to, dragging my feet and beating myself up the whole way.

Because my Understanding Muscle was also weak at this point in my life, I was too busy feeling victimized to be interested in what my next step truly should be. As a result, I didn't consult my inner wisdom or intuition to help me decide what I should do next.

And without a strong Take-Action Muscle, I let outer influences act upon me—in this case, my parents' suggestion and the proximity of the business school. There was no inner drive propelling me forward; I just chose the path of least resistance. Sadly, being swept along with this particular current kept me going in the wrong direction for a long time to come.

Playing Small

For the next few years, I used my training to work in various jobs in the accounting field. These jobs paid the bills, but that's about all I can say for them.

At twenty-three, I found myself working in the accounting/ collections department of a very small answering-service company. A number of our customers couldn't keep up with their monthly fees, and part of my job was to get them to pay their past-due bills.

Though I liked talking to people, these phone calls made me cringe inside. Even as I was demanding that our customers somehow come up with money they didn't have, I was all too aware that, despite my best intentions, I had a few unpaid bills of my own. It felt as though my soul was dying a little more each day, but I didn't have a clue how to revive it *and* make a living.

I'M NOT ALONE

Have you ever felt as though bits of you disappeared the longer you stayed in the same place? Many of us spend years playing small, compromising our joy and not really utilizing our true gifts. We can even become so comfortable in our discomfort that we begin to accept it as our life's destiny.

Check one box if you've ever felt this way. Check two boxes if this has happened more than once. Check three boxes if you feel that this is true for you most of the time.

One day, my boss called me into her office and motioned me to sit down. Smiling at me, she asked politely, "Lisa, what's your passion in life? What do you *really* want to do?"

Caught off guard, I hesitated for a moment. Thinking that she was testing my company loyalty, I gave the answer I thought she wanted to hear, though I knew in my heart it wasn't the truth. "I want to do accounting and serve this company," I replied.

I assumed that she would be pleased with my response, but instead she sighed, leaned back in her seat, and shook her head. "Lisa," she said, "you have to be one of the sweetest people I've ever met. I've heard you on the phone, and I can tell that you genuinely love people."

I smiled at the compliment, thinking of all the wonderful conversations I'd had with our clients and the compassion I'd been able to extend to them.

"The only problem is," she continued, "you love them *so much* that if they're going through hard times, you don't want to make them pay their bills. Honey, you're in the collections department! You know from your training that you have to be tough with people, but you just won't do it. It's crystal clear to me that this is not what you are supposed to be doing with your life."

Finally realizing where this was going, I blurted out, "Ma'am, are you firing me?" As much as I hated it, I needed this job.

Her response, though loving, stung. "Lisa, I'm not firing you—you're a great employee. I'm *releasing* you to find whatever it is that you're supposed to be doing in the world, because it is definitely *not* collections, and from what I've observed, I don't believe it's accounting either."

My boss kindly smoothed over my exit from the company, saying she would write me a glowing reference, but inside I burned with embarrassment and humiliation. In my mind, being fired was for losers. This didn't make much sense since I'd hated my job, but haven't you ever felt the pain of being rejected even though you didn't want what you were losing?

As I'm sure you've noticed, people have a tendency to stay in situations even when those situations are uncomfortable. We often hang on to relationships, jobs, and other circumstances that don't really serve us in order to pay the bills, keep the peace, or avoid failure. Then, if we lose our job or if our partner breaks up with us, though we know it wasn't right for us in the first place, we still feel rejected. The experience of being pushed out before we're ready to go is a painful one.

This is because our need to be accepted and approved of often supersedes our desire to be happy. When you're clear that being happy, whole, and complete is really your first and foremost goal, then you can see an involuntary parting of the ways not as rejection but, in the words of my supervisor, as release. You recognize this type of change as the opportunity it truly is—the opportunity to move closer and closer to what's right for you.

Until you develop your Understanding Muscle and your Faith-in-Myself Muscle, it's difficult to see that. It all appears as one rejection after another. What helps is to recognize that whatever it is you were holding on to wouldn't have lasted anyway. When you're in a situation that isn't a fit for you, things just won't line up for you to stay in that space. So whether it's someone releasing you from a job or someone leaving you in a relationship, instead of cursing the change, bless it. It's creating space for what you're really supposed to be doing, for what the universe has in store for you.

Even back then, though I was upset about losing my job, I knew my supervisor was right. I couldn't put any real energy into getting money out of people who had none, and balancing debits and credits just didn't do it for me. Yet that left me even more confused: *now what*?

I had to eat and pay the rent. I had to get another job—most likely doing accounting—no matter how I felt about it. So, the search was on, yet again. Every day, I'd buy three newspapers and carefully circle all the available accounting jobs. But when it was time to pick up the phone and set up an interview, I'd actually get sick to my stomach.

I'M NOT ALONE

We've all experienced at one time or another how frustrating life can be. Sometimes it feels as though *nothing* is going the way we want it to—as though we're heading in the wrong direction faster and faster and can't slow down. What's worse, this can leave us with a negative attitude that draws more of exactly what we don't want into our lives.

Check one box if you've ever experienced this. Check two boxes if you feel like this happens fairly often. Check three boxes if this describes your situation much of the time.

☐ ☐ ☐

After three months of halfhearted searching, I was no closer to getting a job. I was behind on my bills, my unemployment benefits would be running out very soon, and my roommates, Sharon and Kendra, were beginning to get concerned.

One morning, I left the house and couldn't find my car. I walked up and down the streets looking for it, alternately frantic and fuming, and then finally ran into the house to report the theft. I phoned the car-financing company to inform them, too. "Ms. Nichols," the woman on the other end of the line said in a flat, dismissive voice, "your car has been repossessed due to nonpayment."

This was the last straw. Frustrated and embarrassed, I threw the phone across the room. I was mad at myself, mad at my situation—mad at everything! I was mad at *life*.

My Bed of Nails

The next day, feeling disgusted with my situation, I lay in bed, still in my pajamas, the classifieds spread out beside me. I was flipping channels with an attitude when suddenly my attention was caught by a well-dressed African American man giving a talk. His name, Les Brown, appeared on the screen, and he seemed to be a motivational speaker. I had never heard of him before that moment, but intrigued by his upbeat presentation, I put down the remote control and listened as he told a story that would rock my world.

One day, a man walked past a house and saw a little old lady rocking in her chair, a little old man reading the paper as he rocked next to her, and a dog lying on the porch between the two, moaning as if he were in pain. As he passed, the man wondered silently what the dog was moaning about.

The next day, he walked past the house again. He saw the old couple rocking in their chairs and the dog lying between them, making the same pained sound. Puzzled, the man promised himself that if the dog was still moaning the next day, he'd ask the old couple about it.

On the third day, to his distress, he saw the same scene: the little old lady rocking, the little old man reading, and the dog in his spot, moaning piteously. He couldn't stand it anymore.

"Excuse me, ma'am," he called out to the old woman, "what's wrong with your dog?"

"Oh, *him*?" she said. "He's lying on a nail."

Confused by her reply, the man asked, "If he's lying on a nail and it hurts, why doesn't he just get up?"

The little old lady smiled and said in a sweet, grandmotherly tone, "Well, honey, it hurts just enough for him to *moan* about it, but not enough for him to *move* yet."

Startled, I sat up in bed, my eyes wide with surprise. It was as if Les Brown were talking just to me. I almost expected to look down and actually see the nails that I had been lying on and moaning about for the last few months—in reality, for the last few years! Appalled at my own immobility, I decided, *That's it! No more. Today's the day I'm getting off my nail!* I'd quit moaning and I'd start taking charge of my life.

Are You Lying on a Nail?

Do you recognize yourself in that old couple's dog, as I did? Are you complaining about a situation in your life but not taking action to improve it? Sometimes we fool ourselves by thinking that going over and over our problems in our heads or discussing them repeatedly with others is taking action. The truth is, these activities can eat up a lot of time, but they rarely bring us real resolution. (Plus, they drain and deplete us!) Yet it is at exactly this point that many people stay stuck.

Then our egos (or "she-gos") get invested in the drama. We justify our own position and start actively seeking out others who will support us in it. We want to enroll other choir members to sing our "poor-me" song with us—and we always seem to find them. Our fellow singers are usually lying on their own nails and moaning about their plights as well. This is where the old adage "Misery loves company" comes from. But this kind of support just makes it harder for us to get up off the nail.

After a while, we become so accustomed to feeling unhappy about a problem that we accept our unhappiness as normal. As crazy as it sounds, being uncomfortable becomes our comfort zone!

Still, however uncomfortable it may be, we can't break free of that comfort zone until we take the first crucial step: recognizing that we're stuck. Les Brown's story did that for me. I finally realized I was lying on the nail.

To build your Take-Action Muscle, use your pain or discomfort as a signal to review your current course. Why are you moaning but not moving? When you hear yourself complaining, take a moment to become conscious of what's happening inside you. Ask yourself, *What do I want? What would make me happy? What baby step can I take today to move in that direction? What am I afraid will happen if I take that step?* Asking ourselves these questions makes us more self-aware. Self-awareness is a powerful antidote for destructive habits and, as we've seen, developing it is the first step in building *all* of our bounce-back muscles. Knowing more is the basis of doing more.

From Anger to Action

Once we become aware of our situation, it's up to us to take action. Fortunately, the same energy that we've been channeling into our complaining and moaning can be redirected to fuel our transition from stuck to stepping forward.

For me, recognizing that I was lying on the nail was like finally taking my foot off the brake of a car. What I needed to do next was to grab the steering wheel and aim the car where I wanted to go.

Dazed by my epiphany about the nail, I realized Les Brown was still talking. I turned my attention back to the television. The words flowed powerfully from his mouth to my ears: "You are the master designer of your life. It's your job to design the life that you want!"

I could design my own life? I could decide what I wanted to do? Suddenly, I felt filled with a new excitement. It was time for a fresh approach to job hunting.

I jumped out of bed and took a shower. I threw away the three marked-up newspapers. I was no longer that hopeless, helpless person who had circled the same unappealing accounting positions day after day. I took out a blank piece of paper and spent the next hour getting very clear on what I wanted to do, what my gifts were, and what made my heart sing.

I started by making a list of the activities that I thought would bring me joy, the ones I dreamed about doing. Even just thinking about them made me feel alive! Reviewing my list, I felt an excited, fluttery feeling in my stomach—butterflies of hope and happiness I thought had all flown away, never to return. I knew then that I was on the right track.

Next, I prioritized the top four items on the list. They were:

1. I want to talk to people and help them.
2. I want to travel (eventually around the world).
3. I want to carry a laptop.
4. I want to wear a black suit.

Not everything on my list made immediate sense. I wasn't sure why it was important to me to wear a black suit (I think I probably associated it with power and success). I just knew that imagining a life that included all these things filled me with more delight than I'd experienced in years! It gave me a vision of the Lisa I wanted to be and knew deep down inside I could be.

Then I made a bold decision. After running to the closest newsstand to buy a fresh set of papers, I decided to circle only the ads that fit *my* criteria—whether or not they had anything to do with accounting. When I was finished, I'd call the companies in the circled ads and *I'd* interview *them*!

After marking a number of interesting ads, I picked up the phone and started dialing. When I was connected with the appropriate person, the first thing I asked was, "Does this position involve travel and working with people, and does it include a personal computer?" After the first twelve nos, I began to feel a familiar twinge of discouragement.

I didn't want to lie back down on the nail, so I went to the bathroom mirror and gave myself a pep talk. Looking myself directly in the eyes, I said, "This is the only life you get, Lisa, and if you don't fight to give yourself the best, no one else is going to come and give it to you. You got twelve nos—so what! All you need is one yes!" I realized that my new attitude didn't automatically make things easier; it just gave me more conviction to push forward.

Determined, I kept dialing and getting nos to my questions. Then I struck gold!

"Hi," I said. "My name is Lisa Nichols, and I'm calling about your customer service job. I have a few questions I'd like to ask you, if I may." Without giving the woman on the other end of the line a chance to say no, I continued, "Does this position involve working with and helping people?"

"Yes, it does," the woman replied.

"And does this position require traveling?"

"Yes, it does," she replied again.

"Does your company provide a laptop computer for this position?"

"As a matter of fact, we do," she answered, sounding a bit surprised.

I'd never gotten this far before. Excited, I posed my final question: "Can I wear a black suit to work?"

"Absolutely!"

I could tell I had piqued her curiosity, because the next question was hers. "Do we fit your criteria?" she asked with a little giggle.

"Yes, you do," I said, a huge smile on my face. "May I set up an interview?"

I got the job! My new employer was a software company, and my job was to train people in the use of their products. Ten days later, I walked into their offices and began training for the position that I'd been led to by my wish list. I'd gotten off my nail and stepped into my power.

Committed to Movement

Having a strong Take-Action Muscle means you're committed to movement in your life, *no matter what.* If a roadblock looms up before you and knocks you off your path, you get up, dust yourself off, and look around, ready to discover what your next step will be—and to find a new path, if necessary. This doesn't mean you always have to move quickly; it simply means you make it your priority to keep moving. There have been times since discovering my Take-Action Muscle when I could only crawl. Even so, I made sure that I stayed in motion.

There may be situations in your life when, from the outside, it could appear you're not moving, but inside you know you're in motion, gearing up for the leg of your journey that lies just ahead.

This commitment to movement works best when your Understanding Muscle is also strong. As you recall, the Understanding Muscle allows you to see the gift in every situation; your Take-Action Muscle takes it one step further, enabling you to act on that understanding. If you're recovering from a broken relationship, a career setback, a health challenge, the loss of a loved one, or some other personal breakdown, finding the gift or the lesson will allow you to see beyond the chaos of the

present. But it's by taking action that you can experience the
bliss and the breakthrough that await you. In chapter 7, we'll
learn about the Determination Muscle, which works to keep
you going till you reach your goals.

With a developed Take-Action Muscle, you automatically begin
looking for the opportunities an unexpected detour brings. Instead of regretting the past and the loss of Plan A, you fashion
your new plan, Plan B, from the elements and ingredients present in your life *now*. What you find may surprise you!

What you may discover is that Plan B is the universe's or
God's plan for you and that Plan A was *your* plan for you. Plan
A, based on your limited vision and understanding, can't help
but fall short of what God has in store for you with His Plan B.
Looking back, I know that I wouldn't have had the same oppor-
tunity to develop as a speaker and go on to help so many peo-
ple if I hadn't ended up working at the company I found when
I finally embraced and started moving toward my Plan B.

Stop now and think of a situation in your life when a door
has shut, blocking your planned route and what appeared to be
the clear path ahead. Your first response was most likely frustration, disappointment, or fear. Now imagine how you'd feel
if you knew that that door *had* to close because a better door
was opening for you. Sometimes you'll be able to see that it's
better immediately; other times it may take longer. It doesn't
matter; what's important is that you're always looking for the
next, better door to step through, even if it isn't the one you
expected. This is the fastest way to develop your Take-Action
Muscle.

The Path Unfolds

My new position at the software company involved traveling
all over the country (in my jazzy new black suit, with laptop in
tow!), training employees of drug and alcohol counseling agencies to use software designed for their specific needs.

This was in the late 1980s, before personal computers were a part of daily life, and I found that most people were intimidated by computers and everything that went along with them. I approached my boss and suggested that the first hour of my training sessions be strictly motivational, geared toward helping the participants overcome their fears of the unknown and embrace the electronic winds of change sweeping the country and the world. He agreed to my proposal.

It worked like a charm. The employees in my sessions were more engaged, asked more questions, and learned far more quickly once I'd spent time addressing their resistance and uncertainty. But what surprised me was how deeply my students—and I—enjoyed the inspirational segment of the training. Soon they were begging me to do more: to start the afternoon session with motivation and end the day with more of the same.

The focus of these sessions often turned to more personal matters: people's goals, their children, their spouses, their weight, and so on. It was clear that this opportunity to grow and face the challenge of their computers spilled over into every aspect of their lives. I realized that what I was actually doing was helping them get off their own nails and build their Take-Action Muscles.

I looked forward to our sessions as well. Whenever my clients had "aha!" moments, high-fived each other, got in touch with some long-buried emotion, or hugged each other (which was often), I'd get goose bumps and feel the hair on the back of my neck stand up. People were so grateful, and I could see that I was truly helping them. I felt more purposeful than I had ever felt before and knew I had finally found my calling.

My way forward became clearer and clearer. I wanted to do more of the type of speaking that set my listeners, and me, on fire. Slowly but surely, I created a career for myself as a motivational speaker, first offering my speaking services for free while I kept my day job and within a few years working as a full-time motivational consultant to two companies—including the software company that I'd been led to the day my Take-Action Muscle came to life.

I'M NOT ALONE Do you fill your weekends and evenings with activities that thrill your heart—and even dream of turning what you love to do into a career? Once you've had a taste of using your gifts and your abilities, it's natural to want more. Nothing else brings you to life in quite the same way as utilizing your unique talents.

Check one box if you've ever experienced this. Check two boxes if you feel this way often. Check three boxes if this describes your experience perfectly. ☐ ☐ ☐

Les Brown's story ignited a spark in me that has never gone out. In chapter 6, I'll describe the challenges I faced a few years later, when my internal guidance asked me to take a new course of action: to play bigger and share my gifts with a larger audience.

Becoming the Architect of Your Own Life

When you begin to develop your Take-Action Muscle, a wonderful thing happens: crises become chances to go inside, review your priorities, and get back in touch with your true dreams. I meet so many people in my workshops and speeches who, like me, have spent years reacting to unwanted events in their lives with paralysis and negative emotions. Rooted to the spot, they cry, shake their fists, or hang their heads, unwilling to consider even for a moment that it's still in their power to take action to create the life they want. They've stopped believing (at least temporarily) that they, and only they, are the architects of their lives. In these moments of relinquishing their power to the unwanted event, they miss the growth and deepening of self-knowledge that happens when you reach inside and hold tight to your higher purpose for being here on earth.

Don't get me wrong. I'm not telling you to stuff your emotions when your dreams collapse around you or pretend that nothing affects you by putting on a "happy mask." I encourage you to have your tears or your anger-storm! Acknowledging those feelings is very important in your process. What I am saying is don't get stuck there.

Some people would rather cling to their painful stories than try to go for something greater and risk failing. The first option may seem easier, but the cost is far greater in the end. It's true that you'll probably meet with some setbacks and failures if you dare to take action to create a better life for yourself. At times, you may feel embarrassed. People may mock you for having tried to do something great and momentarily fallen on your face. But once you start to take action, you've broken the spell of hopelessness. And once you've tasted the sweetness of your own passion and purpose, nothing else will satisfy your palate but heading toward your destiny—and reaching it.

In my case, once I moved off the nail, I could see that I had been held back more by my ignorance than by my fear. I simply hadn't known that I could reconnect with my inner truth, write down what I wanted in my life, and boldly take action to turn it into my new reality. I'd felt as though I were in a prison, but the prison had been all in my mind. Once I started using my Take-Action Muscle, I realized I could have taken action at any point—if only I'd known I could.

You strengthen your Take-Action Muscle by being 100 percent committed to your desired outcome. I'm not talking about getting the great car or the fabulous house, or having a substantial bank account. Those are simply the small perks of bigger, broader outcomes, such as living in your passion, serving your purpose, having meaningful relationships, and feeling connected to a higher spirit. When you become more committed to reaching those outcomes than to having your plan work out just the way you designed it, at the pace you prefer, and with the people you'd like included, you'll be inspired from such a deep, true place inside that you'll become unstoppable.

Then, watch out! When your clarity meets your conviction and you apply action to the equation, your world will begin to transform before your eyes.

In my workshops, I tell people about the mountaintops and valleys in our lives. When you're standing in your power, loving everything in your life, and your mind is at peace, those are the times you're on the top of your mountain. But when life seems out of balance and you're struggling to deal with your thoughts and emotions, then you'll know you're standing in a valley between the mountaintops. When you find yourself in the valley, the most important thing to remember is **don't buy real estate there!** Don't bring your iPod, your furniture, or any of your clothes. And please don't throw any pity parties there! Your job is to become aware that you're in the valley and then get out as soon as possible. Visiting the valley is absolutely okay; relocating to the valley is not!

It's helpful to learn to recognize where you are more quickly—to distinguish whether you're climbing up toward the mountaintop or getting stuck in one place on the side of the hill or even sliding down toward a valley. Wherever you are, focus on using your Take-Action Muscle to continue making the ascent to your next mountaintop.

You give your Take-Action Muscle a workout by:

1. Recognizing when you're moaning—stuck "lying on the nail"
2. Refocusing on your original goal
3. Being open to other, possibly better, ways to reach it
4. Keeping in view your highest dreams and the ways in which you want to be of service while you're on this earth

When you commit yourself to doing the highest good, living your purpose, and always moving forward, you're setting yourself up for success—*no matter what*!

INSPIRED ACTION STEPS

There's no better way to experience the benefits of taking action than to take action! Each chapter has Inspired Action Steps that develop your bounce-back muscles, but for the Take-Action Muscle, they're doubly important to do. Reading thought-provoking ideas and interesting stories won't build this muscle and transform your life; taking action will.

1. **Identify Your Nails:** Over and over again, I tell people that you must begin any process of personal growth by getting a good strong dose of reality. In this case, it means facing the reality of the nail (or bed of nails) that you may be currently lying on. These are the poor habits, strained relationships, negative working conditions, less-than-ideal health situations, or the precarious financial state that you have been complaining about for quite some time but have yet to resolve. The following exercise will help you to identify your specific nails—the source of your long-term complaints—and start the process of safely removing them from your life.

   - Find a toolbox in your home or visit the local hardware store and get yourself a set of nails of different sizes, ranging from as small as three-quarters of an inch to four inches. You could need three nails of the same size, so be sure to get three nails each of the same size.
   - Think of three areas in your life that are causing you pain or that make you feel as though you are lying on nails. For example, one area could be your debt, another could be your difficult relationship with a family member or loved one, and a third could be your dissatisfaction with your current job or weight. Then take each area and write it down at the top of a sheet of paper (three sheets total). Draw a horizontal line across the middle of all three sheets.

- Rate each issue on a scale from 1 to 5, with 1 being a mild level of discomfort, 3 being a greater, more constant challenge, and 5 being the highest level of aggravation and exasperation possible. Tape the nail you think represents the relative magnitude of each issue to the top of the page. (If they all feel like level 5s, it's okay to attach three big nails! Just be sure you have enough big nails on hand.)

- On the top half of each individual sheet (up to the drawn line), write down in detail the current challenges that make up that issue. You may describe it in paragraph form or make a list of each thing that doesn't work about the situation. Remember, this is about ownership and responsibility, so the problem cannot be all about someone else; you must keep yourself in the equation while identifying what's not working. This will give you more power to influence a new outcome.

- At the bottom of each page, make a list of actions, no matter how small, that you can take to impact and reduce the size of the nail that you have placed on the page. Your number-one goal is to get that nail to its smallest form, and then remove it totally. Ask yourself, *What must I do to handle this issue once and for all?* Again, think small, calculated steps, not huge, impulsive ones. A surgeon operating to remove a foreign object from your body wouldn't rush in and operate with speed and haste, nor should you as you remove this nail from your life.

When you follow through on your actions to improve each of these areas, you'll notice that the size of the challenge becomes smaller and smaller. When that happens, it's time for the size of the nails to get smaller as well. Simply replace the existing nail attached to the problem with one the next size down. Eventually, you should be able to remove the nail

entirely. See if you can remove at least one nail completely
from your chart within two to four months. Some will come
off sooner than others, and you may have a nail that takes
much longer to come off than you expected or planned for.
Don't give up if it takes longer. Just keep flexing your Take-
Action Muscle, and you'll find those nails disappearing in
time. When you're committed to exercising your Take-Action
Muscle, you will safely remove those nails forever.

2. **Reconnect with the Original Goal During or After
   a Detour:** Remember that one of the keys to building your
   Take-Action Muscle is to keep your destination at the forefront of your mind, even when faced with setbacks or in
   moments when you seem to be moving in another direction. For example, let's say you plan an elaborate vacation with your family, and everything goes wrong from the
   minute you get in the car or on the plane. This is when
   it's important to reconnect with the reasons you're taking
   this trip: to recharge your batteries, to spend quality time
   with loved ones, and to experience a different setting and
   try new activities. The sooner you can rededicate yourself
   to your original, greater goal, the less time you'll need to
   spend recovering from your disappointments.

   • The next time you feel that things aren't going the way
     you want them to, see if you can press Pause and focus
     your mind solely on your original intent. Start by taking
     a few deep breaths. Leave the frustrations aside and just
     concentrate on your chief goal. What was your primary
     purpose? Can you find a way to make that happen even
     amid a detour? Pretend for a moment that everything *is*
     going your way and that you are getting exactly what
     you want. Forcing this slight shift in your mind may bring
     about change in how you choose to go about achieving
     a certain goal. You may find, for example, that during

these little side trips, you discover insights that show you other, possibly better, ways to get to the goal line. This usually requires some flexibility, but with practice you can reach that goal no matter how many twisty turns you take to get there.

3. **Don't Get Stuck Moaning and Groaning:** It's human nature to complain, especially when we're feeling pain or discomfort in our lives. But as we already know, complaining won't get us anywhere if we're not doing anything to change our situation. The key is to stay moving forward, despite our complaints. Just as you need to become fully conscious of the nails you're lying on, you must also recognize the accompanying complaints as well as their effect on you. Though many of us don't complain out loud to anyone else—our grumbling is solely our internal conversation and frustration—it still has that same negative impact on our energy. The next time you hear yourself complaining, either inside or to someone else, take on the challenge of shifting your state from complaint mode to action mode. Answer the following questions, and act on your answers:

   ○ What's not working for me right now?
   ○ What do I want that will make me feel better about the situation?
   ○ What baby step can I take today to move in that direction?
   ○ What's the benefit to me when I take that step?

   Once you're aware of what you're complaining about, you can then gain greater clarity about which actions will move you forward sooner and faster. Action follows awareness.

CHAPTER FOUR

Developing Your I-Know-Like-I-Know Muscle
God Is Good, Good Is God. Woo-hoo!

"EVERYTHING WILL BE OKAY."

How many times have you heard these words—or *needed* to hear them? And how many times have you said them quietly to yourself but didn't trust enough in their truth to move forward with real confidence? Imagine knowing that things will work out for the best—even when you can't see any evidence of that and have no idea how it could happen!

Having this true sense of trust is what I call the I-Know-Like-I-Know Muscle, and it comes from being connected to something bigger than yourself. When this muscle is strong, you won't have to try to convince yourself that your highest good is waiting for you, because you'll already *know*.

Notice that I'm not using the word *believe*. That's because knowing is a step beyond believing. Think about it: often when you say that you believe in something, there is a part of you that isn't sure. You're still talking yourself into whatever it is that you're hoping to believe. Knowing, on the other hand, is said and done. You're sold, and now it's nonnegotiable. This is complete and pure trust, the kind of unwavering faith a child has in a mother.

The benefits of a toned I-Know-Like-I-Know Muscle are tremendous. It gives you both the freedom to do and try anything, as well as a unique peace of mind that's impervious to confusion and fear. It closes the door to chaos and anxiety. Picture a glass of oil and water. The oil represents all your doubt and fears, and the water stands for your faith. You know from experience that the two simply don't mix. In the same way, when your I-Know-Like-I-Know Muscle is strong, your doubts and fears can't affect your faith. You know, *without any question,* that you'll be all right.

I first found this muscle during a very dark time in my life. There was very little on the outside to show me things would be okay—in fact, it appeared quite the opposite—so I had to reach inside myself and search for that encouragement and safety, that *knowingness*. I found it through my connection to my Higher Power and then held on tight. But in order to make that connection, I first had to go beyond the concepts of God and godliness I'd formed in childhood.

Searching for God

"Young lady! Just where do you think you're going with those bare, skinny little legs?" Scowling, Sister Brown, my childhood Sunday-school teacher, peered at me as I made my way to my chair.

I froze in terror, momentarily struck dumb. I'd fallen on my way to Sunday school, scraping my knee and ripping and bloodying my clean white stockings. Arriving at church, I'd hurried into the restroom, pulled off the ruined hose, and stuffed them in the trash can. I'd miss class if I went back home to get a fresh pair and figured that God would accept me with or without stockings.

Sister Brown, a large, imposing woman with a voice to match, had a different opinion. Before I could say a word, she yelled at me, "You are disrespecting God's house, and I will not stand for it!" Pointing at a hard, wooden chair in the corner, she said, "Sit there, and I'll deal with you later."

All through the Bible lesson, whenever she spoke of the things we do that displease God, she would stare at me pointedly until the other students looked, too. Seeing the judgment in my friends' eyes was painful and humiliating. After class, while Sister Brown chatted with the parents coming to pick up their kids, I slid out the back door and ran as fast as I could down the alley toward my grandmother's house, crying and asking God why He had chosen such a mean lady to work in His house.

Though I continued going to church (though never bare-legged again), it was the beginning of my powerful aversion to what I called the "Holy Guacamole" crowd, those members of the congregation I felt were "pimp-slapping" me with the Bible—as though I was a heathen from hell who'd never be good enough to have a relationship with God. Instead of being welcomed and embraced, I felt judged.

Still, I definitely wanted a relationship with God. My grandmother Bernice always lived that way, and I saw her walk with confidence and grace as a result. But it just seemed too painful to put up with the Holy Guacamole crew to get there. *If that's the only way to get to heaven*, I thought, *I pass.*

Eventually, the resentment and discomfort I felt overwhelmed me. By the time I was sixteen years old, I'd had enough of the fear and the judgment. I threw up my hands about the whole church experience, hoping that I'd find my connection to God some other way.

For the next few years, I rarely picked up a Bible and only attended church once a year, on Easter. I didn't think much about

I'M NOT ALONE Have you ever felt so judged by a person or group that even though you knew you needed the connection and support they had to offer, you still decided to step away from all of it to protect your heart?

Check one box if you've ever felt this way. Check two boxes if this is or has been a serious issue for you. Check all three boxes if you are currently overwhelmed by this feeling or have been in the past.

spirituality one way or the other, until a long-buried memory brought me to my knees, causing me to seek refuge in God.

A Plea Born of Pain

It started innocently enough. I was nineteen and had already left college. One afternoon, I was sitting with my three cousins, going through a stack of old photos, when I came across a photo of a teenage boy I didn't recognize. Instantly, my heart started pounding and I could barely breathe. It felt as though a blanket of rage covered me.

"Who is this boy?" I said, almost choking on my fury. "Somebody tell me!" When my cousins didn't know, I ran into my aunt's room. "Auntie, auntie," I said, showing her the picture. "Who is this person?"

She paused for a moment, thinking, and then said, "Oh, that's the son of the woman who used to babysit for you and your brother and cousins."

I stared at the picture, my head spinning. *What was going on?* I didn't know him personally, yet I was sure I'd been around him—and that I hated him. Despite my inner turmoil, I kept my feelings to myself.

I took the picture home with me and stared at it off and on for the rest of the afternoon, trying to understand my connection to this person. So he was my babysitter's son. What did that mean to me? At one point, I had an overwhelming desire to wash my body. I turned the water to hot and, stepping into the shower, I scrubbed myself until my skin hurt. Afterward, I grabbed my towel and began drying myself off.

Suddenly, it seemed as though everything slowed down around me. As I touched my body, rubbing the towel over my thighs, I remembered—in great detail—that *he* had touched my body, too. The impact of the memory was like a car smashing into me. I began to shake and cry uncontrollably, my head spinning until I could barely stand.

Still clutching my towel, I fell back onto the toilet seat, frozen in horror as a montage of streaming video ran through my head: The boy in the photo sending my brother and cousins out of the room, unzipping his pants, and then forcing me, just a five-year-old little girl, to put my mouth on his penis. In the next painful scene, he is saying I must never, ever tell anyone what he'd done. If I did, he threatened to beat me up and promised that my parents would also give me a spanking. Though I'm not sure precisely how many times it happened, I'm certain that it happened more than once.

Remembering this, I experienced a taste in my mouth that caused my stomach to churn. Grabbing an almost full bottle of Listerine, I gargled over and over, swallowing much of it, until the bottle was empty.

The pain in my chest was unbearable. I felt like I needed to punch something or speed in a car. I didn't want to do anything stupid, but I knew I had to release my growing rage. Thinking fresh air might help, I went outside. The hurdle my father had set up in our yard when I was in high school was still there. I started running over the hurdle—sprinting about

20 or 30 yards and leaping over the bar, then running back to do it again, remembering more details with every lap. No one was home to see me, so I did this for about two hours straight, until I was too exhausted to be angry. Finally, I went inside and cried myself to sleep.

The next morning, I woke up with a throbbing headache and my eyes swollen shut. My father noticed my red, puffy eyes and slow movements and asked me what was wrong. I told him that I had allergies. I couldn't bear to tell him the truth.

For the next six months, though I didn't actively search for the young man who had molested me, I was on the lookout for him. I'd memorized his picture—he had a large Afro, caramel-colored skin, and a strong, chiseled chin. Every time I saw someone with an Afro walk by, I'd crane my neck to see if it was him. I wasn't sure what I'd do if I found him; I just knew that I wanted to hurt him as much as he'd hurt me.

I'M NOT ALONE

Have you ever had someone violate you in a way that left you filled with hurt, anger, feelings of victimization, or the desire for revenge?

Check one box if something like this has ever happened to you. Check two boxes if these feelings consumed you for a time. Check three boxes if you're still trying to figure out how to get past what happened and the feelings it created in you. (Remember you're not alone; we're checking these boxes together.)

As time went by, I continued to feel rage toward my molester. Consumed with hurt and anger, I felt as if my body, mind, and spirit were all out of sync. I'd heard that being angry at someone who'd hurt you was like drinking poison and expecting that person to die. Yet with every hate-filled thought of him, I took another sip of poison.

One Friday night, I sat in my bedroom, feeling more hopeless than ever. My grandmother used to tell me as a child, "When there's no place to run, go and give your troubles to God, baby. Just go to God, and God will always be there." Remembering her words, I fell to my knees and cried out, "Lord, please help me get through this. I want to be okay with myself in spite of what's happened to me." I was counting on God to accept my direct and honest appeal and not to care that I'd rejected His church and so many of the people in it.

I poured my whole being into my prayer. "Please help me release the vengeance and hatred that's in my heart toward this man and put compassion and forgiveness there instead. I need your help, God; I can't do this by myself."

In that moment, I took the first step toward letting go of the anger and victimhood I'd been holding on to so tightly. It was as though I took my first deep breath in six months. I'd been afraid of my anger and of what I might do. When I opened up and asked for help, I finally gave myself permission to trust myself again.

Opening Up

"Opening up to God." I'm sure many of you have heard that phrase before—but what does it really mean? And how do you do it?

First, it helps to understand what I mean by God. My experience of God is defined by my strong Baptist background, but that may not work for you. Perhaps you refer to God as Nature, Spirit, the Creator, the Universe, Universal Power, Mother/

Father God, your Higher Self, or simply the unnamed owner of your inner soul, your spiritual awareness. Whenever you see the word *God* in this book, know that you can translate that word to whatever feels right for you. The important point to recognize is that there is something higher operating within all of us—and it's operating in our favor. Your I-Know-Like-I-Know Muscle helps you to feel supported and connected to this Higher Power, whatever you decide to call it.

When you use your I-Know-Like-I-Know Muscle, you won't need anyone else to tell you how to link yourself to that divine source of strength. When I made my appeal for help that Friday night, I spoke directly to God, saying, "It's between you and me, God." The Holy Guacamole people were no longer sitting on my conscience, blocking my path to God. Once I entered a one-on-one relationship with God, my connection was pure and direct.

Opening yourself up to your Higher Power is not difficult—in fact, you start by not doing anything at all. To activate your I-Know-Like-I-Know Muscle, let go of all your efforts to solve and resolve your situation and be still. In that quiet, you'll find you're better able to identify what's really going on inside of you.

The next step is to let down your guard, to surrender. This may require a little bit of courage, because you're making yourself vulnerable at a very deep level. But a crucial part of developing your I-Know-Like-I-Know Muscle is realizing that there's nothing to be scared of. God isn't like anyone you've ever met. This divine and universal Power is in a whole other realm. Take any love you've ever experienced and multiply that by a million. Then make it available to everyone, everywhere. Think of forgiveness offered freely at all times, for anything. Finally, picture the sunset, the rain, the oceans, and the mountains—the entire magnificence of creation. That's what I mean by God.

For me, letting down my guard meant trusting that even though I had bad-mouthed the church, even though I'd fallen away from my walk with God, I could still come back—and be welcomed. It meant knowing that a power greater than me would help me with my anger, fear, and pain.

What would letting down your guard mean for you? Admitting that you need help? Or maybe accepting that you deserve love? Whatever it is, to strengthen your I-Know-Like-I-Know Muscle, this is where you begin—by being willing to reach out from where you are, alone and in the dark, to a source of love and power you may not be able to see.

After years of longing and hoping, I finally discovered how to open up my heart to a higher power. Appealing directly to God and feeling that He was there for me was a step in the right direction, but I still had a long way to go to fully "know-like-I-know."

Baby Steps

For the next two years, I lived day by day. I hadn't eliminated all my pain, so I worked hard, partied hard, and had relationship after relationship, hoping to find the experience of true love that could make some of my hurt go away. Though I had reached out to a Higher Power, I hadn't truly formed an ongoing connection.

Then one Sunday, a neighbor invited me to attend services with her. My first thought was, *Oh no, another one of these Holy Guacamole people attempting to save my soul.* Trying to get out of it, I told her that I wasn't dressed properly. (I was in sweats.) She said that's okay, you can go just as you are. That intrigued me. Remembering Sister Brown's meltdown over my stockings, I wanted to see the church that allowed you to attend wearing sweats, so I accepted her invitation.

During the service, my mind was so full of fearful chatter about what a sinner I was that I couldn't hear a lot of what the minister was saying. Yet every time the congregation sang, they'd sing songs I could relate to: songs about imperfection, loneliness, and need. I began to think that maybe I wasn't so different from these people after all, and the wall I'd built around my heart began to slowly crumble. I sat in the pew and cried for the entire service.

Afterward, though apprehensive about approaching the pulpit, I walked to the front of the church. The minister, a woman named Argie Taylor, took one look at my tear-stained face and opened her arms to me. I fell into her embrace, laying my head on her chest as if she were my mother. Pastor Taylor held me tightly as I sobbed, caressing my back and stroking my head. I didn't feel any judgment or ridicule or damnation. No fire and brimstone, just love and acceptance. When I finally stopped crying, she asked me if I'd stay behind until she'd finished greeting the rest of the congregation and meet her in her office.

That day, with Pastor Taylor's help, I embarked on a journey of baby steps that would lead me to a new level of spiritual strength. Pastor Taylor started by asking me if I would be willing to give up the things that were keeping me from having a close relationship with God and to try leaning on Him for all of my needs for the next six months. I thought about the request. It meant saying no to the clubs, partying, and late-night dates that had become the main source of release and pleasure in my life.

"No, Pastor, I'm sorry. Six months is too long."

Then she asked if I would consider leaning on God for thirty days. I thought of all the opportunities to find love I'd be passing up for thirty days. "Sorry, Pastor, that's too long as well."

"Well, Lisa, will you try God for seven days?"

Once more, I deliberated. I was sure that if I changed my lifestyle and put off my friends and lovers for just seven days, I'd still be able to reconnect with everyone if this "lean-on-God-totally" thing didn't work out, so I agreed.

At first it was hard; I worried a lot about what I was missing. But with each passing day, as I studied the scriptures, read the affirmations, and listened to the tapes Pastor Taylor had given me, I noticed that my heart felt good, and I felt stronger than I had in a long time.

The next Sunday, I went to church again. Afterward, I visited with Pastor Taylor, who asked if I would be willing to renew my commitment for another seven days. I agreed.

By the end of the third week, I could feel that my energy had shifted. I walked with more spring in my step, my shoulders were relaxed, and instead of slipping out right after services and running to the pastor's office for refuge, I was sticking around and talking with the other church members. I didn't worry about the partying or the dates I was missing because the feeling of belonging that I'd tried to gain from those activities was now coming from my connection to Spirit and my new church community. That Sunday, when Pastor Taylor asked me if I'd try God for another seven days, I shook my head and said, "No, I won't."

That surprised her—but the startled expression on her face disappeared with my next words. Smiling, I told her, "I'll try God . . . for a lifetime."

I had finally found a way to have a relationship with God.

At first, it took energy to keep this relationship going, like cupping your hands around a flame to protect it from the wind. I committed to opening my ears and my heart to my Higher Power. When faced with choices, I began asking myself, "Would this show people the God in me?" This caused me to clean up my act, though I wasn't ready to change completely. I like to say that I "switched out of the fast lane, but didn't exit the highway." As time passed, though, my feelings of connection to my Higher Power grew more and more steady and soon began to give me energy—and strength—when things went wrong in my life.

I'll Help You Vacuum, Honey!

Too many of us have it backwards when it comes to having a relationship with our Higher Power. We want to invite Spirit into our lives, but we think we have to be worthy first. The truth is, you're already worthy. There are no prerequisites for having a relationship with your Higher Power.

Step number one for me was to let go of the crazy notion that I had somehow wronged God in the past. Not wearing tights in church? Not praying or going to services on a regular basis? I was able to release all these reasons for feeling unworthy when I realized they had nothing to do with my being able to establish and maintain a meaningful connection to my Higher Power.

To develop the I-Know-Like-I-Know Muscle, you need to accept exactly where you are in relationship to your Higher Power and drop the idea that you have to be perfect before you can let God in. The irony is that God is sitting on the doorstep waiting while you think you have to clean house. In reality, He doesn't care if your house is dirty; He wants to help you clean things up. He's calling through the door, "If you let me in, I'll help you vacuum, honey!" He wants to uplift your life.

Your trust in Spirit can help build your I-Know-Like-I-Know Muscle. But remember, though having a strong I-Know-Like-I-Know Muscle definitely smooths the road ahead of you, it doesn't mean getting a free ride. When you submit your burdens to your Higher Power, you remain responsible for the part that you've played in them as well as for creating solutions to them. You *share* them with your Higher Power so you can free yourself from their overwhelming hold on you.

For example, if you are having financial trouble, you can't just give your debts to God. But knowing that things will work out makes it easier for you to take action and accept responsibility for what needs to be done. Do you increase your revenue stream? Do you go out and find new ways to make money so you can clear up your debt? Of course! Though your Spirit will light your path, it's up to you to take the physical steps forward.

You can always tell when you've given something to a Higher Power and you're working with the I-Know-Like-I-Know Muscle, because you act with a sense of peace and clarity. If you're feeling stressed and anxious, it means that you've taken all your burdens back from your Higher Power. You're afraid it won't deliver. When you lose that conviction and are only wishing and hoping for a good solution, the nervous chatter in your head distracts you. You're not in tune with what your steps should be.

Trusting that there will be a good outcome allows you to think more clearly. Once you've opened up to Spirit and have begun exercising your I-Know-Like-I-Know Muscle, all you have to do is listen. You'll hear, "Look, go this way; do this." Suddenly, you'll see a clearer road map to follow as you let your Higher Power step in and help you succeed.

It was knowing—beyond a shadow of a doubt—that God would always catch me that got me through one of the most frightening falls of my life.

I Will Never Leave You

About a year after meeting Pastor Taylor, the luxury auto accessory company I worked for was investigated for embezzling funds from its parent company. My position was at the order desk, and I had unknowingly been a part of a scam that involved placing falsified orders. I did what I was told to do, processing the order slips that came across my desk without question. Though there were criminal dealings going on, I'd been clueless. Yet none of that mattered. Charged with committing fraud, my neck was on the chopping block, and I learned that my innocence might not be enough to protect me.

For as long as I could remember, I'd feared going to jail—or Club Fed, as it was called in my neighborhood—and now it was a real possibility. With each court visit, I became more afraid, and would sit crying the entire time I was in the courtroom, unable to stop. Then one day, a few months into the trial, I heard a voice inside me ask, "Why are you are crying?" Of course, I was scared that I might go to jail even though I was innocent.

The voice inside me said with absolute resolve, "Lisa, when you accepted a Higher Power into your life, you received a commitment from God to never leave you or forsake you. If you go to jail, then guess what? God will go to jail with you, too."

Though I still didn't want to go to jail, when I heard those words, my fear dissipated into the nothing that it truly was, and I was at peace, strong in the knowledge that wherever I went, God would be with me.

Though I found new employment, the case against me and

I'M NOT ALONE

When we hear that still, small voice inside, an overwhelming sense of calm descends upon us that we never could have produced ourselves.

Check one box if something like this has ever happened to you. Check two boxes if this happens frequently. Check three boxes if you can count on that voice of wisdom and comfort to speak inside you whenever you need it.

☐ ☐ ☐

---

my former company dragged on for years. Month after month, I continued to go to court when summoned, but remembering God's commitment to me, I went with a sense of assurance and courage. Then, out of the blue, one of my biggest fears materialized.

One morning as I was getting dressed for work, two plainclothes police officers showed up on my doorstep with a warrant for my arrest. Shocked and upset, I asked why I was being arrested.

"We don't have any details, Ms. Nichols," one of the men replied. "We just have a notice to pick you up because of an FTA (failure to appear) and take you to the local station."

After reading me my rights, the two men walked on either side of me to the unmarked police car parked in front of my house. Despite the knot I felt in my stomach and the tears welling up in my eyes, I was able to maintain my composure.

As we drove, I knew I needed something to help me through this new and terrifying journey I was on, so I began focusing on scriptures I'd learned and affirmations I'd studied. At first, I mentally repeated the phrase "God will never leave me nor forsake me" but quickly decided that I needed something more powerful, something that would engage my heart. A song! I racked my brain trying to remember one of the many hymns that I'd learned, but for some reason, nothing came. I was still searching when we arrived at the Lennox sheriff's station, a small building located just a few miles from my home.

We waited in the parking lot while the officer in the passenger seat hopped out and went inside. He returned a few minutes later and said, "I'm sorry, Ms. Nichols, there are no female officers on site to book you." Something in the way he looked at me as he said this gave me a glimpse of what was next. "We're going to have to take you to Sybil Brand Institute for Women." Sybil Brand Institute for Women was the women's county jail, infamous for its overcrowding, violence, and squalor.

I felt my heart begin to beat a little faster. It was clear I'd have to go to a higher level in my spirit to get through this. As we began the forty-minute drive to the women's correctional facility, I was still unable to remember any song at all, so I created one. My musical talents are slim to none, but the point was to keep myself connected with God. I began to chant in my head, in a singsong rhythm, "God is good and good is God.

God is good and good is God." Closing my eyes, I gave myself over to repeating my new "song." I was amazed at how it filled me, leaving no room for any other thoughts—or fears. I began to feel my body settle into a peaceful place, and before I knew it, we'd arrived at our destination.

Creating a Safe Haven

When you're facing a fear-storm and there's no safe haven outside, a strong I-Know-Like-I-Know Muscle enables you to create one inside yourself. You can do this by visualizing a calming scene, singing an uplifting song (even making one up, like I did!), repeating affirmations that inspire you, or meditating—whatever you need to do to stay connected to the knowledge that everything will be okay. Each person's safe haven will be different. The goal is to find a way to rekindle those feelings of inner well-being and peace.

One very effective way to turbocharge the process of finding serenity inside is by getting the body involved through deep breathing. When we're stressed, we have a tendency to breathe more shallowly or even stop breathing for a moment or two. Think of a time when someone startled you. The first thing you probably did was gasp and then hold your breath. Once you felt safe, you exhaled in relief and began to breathe normally again. Unfortunately, this reaction doesn't help—it actually creates chemicals in your body that raise your anxiety level.

The next time you find yourself becoming tense, tightening up, and holding your breath, recognize your body's fight-or-flight tendency. To calm and center yourself and to become more grounded, begin to shift your breathing patterns by inhaling and exhaling more deeply.

A technique I like to use is to imagine breathing in something I need, whether it's power, humility, or faith, and then breathing out what I want to manifest around me, like peace or love or balance—or exhaling something I need to release, like fear or anger. Either way, this process will connect your mind and your body and allow you to access a deep source of strength inside, which, in turn, will nourish and build your I-Know-Like-I-Know Muscle.

In the Belly of the Beast

Inside the facility, I was escorted to a holding room where there were approximately thirty other women, some wearing their own clothing, and others, blue prisoner dresses. The room was filled with benches, and in the corner was a half-open door that led to a single, filthy commode. I could see the dirt and urine on the floor and the used toilet tissue cascading from the overflowing toilet. I took a seat on a wooden bench and leaned my back against the cement wall. Over and over, I kept chanting in my mind, "God is good and good is God. God is good and good is God." I had a rhythm going in my spirit that kept my body and mind calm; I could actually *feel* God's presence right there in jail.

Then the door to the holding cell opened, and thirty-five of the scariest-looking women I'd ever seen in my life filed in. Wearing orange dresses, covered in tattoos, and with faces hard as stone, they acted as if they owned the place. Some of them were more masculine than men I've known. They were cursing at one another and then began cursing at the rest of us. I learned later that those in the blue dresses were from the correctional facility, and those in the orange dresses had been brought down from the federal prison—women who'd been convicted of murder, sexual assault, drug trafficking, and robbery and who were serving twenty years to life.

I felt my fear rising and knew it was time to turn up my God volume. I closed my eyes and practically screamed inside my head, "God is good and good is God," and then I added something to give it more juice: "*Woo-hoo*!" "God is good and good is God. *Woo-hoo*! God is good and good is God. *Woo-hoo*!" I liked it. Now all I needed was for it to start working.

I kept my eyes closed and began to bob my head and tap my foot to my inner chant. I could feel my spirit rising again. God's presence was still with me, and there was a growing sense of peace inside. After a while, the noise in the room faded away. I don't know if the others stopped talking or if I just stopped hearing them. I was in a full-blown concert featuring my one-line song. "God is good and good is God. *Woo-hoo*!"

I'd been singing for what could have been hours or minutes, I wasn't sure, when suddenly I heard a voice close to me say, "Give her back her motherf----g sandwich!" I opened my eyes and saw to my surprise that lunch had been served. A small bag had been set in front of me and an inmate in an orange dress had helped herself to my sandwich. Another orange-clad inmate was standing up for me, demanding that she return it. "She ain't botherin' nobody. All she doing is singing that damn 'God is good' song. Give her back her damn sandwich *now*." Her comment about my song startled me; I wondered how long I'd been singing out loud.

The tall, mocha-skinned woman reluctantly turned around and tossed my sandwich back.

I wasn't hungry, so I gave it back to her and closed my eyes. "God is good and good is God. *Woo-hoo*!" I chanted mentally. Every time I sang it, it put something in me that I felt no one could penetrate. I kept singing.

Then I heard, " 'Scuse me, 'scuse me," in a loud voice. I opened my eyes. It was the inmate who'd worked to save my sandwich. "Why you keep singing that damn song, anyway?" she asked.

I noticed the women all shushing each other. In seconds, all sixty-five women in the holding cell were silent, watching me and waiting to hear what I would say. I guessed they had all been listening to me sing for quite a while and wondered what my story was. With more confidence than I thought I'd ever have in a situation like this one, I said, "Because I want to stay connected to God right now."

Then, not caring if they thought I was crazy, I closed my eyes and silently resumed my song, "God is good and good is God. *Woo-hoo!*"

" 'Scuse me, 'scuse me," the inmate said again.

I opened my eyes.

"You seem pretty damn calm to be in a place like this. Anybody can tell that you don't belong here, and you ain't even scared. What's up with that?"

I smiled and replied, "God said He would never leave me or forsake me." Then, before I knew it, I was telling her how I had the armor of God around me, and how nobody, I mean nobody, could harm me because God was here with me.

"Well, *damn*, what did you have to do for God to give you that kind of strength?" she said. "Because you know I done some bad things. I killed people, I prostituted myself, I robbed people." She lowered her voice so the others couldn't hear her next question. "Do you think God would do that for somebody like me?"

Staring into her hardened face, with her tattoos and don't-mess-with-me-I'm-the-roughest-woman-in-here energy, I could see the little girl in her still wanting to be protected. I leaned toward her and she leaned toward me. I said, "No matter what you've done before today, you still have the right to God's comfort and grace."

I could see her clinging to those words. Then the moment passed just as quickly as it had come. I gave her one last smile, closed my eyes, and went back to my safe space. "God is good and good is God. *Woo-hoo!* God is good and good is God. *Woo-hoo!*"

By the time they began to book us, I'd been in that holding cell for at least eight hours. I was fingerprinted, photographed, and handed a blue dress, stiff and scratchy and at least two sizes too big, to put on. When we were all processed, a tired-looking officer led us into a new, much larger room that held about three hundred women total—a spotted sea of blue and orange dresses.

We arrived just in time for dinner. I got my tray of food and found an empty bench to sit on. Looking up, I saw the inmate who had saved my sandwich walking toward me. "I'm Andrea," she said, sitting down. "What's your name?"

"I'm Lisa."

"Lisa, you going to actually talk during dinner, or you going to sing that damn song again?" she said with a smirk.

Her question made me laugh. Suddenly I realized that I *had* the peace I'd been seeking with my song—I had it with my eyes open, while speaking and interacting with another person. I smiled at her. "No, I'm not going to sing. I'd like to talk if you'd like to."

She gave me the first smile I'd seen all day. "Yeah, I'd like to talk."

She quizzed me about myself, and I answered: no, I wasn't married; no, I had no children; yes, I had a job, one I liked. I told her that I had worked for a company that was being investigated for fraud, and that I didn't quite know why I was here. I learned from her that she had been a prostitute for more than seven years, had murdered a john who had gotten too rough, had been addicted to drugs, and that she would spend the rest of her life in prison.

As we both peeled back layers of our lives, other women began to gather around us. Before I knew it, there were at least fifteen of us laughing, talking, and sharing stories. They'd nicknamed me "Little Oprah" because I asked so many questions of each person.

These were the same women whose appearance and behavior had scared me half to death just a few hours ago, and now here we were, actually enjoying each other's company. Accessing my Higher Power had opened my heart and made me less judgmental. I saw that these prisoners had the same fears, joys, and hopes that I did. Underneath our dissimilar exteriors, we were far more alike than we were different.

I was released the next morning, after a brief hearing with

I'M NOT ALONE

How many times in your life have you missed the opportunity to connect with other people because you've judged them by their outer appearance? Often we conclude from someone's demeanor, expression, or clothing that we couldn't possibly have anything in common with him or her—and then discover that we were wrong.

Check one box if you've ever had this experience. Check two boxes if you've made this mistake many times. Check three boxes if this is a bad habit of yours and is costing you feelings of connection.

a judge. He determined that the summons to appear in court had gone to a previous address and never reached me. I walked out of that dingy, concrete building crammed full of women who were sad, angry, or hostile—most of them a combination of all three—filled with relief and wonder. Although it was one of the experiences I had feared most in the world, I knew that my twenty-seven hours in Sybil Brand Institute for Women had been a gift. It was the first time in my life that I had felt peace in the very midst of a storm. There had been nothing in my surroundings to give me joy or serenity in my heart, yet I'd had them anyway. My smile and my laughter had been real.

Best of all, my greatest fear—the boogeyman of all the things that could go wrong in the unknown future—had disappeared.

In its place, I felt courage and a certainty that I could handle whatever was around the corner, *no matter what*!

Gratitude: A Direct Line to Your Higher Power

When you feel "I know like I know," you don't have to examine the trouble you face to determine if you can get through it. You don't have to measure how dark it is or how deep it is. You already know from inside that the outcome is going to be just fine, regardless of what you have to do or endure to get there. You feel, "I know like I know *like I know* that I'm going to land on my feet—even if I can't see how or when!"

You may be saying to yourself, *That sounds great! But how do I make that kind of spiritual certainty a reality in my life?* The answer is simpler than you might think: gratitude!

Taking time each day to feel grateful for what you've been given is like having a direct line to your Higher Power. It opens up an ever-widening channel for divine energy to flow into your life. But your I-Know-Like-I-Know Muscle isn't just for getting you through the hard times. It can also direct your steps toward having all that you desire in your life. Gratitude plays a part here, too.

Gratitude anchors you to the source of blessings and comfort and gives you confidence that you'll always be taken care of, aided, and guided. You move forward in your life fearlessly, with joy and excitement. You know that you're going to have *even more* to be grateful for as time goes on.

This is another benefit of gratitude. When you consciously appreciate the gifts in your life, no matter how large or small, it lays the foundation for more blessings to come to you.

A lot of people think that using the Law of Attraction to manifest their desires in life means simply imagining over and over what they want. That's only one part of it. What's more important is that you look for whatever parts of your dreams *already exist in your life* and feel grateful for them. This gratefulness cements the reality of that experience in your heart, drawing in more of the same. Then you can *know*—not merely wish or hope—that you are moving in the direction of your cherished goals.

———————————

Walking with confidence and trusting in your Higher Power isn't just for the lucky few. In this chapter, we discovered four processes anyone can use to develop their I-Know-Like-I-Know Muscle:

1. Opening yourself up to God, Spirit, Nature, the Universe, or whatever you call your Higher Power
2. Inviting that Higher Power into your life now (don't wait to be perfect)
3. Learning to access that larger source of strength at will through meditation, breathing, or prayer
4. Feeling the constant presence of your Higher Power in your heart through gratitude

Remember, it doesn't matter what you call this Higher Power; it doesn't matter if you come to Him or Her through a certain religious framework. What's important is to feel that you are a part of a larger whole and that that whole is on your side.

INSPIRED ACTION STEPS

Having a strong I-Know-Like-I-Know Muscle supports the Faith-in-Myself Muscle we explored in chapter 2. You "borrow faith" from the highest and biggest power there is. The exercises below will help you do this. The ultimate payoff is huge and can be life-changing for more than just you. When you have a strong, unshakable I-Know-Like-I-Know Muscle, you become a lighthouse for others. Your life takes on a larger dimension.

1. **Giving it Back to Spirit:** When we give our challenges to our Higher Power, we are free to resolve them without the anxiety that comes from uncertainty about the outcome. If you're not at peace about a situation, then you haven't fully given it to your Higher Power. In this action step, you'll design a releasing process, a physical or mental practice to help you let go of any negative feelings attached to a situation, even if you are still working on it.

   - Think of at least one situation from the past or present that you thought you had given to your Higher Power but now realize, based on your level of worry, hurt, anger, or fear, that you have taken back.
   - Write down the situation on a piece of paper. It doesn't matter whether the experience occurred recently or long ago; what matters is that you are still holding on to it and the feelings attached to it. Write down any details you need to in order to get the entire experience out of your head and down on paper. Explain it the way you would in a conversation or in a letter to someone you trust.
   - Now get a bowl, basket, envelope, or even a lockbox and label it "Peace of Mind." This is where you will put the paper to release your situation to a power greater

than yourself. By placing your paper in this container, you are declaring that you trust that this situation will work itself out and that you are choosing to move forward with joy in your heart. It's like mailing a letter; once you place it in the mailbox, you can relax and know that it will be delivered.

- If you prefer, once you've written down your troubling situation, go to the ocean or a lake or a river, and using an environmentally friendly object like a leaf, a rose petal, or a stick to represent your challenge, throw it into the water as a symbol of your release. Feel the peace in your heart that comes from recognizing the larger forces at work in the universe.

2. **Ground Yourself in Faith:** Think of three affirmations that remind you of your power. For example, "I've been created to handle anything and everything that comes across my path." "Situations only arise to allow me to prove my strength and my faith." "I'm the designer of my destiny." Write them down on index cards or Post-it Notes. Take five to ten minutes and repeat any one of them over and over again (similar to my song) with your eyes closed. Revisit this process as often as you like, each time choosing a different affirmation that serves you.

3. **Declare Your Victory:** In the morning when you look in the mirror, complete each of the following sentence stems with three different endings:

   o Today I feel more powerful and prepared because . . .
   o I know victory is mine because . . .
   o I choose to celebrate this day because . . .

4. **Cultivate an Attitude of Gratitude:** For the next twenty-one days, before you get out of bed, lay still and

think of ten things that you can be grateful for right now. They can be tied to material items, like having a nice car or a comfortable place to live, or something simple, like having a meal cooked for you or receiving an act of kindness from a stranger. Stretch yourself to find all the ways that God demonstrates His love for you through other people. (I suggest twenty-one days because experts say it takes twenty-one days to turn a behavior into a habit.)

CHAPTER FIVE

Developing Your Honesty Muscle
Keeping It Real

IF YOU WANT TO GET ANYWHERE IN YOUR LIFE, HONESTY ISN'T JUST the best policy, it's the only policy—especially honesty with yourself. Though it's common knowledge that lying to others isn't acceptable, many of us consider lying to ourselves perfectly fine.

Often we coast along in life, reluctant to face the truth—even actively avoiding it—and as a result, we repeat old, destructive patterns of behavior, which in turn compounds our mistakes. Instead of creating success, we make a mess.

Think about it. If you aren't willing to look at where you are, how can you get to where you want to go? When you're navigating with a map, you can't figure out how to get to your destination unless you know the location you're starting from. In life, this means acknowledging your present situation fully—which requires a level of honesty many people don't choose to embrace.

Having a strong Honesty Muscle is particularly important if you want to make progress in your life *no matter what*. When you're having difficulties, the first step is to look unflinchingly at your circumstances: face reality, no matter how unpleasant or painful that may be. Then, once you've got a crystal clear picture of your current position, the next step is to recognize how you have participated in creating it and own your piece without any excuses or blame. Only then can you successfully plot a course to a higher level of success, joy, and accomplishment.

Don't confuse being honest with yourself with beating yourself up. This is why so many people shy away from self-honesty. They're afraid to admit their mistakes because in their minds, it means they're weak and deserve to be shamed and blamed. But true honesty includes compassion, which involves acknowledging the good in yourself along with your shortcomings. **A strong Honesty Muscle allows you to identify and own the habitual patterns of thinking, feeling, and behaving that don't serve you and then to be willing to honor and celebrate yourself in preparation for shifting those patterns.** In this chapter, we focus primarily on identifying and owning your patterns. In chapter 9, we'll address the muscle responsible for choosing new and healthier behaviors.

When your Honesty Muscle is fully developed, you're able to be honest with other people about your life, too—even in the areas that you're still working to improve. You don't have to hide who you are and what you've been through. You can tell others your truth without fear, because you realize that other people's opinions of you don't define who you are and in fact aren't even any of your business. You can begin to stand in that powerful yet humble place of self-acceptance and finally show the world who you are: unadulterated, unrestricted, and totally free.

For me, the place I found it hardest to tell the truth was in the area of my relationships with men. I spent years engaging in self-destructive patterns by "looking for love in all the wrong places," and then fabricated stories with just enough truth around the edges to make myself believe that I was being honest. I was comfortable discussing my friends' men issues with them but conveniently avoided the same topic when the conversation came around to me.

Unfortunately, if we won't face things voluntarily, the situation usually gets worse and worse until at some point, the results of our past choices are staring us in the face and we're forced to deal with them. In my case, those results were so obvious and so life-changing, there was no possible way to ignore them.

The Room Called Love and the Door Called Sex

Things were going well for me. At twenty-five, I was enjoying increased professional success and building a strong spiritual foundation in my life, but as wonderful as those experiences were, they didn't warm my feet at night. The lack of self-love I still felt deep inside drove me to look for validation and love outside myself—especially in the arms of a man. I truly believed that the room called love had to be entered through the door called sex. I didn't want to say no to sex because I thought I'd be saying no to the potential for love.

The worst part was that I wasn't ready to admit that it was my lack of self-love that caused me to seek this acknowledgment from the men I encountered. I've always had the gift of gab, so I could tell myself and everyone else a good story about why I so often mistook sex for love. Initially, I blamed the men I was dating, claiming that they were all up to no good. Instead of being the Prince Charmings they portrayed themselves as, I said they were really dogs just looking for a bone. I couldn't face the fact that my need for validation had caused me to lower my standards. If I constantly ended up with dogs, it was only because I went looking for love in the dog pound.

I made it look as though I actually enjoyed the dating scene: being in and out of relationships, playing the field, and moving on when things just "didn't work out." I gave the impression that I wasn't fazed by a breakup or a man's failure to call me back. And in a way, I wasn't. On some level, I didn't respect myself enough to expect someone else to treat me well. But my undeveloped Honesty Muscle caused me to fool myself and others into believing that being a "player" was what I really wanted.

I'M NOT ALONE

Where in your life are you hiding? Are you glossing over problems in a relationship or a job, or ignoring a deteriorating financial or health situation? Sometimes we close our eyes and stick our fingers in our ears, steering clear of the truth at all costs.

Check one box if you've ever done this. Check two boxes if you've done it many times in the past. Check three boxes if you're a pro at denial.   ☐ ☐ ☐

I was always on the lookout for the perfect guy. One day, when our computer systems crashed at work, one of my colleagues suggested we call a computer repairman that she knew. When he walked through the door, the first thing I noticed was his stunningly gorgeous face and then the outlines of his six-foot one-inch frame beneath his crisp white shirt, striped tie, and perfectly pressed slacks. The man I'll call Isaac captured my attention so completely that I nearly forgot that my computer was ever broken. We were immediately attracted to one another, so the next day, when he called the office and asked me out, I quickly said yes. Though I wasn't willing to admit it, I hoped he would be my ticket to feeling loved and desired.

And he was. Isaac and I enjoyed thirteen months of frequent

laughter, wonderful dinners, memorable nights, and a special bond that served us both. I didn't fully understand it at the time, but I found out later that Isaac needed someone to lift him up out of the underground world of danger and crime that he was sinking into. As for me, I didn't stop to ask myself if he was really the best man for me; I needed to feel wanted, to have someone enamored with me. Isaac might not have been Mr. Right, but he was a great Mr. Right Now.

Then I learned I was pregnant. I was horrified—this wasn't what I had planned—but worse, Isaac was not the man I wanted to have a baby with. Though I had no direct proof, I'd overheard enough scraps of conversations to suspect that Isaac wasn't exactly an upright citizen. Once when Isaac was visiting my house, he asked to use the phone. When he began discussing things that didn't sound like normal business, I quickly headed for the bathroom, jumping in the shower so that I could drown out the truth. I wanted to stay in the relationship and convinced myself that his shadiness couldn't be that serious because he had a good job. I hid behind the belief that I could inspire him to clean up his act. Now there was nowhere to hide. I was twenty-seven years old and having a baby—Isaac's baby.

I thought about having an abortion but couldn't bring myself to do it. As soon as I told Isaac of my decision to keep the baby, our relationship began to fizzle. I saw him less and less, until one day he simply disappeared, leaving me to figure out my future on my own. My emotions were all over the place. I felt angry, hurt, rejected, and stupid, but mostly I felt abandoned. Though I didn't want to marry him, I still cared deeply for him and wasn't ready for the relationship to end. But none of that mattered; I'd made my bed and now I had to lie in it.

In those early months of my pregnancy, I beat myself up on a daily basis, reminding myself how different life was going to be with a baby in tow. *So much for my big dreams—I'll be stuck here in the neighborhood,* I thought. Though they realized it wasn't the ideal situation, my mother, father, brother, and extended family were confident that I would make a great mother and greeted my pregnancy with great joy and excitement. Riddled with guilt and shame, I couldn't wait for some of that excitement to rub off on me.

I'M NOT ALONE

Have you ever been so deep in your "misery story" that even when others in your life could see the positive in your situation, you remained stuck in your despondency and gloom? Sometimes we hide from the truth by ignoring the light—by staying in a dark place, rejecting the outpouring of support from others, and even distancing ourselves from them to avoid feeling their love and care.

Check one box if you can relate to this feeling. Check two boxes if you've been in this situation on a number of occasions. Check three boxes if this is something that you experience a lot of the time.

As my stomach began to grow, I worked hard to lift my spirits, but without much success. It was in my fourth month of pregnancy, during one of my West African dance classes, that something finally began to shift. That day, I stood to the side, preparing to stretch, when the instructor noticed my watermelon belly. Bounding over to me, she asked in her beautiful Nigerian accent, "Sister, are you with child?"

My head dropped, and I replied in a barely audible whisper, "Yes, ma'am, I'm pregnant." I braced myself for the scolding I imagined was to come.

"Sisters, brothers, gather around. There is something to share," she exclaimed with joy in her voice. "Sister Lisa is with child! We must cover her steps with prayer and give her our shoulders to lean on."

She looked me in the eyes and said the words that would begin my new journey of self-acceptance and even celebration: "Sister Lisa, you have been blessed with the assignment to birth a royal child. Take heed of your thoughts and your feelings, for this little one is connected to you in every way. God hand-picked you for this particular child, and He is *always* right."

Then the drummers began to drum intensely and the dancers to dance and bow in front of me. My soul leapt to the beat, and a joy—foreign but welcome—enveloped me. I felt my sense of dignity being restored. For the very first time, I experienced my baby moving inside me. It was as if he or she were responding to the drums and the love.

For the next five months, I arrived early to the dance studio so the sisters could wrap my belly in a special way to secure my baby. Then I'd celebrate myself and my child, dancing to the drumming with unbridled love and enthusiasm. This excitement began to spill over into every aspect of being an expectant mother. I soon gathered all of the parenting books I could find, watched any baby program that aired, and happily attended birthing classes with my mother and a close friend by my side. I wasn't certain what motherhood would be like, but I'd decided to dive in headfirst.

It's sometimes easier to be led to the truth by someone else than to blaze that trail alone. Other people's involvement in our lives can help us to not only face reality but to embrace the goodness that can emerge from even the toughest situations. I'm not sure how long it would have taken me to wholeheartedly accept my pregnancy had it not been for my dance class friends, but it certainly helped to have them open me up to a different, loving perspective. They allowed me to be completely honest about my situation—including how my pregnancy was truly a blessing.

There may be people in our lives who see and point out

what we aren't willing to look at and then offer support and encouragement for us once we do. This presents us with the opportunity to embrace our truth and take the necessary steps to face our future fearlessly and responsibly.

To boost the development of your Honesty Muscle, instead of ignoring, resisting, or "shooting the messenger," start listening to the feedback from the people in your environment who have your welfare and best interests in mind. This will help you learn to pay attention to your own inner wisdom and truth.

A Wake-Up Call

When the baby was born, Isaac decided to drop by the hospital to visit me and meet our new son, Jelani. I was cordial to him, but I'd had a C-section and was heavily medicated, so it may have been a case of the morphine talking more than me. In any case, I didn't express any of my feelings about our situation to Isaac. My Honesty Muscle was so undeveloped in those days that I hadn't let myself think much about it. I certainly wasn't ready to confront him or try to pin him down about his role in Jelani's life, so it was easier just to avoid the whole topic altogether. I allowed Isaac to hold Jelani as I answered his questions about the birthing process. We were both a little stunned by the reality of our baby and our new parenthood.

When I went home, my mother and the rest of my family jumped in to help me, and with their assistance, life settled into a new but exhilarating routine. The discomfort I felt about being a single mother was almost completely displaced by the overwhelming love I felt for my baby. Still, I wished that the situation could have been different and that I had the right man in my life, one who would share the joys and responsibilities of parenthood with me. When Isaac began coming over to my house once a week to spend the afternoon with Jelani, I resigned myself to his level of paternal involvement. Though it wasn't much, it was better than nothing.

Then, one afternoon when Jelani was eight months old, I realized that I hadn't seen Isaac in about two weeks. Another two weeks went by with no visit or a call. When he missed his fifth weekly visit, I knew something was wrong. I hoped he was just being flaky, but my heart raced at the thought of some of the things that, despite my best efforts to ignore, I suspected he was involved in and how they could end up. At that moment, the phone rang, interrupting my anxious reverie. "Hello, this is the operator. I have a collect call from Isaac. Will you accept the charges?"

Both relieved and confused, I quickly replied, "Yes, yes!"

The next voice I heard was Isaac's. "Hey, Lisa, I don't know how to tell you this, but I'm in jail. I know that this was something you *never* wanted to be associated with, so I hope you can forgive me."

Devastated, I fell back onto the sofa and sat speechless while Isaac attempted to explain. "They've charged me with grand larceny . . ." His words faded as my internal chatter got louder and louder. *Noooo! I can't believe this is happening. My son's father is in jail, and the criminal justice system is a part of my world now. What more can I be ashamed of?*

I was torn. I didn't know whether to sympathize with him since he no longer had his freedom or to scream and yell the obscenities that were flying around in my head. I kept saying to myself, *This is the very thing that I've worked so hard to avoid. I've tried to be careful about who I date just so I'd never find myself in a situation like this. How could I have ignored the warning signals?*

When I was growing up, our house was across the street from a police station. Sitting on our front porch, I often saw the police officers unloading the gangsters from the paddy wagon. Again and again I promised myself I'd never be a jailhouse girlfriend or a thug's "baby mama." I wanted more from my life.

But now here I was, a single mom whose baby's father was in jail. I did my best to block out this new reality, but it seeped in anyway, dragging down my self-worth. My sense of disgrace was so deep, I kept Isaac's whereabouts from everyone, including my family; it was my dirty little secret.

At the time, I didn't realize how secrets drain a person's energy. I'm sure you've experienced in your own life how much effort it takes to keep a secret, whether you're telling lies or simply withholding the full truth. This is because on the deepest level, living dishonestly is actually harder than living in integrity. You're going against your true grain.

Plus, when you're out of integrity, there's no way to grow or expand. The energy you use to keep your secret in place is the exact same energy you'd use to propel yourself forward in life. You can't expend energy in two places simultaneously. So for every moment you spend suppressing your truth or creating and living a lie, you're taking time, energy, and resources away from developing your power and expanding who you are. And you can't get that time back—once you've relinquished it, it's gone.

What's worse, when you hide the truth about yourself for too long, that truth becomes foreign to you. You begin to lose sight of who you really are. How can you live in your light when you're concealing yourself in the darkness of deceit?

I'M NOT ALONE

Have you started believing the stories you sometimes tell to make yourself feel better? When we rewrite history, we lose the opportunity to learn from the past.

Check one box if you know what I'm talking about. Check two boxes if you do this more often than you care to admit. Check three boxes if this is a real issue for you.

☐ ☐ ☐

In my case, it took another dose of abrasive reality to finally rouse me from my state of denial and passivity.

Into the Belly of the Beast—*Again*

Jelani was just approaching his first birthday when Isaac called again. "Lisa, I want to see my son. I know that I don't have the right to ask you this, but would you please bring Jelani to visit me here in jail?"

It felt as though I had swallowed expired milk. The idea of bringing my baby to the jailhouse made my stomach lurch. This was a huge request, and Isaac knew it. After agonizing about it for days, I reluctantly decided to go.

A week later, Jelani and I arrived at the Los Angeles County Jail. We sat in the waiting area, surrounded by the other visitors: most of them cursing, smoking, and arguing. I held Jelani close to me.

"Lisa Nichols for inmate Isaac Randolph." The booming voice of the police officer made my heart skip a beat.

"Open your purse," he said gruffly. Satisfied I had no weapons, he motioned Jelani and me through to the next room.

Next, a female officer firmly patted me down. Then, to my horror, she took my baby out of my arms and, unwrapping his blanket, patted *him* down. Handing him back, she instructed me to take off his diaper in her presence so that she could confirm I wasn't smuggling anything into jail. I did as she asked, my head spinning. I couldn't remember ever feeling so violated, angry, and ashamed.

Seeing Isaac in his "county blues" was a shock. Though I still cared for him, I was disgusted—with myself and with him. During our entire visit, though we kept our conversation superficial and focused on Jelani, inside I kept asking myself the same questions: *How did I end up at this low place in my life? How did I get here?*

As I drove home, I replayed the whole distressing experience over in my mind: sitting with the other visitors, being patted down by the guard, removing Jelani's diaper, and perhaps worst of all, watching my baby gaze solemnly at his father through three-inch-thick bulletproof glass. I glanced at myself in the rearview mirror and noticed that my eyes had lost a bit of the life they'd had before I went to the jailhouse.

I looked past my own reflection and into the backseat, where my beautiful son lay in his car seat, catching a nap as we drove home. I smiled at his chubby cheeks and his puckered lips, always ready for me to kiss again and again. Shifting my gaze back to my own eyes, I told myself, *Things have to change, and they have to change quickly*. I decided that it was time to have a heart-to-heart with myself.

For the first time in many years, I took a good, hard look at my life and my role in creating it. I spoke to myself out loud. "The reality is that you have a beautiful baby boy whose father is in jail. Although you like to think *you* are the victim and tell others that story as well, the truth, *the total truth*, is that you're in this situation because of your own choices. You're the one who is responsible here."

Hearing such blunt and open candor coming from my own mouth was shocking. Yet even though it stung, in a strange way it felt better than the half-truths and outright lies I had been trying to sell myself. With tears rolling down my cheeks, I continued to stand right in the center of my truth. "Lisa, you're better than this. You're making decisions from hurt, pain, and fear instead of from who you really are. So you made a mistake in the past; it's not too late to change what happens next. Let's bounce back and keep movin'." It felt as though I were pleading with myself to save my own life!

This acknowledgment opened a door inside, allowing the healing in my soul to begin. I'd been holding on so tightly to my mind's rationalizations and excuses that it had affected my body as well. When I finally let them go, even my grip on the steering wheel seemed to relax. I was ready to accept my reality and everything that came with it. With this honesty came a new sense of power.

I'M NOT ALONE

Have you ever hit rock bottom or someplace close to it and known that the only way you were going to stand back up and turn things around was to get to the nitty-gritty, undiluted truth—with yourself and about yourself?

Check one box if you've ever been in this space before. Check two boxes if you've gotten stuck there for a while. Check three boxes if you feel that you're in this place right now. ☐ ☐ ☐

Find the Dot: "You Are Here"

Picture yourself at a mall. You're standing in front of the kiosk with the giant map of the place, looking for Macy's. Once you find it, what do you do next? Find the dot that says "You Are Here," of course! Only then can you make the connection between the two spots and navigate your way.

I like to use this analogy when I talk about the Honesty Muscle because everyone can relate. Macy's may be having a huge sale—85 percent off everything in the store—but the only way you can take advantage of all those great deals is by knowing where you currently stand. In the same way, you have to find your dot in life before you can move ahead and really get to where you want to be. And that means being able to take an honest look at yourself and your situation.

Doing the work to locate the "You Are Here" dot can be very sobering and uncomfortable. That's when the people in my workshops sometimes look at me with twisted expressions and say, "I came here for motivation. Get to the motivation part."

I tell them, "All the motivation in the world won't help you if you don't have a specific course of action—and that includes a clear-cut starting *and* ending point."

But too often we don't want to discuss where we are. We think that's too private, too personal, or too painful. And yet this is exactly what will support our journey toward our goals.

So how do you do this, exactly? Just like I did: take a minute to stop and look in the mirror, even if only figuratively. Identify what's going on in your life *without judgment*. After that, you can begin to recognize your patterns—both the good and the not-so-good—and own them, especially the ones that can have consequences.

Owning the role that you play in your life, whether that role is right or wrong, happy or sad, is the most empowering action you can take. Though it can be uncomfortable and sobering—sometimes even excruciating, depending on your level of honesty and the outcomes that you've created—it's what begins to slide you from the passenger seat of your life back into the driver's seat.

Once I faced the facts, the first step was to figure out what I wanted to do about Isaac. I knew it was time to acknowledge my part in our relationship more accurately. To start, I decided to stop blaming him for deceiving me and take responsibility for the fact that I was the one who'd put the blinders on. I'd been very careful to avoid seeing the truth about him so I wouldn't have to address the things that were not okay with me. I saw that by not confronting him, I'd enabled and supported him to some degree in continuing his criminal lifestyle.

I also admitted that even though we were having protected sex when I got pregnant with Jelani, having an intimate relationship with a man I never wanted to have a child with was not a smart choice on any level. I recognized that if I'd been honest with myself about what I felt I deserved, about my worth, and about my true standards, I wouldn't have been with him at all.

After my visit to the jail, I was even ready to tell my family about Isaac's "new address." And of course, none of them judged me as I'd feared. This total disclosure on my part allowed them to support me more fully than ever before.

Facing the facts about my relationship with Isaac also freed me from a lot of the crippling guilt I'd been experiencing and allowed me to make a healthy distinction between my choices and those of Jelani's father. Without all the self-loathing and regret, I could think more clearly about what was best for Jelani and for me. I decided I wouldn't be frequenting any jails, but that I'd encourage any relationship Isaac wished to have with our son. I also asked my father and brother to spend time with Jelani so he could have men in his life who could be role models. And I made a decision to take a break from relationships for a while, to invest time in me and in being a mother.

Before, when I'd just swept the whole topic under the rug, I'd felt a generalized sense of shame and failure. Now I could see that Isaac was the one in jail, not me. I was free—free to begin a life with my new child and my own dreams.

Freedom and honesty go hand in hand, so although it isn't always easy to be truthful, it's worth striving for. The feelings that come up when you bare your soul to yourself may be uncomfortable. Nonetheless, you can still make the decision to move forward by meeting your emotions head-on and accepting where you are. As soon as you break through the barrier of avoidance and denial, the way ahead will become clearer. A strong Honesty Muscle engages your Take-Action Muscle. When you remove unnecessary emotions from the equation, stop beating yourself up, and reconnect with your goals, you'll know what your next steps should be.

Honesty Out Loud

As time went by, my Honesty Muscle continued to develop. I became more accustomed to being honest with myself and felt less need to hide my truth from others. I found I could be authentic with the people around me, both at home and at work. Still, telling my family about Isaac's situation was easy compared to telling Jelani. But I knew that being honest in my life meant no exceptions. So when Jelani was eight, I told him in simple and straightforward terms about his dad. Because I'd made peace with my part in the drama, I spoke without any defensiveness and was more detached than I would have thought possible. I answered his questions truthfully and completely as we talked about crime, prison, bad guys, and good guys.

Even so, I worried that having a father in prison would be traumatic for my son. I didn't want him to feel ashamed. He didn't *seem* upset, but I couldn't be sure. Then one day, I overheard a conversation he and his friend Jesse were having about their absent fathers.

It was right before Christmas. The two boys were sitting in the backseat of the car as I drove. Jesse told Jelani that he'd be willing to trade in all his presents if he could only see his dad again. My eyes filled with tears when I heard Jelani say he'd do the same thing. Then Jelani asked, "Where's *your* dad?"

Jesse said his father had died in a motorcycle accident. Then Jesse asked Jelani why *his* father wasn't around. I hardly dared to breathe. Would my boy lie?

Without any hesitation, Jelani explained calmly that his daddy was in prison. He summed it up: "My daddy's a good man who made a poor choice, so he's on a long-term time-out."

I breathed a huge sigh of relief. Clearly, Jelani had taken in all I'd told him and had made his own peace with the situation. I saw that being honest with him had given him a head start in strengthening his own Honesty Muscle.

My ability to speak my truth, anywhere and to anyone, has

also served me in my career, helping me to make a difference in the lives of thousands of people. The true strength of my Honesty Muscle was put to the test during a teen workshop I gave a number of years ago.

I'd asked the group to consider releasing their anger about past hurts, when one of the participants, a teenage girl, challenged me. "Miss Lisa, I bet you would stay angry if someone touched you all up and molested you. Wouldn't that make you angry?"

I was quiet for a moment as a battle raged inside my head. I knew it would be selfish to avoid this opportunity to help her, but I didn't know if I was ready to reveal that part of my life. Then I looked her straight in the eye and said, "As a matter of fact, I *was* angry when I was molested."

A shocked silence fell over the room as kids straightened up in their chairs and stared. I went on to explain how being molested had affected me, how ashamed and angry I'd been, and how it had caused me to look for love in unhealthy ways. My voice was shaky and tearful as I forced myself to keep taking deep breaths. It was the first time that I'd ever shared the story of my molestation with anyone.

As they listened, the energy in the room shifted again. The teens, who hadn't known one another before, began to bond, hugging each other for comfort, crying openly, reaching for tissues, and then handing the Kleenex box around to the others.

After the session, the hugs and whispered thanks I received as teen after teen came up to me convinced me I had done the right thing. Since then, although it isn't stated on my curriculum, I share that story whenever necessary. It's been the number-one most liberating piece of work I've done for both men and women.

Where in your own life could you be more authentic with others? And what's stopping you? Stretching your Honesty Muscle by revealing your truth to others can sometimes be hard and, like working out a physical muscle, can even make you feel a little sore. This is because it's human nature to be affected by how other people perceive us. We want to feel accepted, loved, and admired—despite our flaws. The funny thing is that when you're honest with yourself and have compassion for your own weaknesses, you naturally begin to love yourself more. This in turn makes it easier to be honest. Self-disclosure and self-love feed each other. It's up to you to begin the process.

Standing in your truth is a concrete demonstration of self-love. An even greater demonstration is when you're willing to tell the hard truths out loud and understand that you're whole and complete, no matter what anyone else thinks of you. Remember this: Someone else's perception of you doesn't determine who you are. It is simply an opinion. When you're able to affirm and confirm yourself, other people's negative perceptions and opinions of you become meaningless and have less of an influence on your behavior. In fact, what you'll find when you share yourself fully with those around you is that their love and admiration for you expands. Your truth becomes a liberation for others. It frees them to find and share their own truth.

A lot of us walk around as if blindfolded and gagged, too afraid to see or speak the truth, and this fear has paralyzed our growth. In this chapter, I've shared these particular stories—about having a lot of sex when I was looking for love and about my son's father—because they're the most uncomfortable for me to tell. But I did it anyway, knowing this was just one more opportunity for me to build my own Honesty Muscle as I encouraged you to build yours. I want to show you that when you tell yourself the truth and love yourself enough to share your truth with others, you find peace—and the wisdom to avoid going down that road again. Knowing which part of your history you don't want to repeat, fearlessly addressing it, and then giving yourself permission to move on allows you to begin an adventure on a whole new road filled with far more freedom and joy than you could ever imagine.

I suggest that you make a daily practice of "finding the dot." Each day, get up and identify where you're starting from in the areas of your thoughts, feelings, spiritual life, relationships, health, finances—everything! Some days you may be excited about where you are. Other days might not be as comfortable. Love yourself through whatever that looks like, and use the other muscles you've been working on, your Understanding Muscle, your Faith-in-Myself Muscle, your Take-Action Muscle, and your I-Know-Like-I-Know Muscle, if necessary.

When I drive to work or to run errands, I don't listen to the radio or to CDs. From the moment I pull out of my driveway until the moment I get to my destination, I have a long conversation with Lisa. I spend time really taking stock of where I am, facing my challenges, and celebrating my "wins."

It's important to remember that being honest with yourself has just as much to do with accepting your *breakthroughs* as it does with accepting your *breakdowns*. Looking at myself in the rearview mirror was a pivotal moment in my life: I was not only finally willing to face the truth about my situation but to begin to accept more of my greatness as well.

We lie to ourselves when we play small in our lives, when we play it safe by settling for less than we know we can be and have. We end up hiding our dreams and aspirations behind a mask of mediocrity, people pleasing, and conformity. In the next chapter, I share with you how this mask became increasingly uncomfortable for me to wear, eventually making me feel as if I were the size of Godzilla and living in a studio apartment. I was cramped in my own world.

Developing your Honesty Muscle requires courage, but no matter what you've done or not done in the past or what challenges you're facing now, it's truly the only way to build a strong future. Hiding from the truth by living in denial—telling yourself partial truths or lies—gets you only so far. Sooner or later, you run into a brick wall.

Strengthen your Honesty Muscle by:

1. Being willing to take an unflinching inventory of what works and doesn't work in your life
2. Taking responsibility for your part in creating your situation
3. Addressing the things that don't work with detachment and clarity
4. Embracing yourself enough to share your truth with others

The Inspired Action Steps that follow will guide you through this process.

INSPIRED ACTION STEPS

Honesty begins with self-awareness. When we are unaware of the feelings and beliefs running our lives, our ability to be honest—and to make choices about our future—is limited. The following action steps are designed to help you shine a light on your current situation and then to look at it from many different angles, allowing you to become more comfortable in your own skin and eventually to share yourself more deeply with others.

1. **Make a "Quality of Life" Chart:** This exercise will help you see areas in your life in which you are strong— where you feel balanced and fulfilled—and will also allow you to identify areas that could use improvement, areas that are out of balance or that lack attention or growth. This exercise ultimately helps you to get an overall picture of what is and is not working optimally in your life.

    • Start by taking a piece of blank paper. Draw a vertical line along the left side of the paper. At the bottom of this line, write "1," and at the top, write "5." Let 1 represent feeling stuck and unhappy. Let 5 represent feeling very functional, satisfied, joyful, and at peace. And at 3, you're in the middle—average. Now look at the following categories and rate them based on your level of satisfaction and fulfillment with each one:

        ○ Health
        ○ Relationships and Family
        ○ Finances and Career
        ○ Emotional
        ○ Spiritual
        ○ Intellectual Development
        ○ Service
        ○ Play

- Now write these areas of your life next to where you think they go on the vertical line. It's okay if more than one area is in the same place. For example, you may rate your health at a level 3, as well as your finances and career. The goal of this exercise is to visually experience how each of these important areas in your life measures up today. This allows you to prioritize which areas need your immediate attention so you can up-level your entire quality of life. Look at the chart and ask yourself the following questions: Where are you strong? Where are you weak? Are you sacrificing the quality of many of these areas for just one? Which of these do you feel are important? Unimportant? Why? Take some time to discover your real priorities.

2. **Play the Reversal Game:** All too often when we are angry at someone, something, or some circumstance, we hear ourselves saying, "I can't," or "I don't," or "Nothing is working for me," or "I wish." Statements like these set us up for impossibility rather than possibility. We try to place the blame on anything but ourselves for our situation, even if we're simply blaming the world or the universe in general. The Reversal Game will get you to shift that perspective—to see your part in creating a situation and then take control of it. Here's how you do it.

- Think of a problem you're having in your life or something that makes you irritated. It may have been something you've already written down in a previous exercise. For example, you cook for your family and feel frustrated that you can't lose extra weight, or your daily to-dos are so demanding and exhausting that you never have time for self-care.
- Write these annoyances down as you think of them. In the first of the above examples, you'd write "I can't lose

weight because I never have time to work out and I have to cook all the meals for my family."

- Now consider the *reversal* of these statements. Remove any "can't," "never," "no," or other negative word, and change the sentence around so it reads in the positive. There are no limitations. In the previous example, you'd write "I *can* lose weight because I *can* find time to work out and cook all the meals for my family."

- Notice how these reversal statements create a different energy in you. They empower you. Repeat these statements five times and watch how your energy shifts, and how your stress is naturally reduced. You may even find that the paths to get what you want will open up for you in unexpected ways.

Another way to do this exercise is to reverse a problem in the following manner: Let's say you feel that you aren't being appreciated by your spouse. Write the sentence: "My wife or husband should appreciate me more." Now write the exact opposite of that sentence, as in: "I should appreciate my wife or husband more" or "I should appreciate myself more." Can you see that these are true, too? How does it feel to look at what you can do in these arenas rather than how you're being acted upon?

3. **Be Your Own Counselor:** Look at the sentence or sentences you wrote in the last action step—the statements that identify the problems, the discomforts, and imbalances in your life. Pretend that a friend has come to you with one of the exact same problems you have. Though your friend feels like he or she has tried everything to fix or resolve the problem, your friend continues to feel stuck or off track. You, as a good friend, know in your heart that the person can move past this challenge. It's not something that will keep your friend sidelined forever. He or she simply needs to look at the situation differently, and you can help your

friend do just that. What would you tell this person? What thought would you have your friend focus on, other than the problem?

Oftentimes we are able to see clearly what others should do. Apply this clarity to your own situation; once you've identified the action your friend should take, try acting on your own advice. This process allows you to first detach yourself from the emotional charge that comes with your personal experiences. It further allows you to force a shift in perspective that can bring to light the logical next step to take to get back on track.

4. **Share Your Truth:** Find a Rocket Booster friend and share with the person something you've been keeping to yourself for fear of judgment, embarrassment, or ridicule. The toll this has already taken on your energy has been huge, and now you've chosen to end this discomfort or at least reduce the impact it's having on you. It's okay to start small, based on your comfort level, and continue to progress toward bigger issues. What you'll find is that you're not alone and that there's great relief on the other side of being honest out loud. Feel the freedom that comes with being transparent.

CHAPTER SIX

Developing Your Say-Yes Muscle
Being Willing to Play Full Out

Take a minute right now to say the word *YES* out loud. Say it with spirit, the way you would in a moment of triumph—when you lift your arms in victory, punch your fist above your head, or high-five a friend. Feel the power of "Yes!"

Saying yes to your own dreams and aspirations opens something up inside you and connects you to the force of life itself. When you say yes, you go beyond your fear and smallness and give yourself permission to hear, acknowledge, and move toward what life is calling you to do—those activities that make your heart sing and give meaning to your time on this planet.

A lot of people are stuck in their comfort zones, playing small because they're afraid to say yes to something bigger. When you continually choose to play it safe, life is mundane and repetitive—it doesn't have any flavor or depth to it. Developing a strong Say-Yes Muscle allows you to embrace your passions and share your gifts with the world. You can be more creative, more enthusiastic. Life becomes more fun!

Sometimes saying yes means saying no to distractions—the people, places, and events that don't serve you and take you away from your goals. At times, this can even include *you*. Sometimes your own behavior, habits, and choices are counterproductive to your success. Saying no is a potent force for good when you want to set a boundary or rise above a bad habit that's dragging you down. Just don't get stuck in *no*. Once you've said it, find your way back to *yes*.

I'm not suggesting you become a doormat and say yes to everything. You have to use your common sense and your best judgment when deciding what to do. But when you say yes to the right things—the right people, opportunities, and choices—it keeps you open and growing. It's the engine that drives the Law of No Matter What and moves you toward your destiny, toward your highest good.

Though I'd learned to say yes to some degree in my life, when I was asked to step up to a higher level of performance, one that challenged my beliefs about what I could achieve and disturbed my tidy state of affairs, I found myself resisting. Developing my Say-Yes Muscle had two stages: first I had to accept *what* I was being called to do, then I had to say yes to *doing* it.

God Had Me on Redial

I was flying high. The muscles I'd developed so far—my Understanding Muscle, my Faith-in-Myself Muscle, my Take-Action Muscle, my I-Know-Like-I-Know Muscle, and my Honesty Muscle—had helped me create a good life for myself. Two-year-old Jelani and I were thoroughly enjoying the mommy/son experience, and my career had taken off. I'd progressed from my training position at the software company to being a consultant to two large agencies that promoted economic development in Central Los Angeles. It was my responsibility to assist in the coordination and strategic planning of programs that helped local residents keep their kids in school.

The assistance we provided was comprehensive, including health, education, transportation, and housing programs.

Whether it was a mother who needed a bag of free groceries from our pantry, a student who had no bus tokens to get to school, or a child who required immunization or medical care, we were there to help.

One day, Stacy,* a divorced mother of four, came in crying, explaining that her fourteen-year-old son, Thomas, had recently joined a gang. Thomas had confided to her that he really didn't want to be in the gang but didn't know of any other alternative for keeping himself and his three younger siblings safe. Stacy was afraid for him and begged me to help.

My heart went out to her. I had never been approached before by a mother whose child had mixed feelings about being in a gang. Most of my experiences were with kids who were already totally consumed by that lifestyle. But the way that she described her son made me feel that it wasn't too late for him.

I spent the next few months searching everywhere for a teen program that could do three things: be a safe space where Thomas could open his heart and be listened to; provide him with new tools and techniques that were instantly applicable to his current life situation; and radiate such a great energy that he would want to come back again and again, thereby becoming his safe haven. I was shocked to learn that a program like this simply didn't exist. More than 90 percent of the programs I found were for kids ages five to twelve, and the few functioning teen programs I did locate had very loose structures. They provided a place for teens to hang out but didn't offer the emotional literacy tools I was hoping to find.

While I was conducting my search, I met with Thomas once a week. We became good friends, talking for hours while he did volunteer work around the office. Each week, he told me more and more about himself. I learned that he was smarter in school than he let on (because he didn't want to get hurt by the rough kids who beat up the good students), that he

---

* Many of the names in this chapter have been changed to protect privacy.

resented his dad for leaving his mom, and that he dreamed of being an engineer. I shared with him my childhood experiences of living between two gangs. I told him that I saw gang members as sad people looking for a sense of connection, and that I believed there was another path for him. I explained that the strength and intelligence I perceived in him were going to lead him to a better future.

We often played a game, going back and forth describing the possibilities we saw for the other. I'd say, "Thomas, what I see for you is a great career as an engineer," and he'd respond, "Ms. Nichols, what I see for you is someday you'll be a really successful speaker," and so on. We were painting pictures for each other, which helped him to visualize something bigger and better for himself. I found that his words were healing and inspiring to me as well.

When I observed how good he was at repairing things, I asked the building maintenance men to leave the things I needed fixed around the office for Thomas to take care of. We put little signs on the things he'd repaired: Fixed by Thomas. He loved the visual acknowledgment of all his successes and actively looked for things to set right. You could see the sense of pride and self-worth growing in him as he owned all his talents and accomplishments. As time went by, it became clear to me that until I found another place, my office was going to have to serve as Thomas's safe haven—though in the limited time we spent together, I couldn't do all the things I knew would help him. I could see he wanted to make a break from the kind of life he was heading for, but in between our visits, he still ran with his new gang.

Then, six months after Stacy's initial visit, I received the phone call that would cement my purpose and change the course of my life.

"Ms. Nichols, this is Stacy, Thomas's mother." I could tell that she had been crying, and I felt my stomach tighten with fear. "Last night Thomas was shot and killed by another gang."

Ring, Ring

Sometimes wake-up calls are gentle taps on the shoulder, other times they can knock the wind out of you, and on some occasions they're bombs dropped directly over your head. Certainly you've had moments like this, too. Whatever the intensity, these events make you stop, giving you an opportunity to examine your life and the effect you're having on the people around you.

Learning that Thomas had been killed was like a bomb. I remember gasping, slumping forward, and covering my mouth with my hand. I just couldn't believe it. Once I was able to respond, I managed to stumble through my condolences for her loss and an offering of my prayers, and then I asked what I could do to help. She asked if I would speak at the funeral, and I agreed.

I was about to say good-bye when Stacy said, "Ms. Nichols, I want to tell you something else. Just yesterday morning Thomas said to me, 'Mom, it seems like Ms. Nichols is the only adult that really understands me. She's spending a lot of time looking for a program for me to go to, but I think she should just start her own. She's already doing it for me, and I'm sure it would work for other people.' I just thought you'd want to know."

Those words ripped through me like another bomb. I'd done what I could to help Thomas, but it had been too little, too late. I sat at my desk and cried—for Stacy, for Thomas, and for myself.

The funeral was tough. I gave my speech, trying to uplift his family and friends, but the whole time I felt so helpless and guilty. Afterward, Thomas's words stayed in my mind for weeks, gnawing at me. I had to face the truth of what he'd said, and I kept pondering my part in his fate.

My inner turmoil intensified when my Higher Power began to whisper into my heart, calling on me to be part of the solution for teenagers like Thomas. I did my best to ignore the inner signals I was receiving, but God had me on redial—repeatedly asking me to touch, inspire, and transform teen lives.

Each time I felt this calling, I made the same excuses: I wasn't qualified. I didn't have a degree, certification, or even the proper skills. I'd be starting from scratch to design programs where there were none. And of course, the biggest one: As a single mom, I needed the job security I had. But these excuses weren't cutting it.

Again and again, I felt God nudging me to stop playing it safe. He had brought me through those tough years for a reason: He wanted me to reach back and grab a few teens—or a million or ten million—and teach them how to make it through the dark times, just as I had learned to do.

Responding to Your Call

Are you being nudged from inside to do something different in your life? Is there a greater future beckoning to you? If so, how do you respond? If your Say-Yes Muscle is weak, you are probably doing your best to ignore these promptings. You may be letting fears of failure and of losing security or other people's skewed perceptions get in your way, just as I did before I was finally willing to embrace my destiny.

A lot of people have security and stability in their lives from a financial standpoint but very little peace of mind or deep satisfaction. If you're working at a job that pays the bills but doesn't excite you, you know exactly what I mean. You go through the motions day after day, but your heart's not on fire. Deep down you know what you should be doing, but for whatever reason, you believe you just *can't*. And sometimes the truth of what you should be doing is buried so completely, you don't even know it's there.

Eventually, that inner voice will refuse to be ignored any longer. No matter what you do, you won't be able to escape it.

It will be there in your quiet moments and may even keep you up at night. The first step in strengthening your Say-Yes Muscle is opening yourself up to listen—saying yes to at least hearing what your heart and soul have to say.

Pretend you don't have to change at all and just ask yourself, *What am I called to do?* Put your fears on hold for now and take a good look. Maybe you haven't a clue what your calling is yet. For you, saying yes is simply answering the questions: "What are my gifts? What am I good at and how can I serve others?" Tune out the external noise streaming in from your life and listen. Allow clarity about your life's purpose to emerge from within.

When you finally get clear about your calling, it's possible that the people around you may not understand it. Why? **Because your calling wasn't given to anyone else! It was given to *you*.** It's as though you've been given a very special assignment that can only be accomplished by you. And it's your job to nurture that calling, to grow it, to be protective of it, and to plan for it so that you can make the contribution you were meant to make to this world.

When I first contemplated working with teens, no one else shared that vision with me. When I told people, "I want to teach teens how to fall in love with themselves and how to make integrity-based decisions," they all said, "Eek!" They thought I was crazy to consider working with teens, and most believed it would be a waste of time to even try.

In your own life, you may sense a calling to do something that may also seem "crazy" to others. Maybe it's starting your own business, counseling the homeless, or moving to a new city for a life-changing opportunity. Whatever it is, embrace the passion and enthusiasm you have, and don't let anyone else's disapproval discourage you. When you're willing to own and accept your calling, *no matter what* it is, you can begin to develop and grow your Say-Yes Muscle.

Testing the Waters

Though I wasn't quite ready to say yes to helping teens in a full-time way, I was willing to stick my toe in and test the waters. I began volunteering to speak at local YWCAs and Girls Clubs. I also facilitated teen workshops through Income Builders International (IBI), a networking and coaching organization for entrepreneurs that was a vital support system in both my personal and professional life.

Just as I'd experienced when I first began training clients at the software company, it felt so good to be having a positive impact on others. I loved spending time with the teens, and I knew I'd found an effective way to reach them by the way they responded to me.

Over and over I saw that I could make a difference in a young person's life. When I met Heather, a rebellious young girl of fifteen, she was already in juvenile detention for serving as an accomplice to an attempted murder. Heather's mother, whom I met at an IBI event, pleaded with me to intervene and help her daughter. Over the next year, I worked with Heather, helping her to confront her demons, take responsibility, and finally find freedom, direction, and the ability to make healthy choices in her life.

Then there was Tamara, who in many ways reminded me of myself at her age. She was student-body president, had an impressive 3.8 GPA, and served as a peer counselor. One night in late May, she called my house. "Ms. Nichols, you don't remember me, but I heard you speak two years ago at the YWCA. I've been accepted to six universities but I don't plan to attend any."

Surprised by both the call and her statement, I asked why.

"Because I'm sitting here looking at my suicide letter. I'm calling because I thought *just maybe* you could help me; you're my last hope."

Remembering Thomas, I knew I had to try to save this girl's

life. I asked if I could meet with her the next day. The next afternoon, looking out my office window, I noticed a sweet-faced young woman standing outside the building looking uncertain. I ran outside. She was turning to leave, so I called out, "Tamara!" The startled girl allowed herself to be led inside. She told me that she had been molested when she was ten years old, repeatedly beaten by her mother, and that she'd tried to drown her pain in alcohol and sex, but neither had eliminated her personal turmoil.

Together, we began a journey of healing: Tamara attended my teen workshops, did forgiveness and self-love work standing in front of my bathroom mirror, and allowed me to accompany her to register for college. Out of that shell of hurt and pain a beautiful, confident woman emerged, graduating from college with a degree in psychology and a desire to counsel at-risk youth.

During that period, I also reached out to women in recovery. My first paid speaking job was to a group of cocaine-addicted lesbian women. Sharing my own hard-earned lessons, I discovered two important facts: even though I had been wounded, I could be a healer, and certain truths applied to everyone—for example, your past doesn't equal your future; it's your birthright to be happy; and you don't have to keep paying for your mistakes. Though I wasn't in recovery or a lesbian, I saw myself in each of these women, and they saw themselves in me; all of us were working to accept our journey and create a better future.

These experiences, and many more like them, filled me with enthusiasm and confidence, erasing any doubts I had about my abilities. They also made it harder and harder to say no to what I knew in my heart was my life's true purpose.

Start with Little Yeses

Developing your Say-Yes Muscle begins with just one little yes. First, you acknowledge the call, and then you do something about it. One yes leads to another and another. And saying yes isn't all or nothing. You don't have to stop everything you've been doing, quit your current job, and plunge yourself into a whole new endeavor. The secret is to start experimenting with your dreams without disrupting your livelihood.

Flex your Say-Yes Muscle by finding ways to lay the groundwork first. You can volunteer in the field of your calling like I did or take courses that relate directly to it. If you feel that you're destined to be a writer but you've never taken a writing class to teach you the basics, set aside time each day to write, and look into enrolling at a local college or adult education center that offers courses. If the idea of teaching elementary school children makes your heart sing, spend twenty minutes a day researching what qualifications you need and think about volunteering part-time at a nearby school in whatever capacity you can until you get the right credentials. Small yeses allow you to do the research and homework that are a must before jumping ahead.

The point is, do something—*anything*—that lets you tap into your calling, even if it's only a baby step. Just a nudge in the right direction can have a great impact. Your confidence builds. You push past fears—at least the ones that are initial roadblocks. With each experience, you gain the clarity and confirmation you need to keep moving forward toward your ultimate goal. Then, as it happened to me, you'll start to see miraculous results. This is the universe saying, "Yes, yes, *yes* . . . now go for it!" And deep down you'll know you are doing something so important that no one can tell you otherwise.

There's a second level to developing your Say-Yes Muscle, too. Your calling in life isn't just about discovering your life's purpose. It's also about finding your passions, those activities that bring you immense joy and add to a fulfilling life. For me, doing African dance allows me to stay inside my bliss. For a variety of reasons, I'd stopped dancing when my son was born—there was no time, I'd gained weight, and so on. Recently, when I realized that for the last thirteen years my heart had been crying out to dance again, I took the opportunity to keep developing my Say-Yes Muscle by scheduling a dance class once a week.

What does your heart cry out to do? Maybe it's committing to practicing yoga on Mondays, taking hikes on Tuesdays, and cooking dinner with your best friends on Fridays. Your passion may say, "Take ten minutes to draw," or "Go and sing outside in the backyard," or "Turn the music up and dance this evening." Never lose sight of those things that make you feel wonderful and come alive. The goal is to spend your days engaged in activities that you find absorbing and satisfying, that you feel you're good at, and that celebrate you.

All my little yeses with the teens and women in recovery were preparing me for the big yes. Eventually, suppressing my larger dreams and playing small became so uncomfortable that I couldn't do it a minute longer. The truth of who I was and what I was born to do literally burst out of me—in a particularly public arena.

Saying Yes to My Dream

As an instructor at IBI, I was able to sit in on many of the inspiring classes that the organization offered. One day, the instructor of a workshop I was attending asked us to close our eyes and listen to the words of Dr. Martin Luther King's "I Have a Dream" speech so that we could get in touch with our own dreams. This exercise was so uncomfortable for me that I burst into tears and ran out of the room.

Sitting in the hall, I tried to understand why Dr. King's message upset me so deeply and quickly realized that it brought up all my fears about living my own dream. But as I searched deeper inside, I saw that if I didn't pursue my calling and stayed in my safe little world instead, my life would always remain mediocre. That wasn't what I wanted at all, and that realization brought an even greater discomfort.

I'M NOT ALONE

When you project your present state into the future, how does it feel? Is that the life you want to live? We try to play it safe, though it costs us our joy, but eventually the thought of remaining small becomes scarier than taking the risk to grow.

Check one box if you've ever felt this way. Check two boxes if you've wrestled with this dilemma a few times in your life. Check three boxes if this experience is all too familiar. ☐ ☐ ☐

Unable to bear the pain of saying no to my own dreams any longer, I took a deep breath and said yes. The relief was overwhelming. There was tingling all over my body as tears—this time happy ones blended with tears of excitement—streamed down my cheeks. It was as if the weighted boots I'd been wearing were gone, and I had wings instead! I had opened a door and stepped into a world that dazzled me with its joy and promise; I wasn't going back. Now all that was left to do, as Thoreau would say, was to supply the foundations for my "castles in the air."

Committing to Yes and Jumping In

A strong Say-Yes Muscle pushes you past your preconceived limits. When you say yes fully—and I mean fully—you let go of all your excuses and doubts and you accept the truth of your calling; you make yourself available for all that's possible.

You don't just stumble into yes, and you don't fall back into yes. Yes is a deliberate action. It's intentional. Every great musician, athlete, artist, doctor, parent, and business owner had to say yes with intention. When you say yes to *your* vision, it must be just as intentional.

A yes at this level means, "I want to play full out!" Life has just called you into a game that you were born to play. You might not know all the rules and strategies to win yet, but that will come with time and experience. All you need at the start is commitment and the confidence that you'll figure it out as you go along. This means engaging your I-Know-Like-I-Know Muscle, too, because you're setting out on an adventure without necessarily knowing the exact outcome.

Saying yes doesn't mean the fears will go away. Saying yes means giving yourself permission to play bigger than you've ever played before—*even if your knees are knocking and your teeth are chattering.* True commitment is looking in the face of fear and saying yes anyway. Then you embody the no-matter-what energy: *No matter what,* I'm going to do it!

Planning to Live the Dream

With my new level of clarity and surrender, I began to plan ways to launch my new company, which I'd named Motivating the Teen Spirit. First I set about creating a business model. I was a beginner in this area and didn't know a projected cash flow from a cash register! So I started small. I knew I needed materials to send out to potential clients and investors, so I approached a good friend, a graphic designer who supported my mission to serve and inspire teens, offering to cook several great dinners in exchange for some new business cards and trifold brochures.

Then I opened up a separate bank account I labeled the "Living My Dream" account and each pay period, after depositing my paycheck from work into my regular account, I wrote checks with "Funding My Dream" written in on the memo line for every penny I could spare—sometimes up to 40 percent of my paycheck. I cut every corner I could to deposit as much as possible into the account. I began to do my own hair and nails. I bought bulk foods and committed to cooking and not going out to dinner. I even took a new route home from work to avoid "the golden arches," which Jelani loved so much. I traded in my stylish car for a more economical one with no payments.

This strategy served me in many ways. In addition to saving money to start my own business, it also gave me a new perspective on my existing job. Before, I'd viewed it as an obstacle standing between me and what I really wanted to do because it offered me security. Now I considered my job the first investor in my business, providing me the resources to secure my future. This created a huge shift in my energy: I was working each day not only to pay the bills but also to fund the dream. I saw both a long- and short-term payout for my hard work. My attitude at the office was already good but got better with this new realization.

Over the course of two and a half years, I was able to save $62,000. Prepared to live on $31,000 a year for the next two years while I got my company up and running, I made the leap—leaving my job and my six-figure income, health benefits, and paid vacations behind.

For the next twenty-four months, I worked long before the sun came up to long after I put Jelani to bed, creating my new business. I spent a great deal of time learning from professionals in the areas of finance, investor development, and marketing. I was like a sponge, soaking up everything I could to bolster my very rudimentary knowledge in those subjects. Initially, it all sounded like Greek to me, and I had to press the stop button many times on my negative chatter that told me I would never understand the investor language of PPMs (private placement memorandums), term agreements, and ROIs (returns on investment).

I'M NOT ALONE

Have you ever set out to start something new and realized just how much you *didn't* know? When we don't manage our negative self-talk, we may hesitate to ask for help, or even worse, put our dreams back on the shelf for now—or maybe forever.

Check one box if you've had a taste of this feeling. Check two boxes if you're aware of this fear often. Check three boxes if your negative chatter about a new venture is overwhelming you.

☐ ☐ ☐

I knew raising capital was my next step so I asked my attorney if could sit in on meetings in which he explained the investor development process to other new business owners like me. It took thirty-three meetings before I understood enough to string the words together into sentences that actually made sense.

I used my newly learned skills to make presentations to potential investors, offering them the opportunity to invest in a business that taught teens how to fall madly in love with themselves and make integrity-based decisions. By the end of the two years, I'd raised more than $530,000 for Motivating the Teen Spirit. I was ready to take my commitment to impact the lives of teens to the next level. It was time to say yes to empowering teenagers not just on a local scale but on a national one.

Plan Your Passion and Grow into Your Calling

Saying yes to your calling doesn't mean saying yes to a life of scarcity, lack, and fear. Honor your passions and pursuits, but also respect your basic needs. Think about it: you can't be creative and open to your highest good if you're hungry, or the lights are off, or your bills aren't paid. Without those necessities taken care of, you won't be able to accomplish what you're truly here to do.

I'm sure you've heard the saying, "When you fail to plan, you plan to fail." Once you've said yes to going for your dreams, give yourself all the tools and resources you need, which begins with a plan.

A plan has three levels: goals, milestones, and steps. You start at the broadest level by defining your *goal*—the big dream you want to make come true. Then, you identify the *milestones* along the path to that goal's achievement. Examine the work necessary to make your dream real, and "chunk it down" into more manageable, time-bound tasks. Then, move on to laying out the *steps* necessary to reach your milestones: smaller specific daily or weekly "to-dos" that can be checked off when complete. All three levels of your plan must be clear and concrete—fuzzy targets don't inspire action.

When you consistently take the necessary steps, they add up. Over time, you can't help but reach your milestones. And when you achieve a milestone, take that opportunity to celebrate your progress toward your goal.

Set a doable time line to hit the mark. If you think you can do it in twelve months, allow yourself sixteen. Give yourself breathing space. The rest of your life doesn't stop while you pursue your calling. Choose a time line that allows you to give attention to other areas while you're making your plan happen. Then begin to take the steps.

Planning is not something you have to do all on your own. It helps to reach out to others who can offer guidance, support, and insights. Ask advice from people who have already been there, who have done what you are doing and are farther along the road. Too often, out of comfort and convenience, we spend all our time with the people who are nearest to us on the path—those who are at the same stage of accomplishing their goals as we are. Reach out to people who've already arrived by seeking mentors, coaches, advocates, and role models. Some of these people you have access to, others you can find out more about through research. Learning from their choices, both good and bad, can save you thousands of dollars as well as hundreds of hours of work, stress, and worry.

For maximum velocity, join organizations and networking associations that can function as support groups. On top of giving you encouragement and valuable connections, they also serve to keep you accountable. Voicing your deliverables to the group—I'll do X by a certain date—helps you to stay on track.

Saying yes also means saying no to the things that will move you away from your goal. For seven or eight years, when I received invitations to participate in new projects, if they didn't have to do with empowering teens, I replied with a loving no. Saying yes meant birthing my dream and being there for the long haul. I watched, cuddled, cared, and nurtured it until it was real, and I didn't allow myself to become distracted by anything that moved me away from that process.

I've also found that writing down goals and keeping a journal of accomplishments can be very powerful for keeping you on course. Use your No Matter What journal as a Yes journal, too—the place where you record the yeses you want to say and the ones you've already said as you move ahead with your plan.

You'll be surprised at how life jumps in to support your

plans once you take the initiative. Whenever you take action toward your highest good and the highest good of the people around you, the universe acts and operates with the same level of commitment that you do. The people, events, information, and resources you need begin to move toward you as you move toward them. It feels like magic, but it isn't; it's your focused attention and actions that draw them to you. You are the catalyst that gets the ball rolling. When you say yes and move forward with energy, clarity, and enthusiasm, the universe joins hands with you and becomes a willing partner.

Finally, your plan may need to be amended and changed as you go along. For this reason, saying yes also means saying yes to being fluid and flexible. There will be some days when you can sit well-grounded and steady in your vision, and there will be other days when nothing in your strategy seems to be going the way you planned it. You may need to get more money; you may need more time than you'd originally expected; you may have to change direction; you may even have to change partners. It's all okay. A strong Say-Yes Muscle helps you ebb and flow, expand and contract, and give and take as required.

———————

Your Honesty Muscle helps you embrace the truth of your past and your present; your Say-Yes Muscle helps you embrace the truth of your highest and best future. Each time you say yes to the inspirations coming from your soul, you take another step toward your destiny—your purpose for being born on this planet. With every yes, you pour a little more determination into your tank. You pour a little more assurance, a little more clarity, a little more passion and enthusiasm in, until you look up one day and all your yeses have placed you in a space of overflow. Then your life affects others' lives, enabling you to make an imprint on the world that will outlive you. With a strong Say-Yes Muscle, you experience a life of magnificence and joy, rather than just joyful moments here and there. This is why I believe that saying yes is the key to being truly alive.

To strengthen your Say-Yes Muscle:

1. Hear and acknowledge what life is calling you to do
2. Test the waters by saying yes in small ways
3. Commit to playing full out
4. Formulate practical strategies to live your dreams

The following action steps are designed to jump-start this process.

INSPIRED ACTION STEPS

Everybody has a higher purpose deep inside, but it can sometimes get overshadowed by the everyday routine of our lives. The following action steps will bring your higher purpose front and center and then help you lay out a plan for actualizing that purpose at your own pace.

1. **Imagine That:** Think of anything and everything you've ever wanted to do. Let your imagination run wild, and don't self-censor or limit yourself to "serious" activities. Following are some categories to consider:

   - travel
   - humanitarian service
   - the arts
   - education
   - sports
   - professional/career
   - play/leisure
   - love
   - personal image
   - health
   - . . . whatever!

   Just keep writing, and don't worry or even think about how you're going to go about doing these things. For example, don't deny a craving to travel and see the world or a desire to explore your talents in a more public manner just because you can't imagine how you could make those dreams come true. Come up with five things that absolutely get you excited just thinking about them. Notice how they make you feel alive. The purpose of this exercise is to allow you to feel the positive power and force that comes with acknowledging what's calling you—what's speaking to your heart.

2. **Say a Teeny-Tiny Yes to Start:** Look at the dreams and the desires of your heart that you just wrote down. Whether you ever accomplish them or not, you now have a clear portrait of your soul's character. This acknowledgment of your true self is a powerful step in and of itself. Now, to start the process of living the life of your dreams, look for ways to move toward any of these. If you wrote down singing, instead of just singing in the shower, consider singing at a supper club once a week (or at least doing karaoke). If you wrote that you wanted to be of service to others, instead of writing a check to charity, consider spending time at a children's hospital comforting terminally ill kids or visiting a seniors center and keeping someone company. Give yourself permission to explore the opportunities for fulfillment all around you.

3. **Go for Your Dreams:** Once you're clear about your five top goals and have decided to dip your toe in the water at least a little, it's time to commit to each one of them full out. One way to do this is by creating a vision board or book that includes all of your goals. A vision board is simply a colorful collage of images, pictures, photos, quotations, statements—basically anything you feel reflects what you want to do or achieve. Some things you can use to put this together include magazines, photographs, travel brochures, mementos, objects, lucky charms, affirmations, and even Post-it Notes or pieces of paper on which you write words, doodles, or drawings with a pen or marker. Again, this is where you can also let your imagination run wild. The mere act of creating a vision board or book is fun and exhilarating, and will tap into a part of you that will serve as your inner fire. Even more ideas will surface. The vision

board is your physical, real-life declaration of your intention. It also helps you keep the end in mind as you begin to work on the details.

4. **Plan That:** While you can certainly plan out all five things in detail now, you can choose to do just one or two to begin. First, determine what your goal is and identify what the milestones are to reach that goal. Milestones are the larger target markers that move you closer to your goal and are made up of a number of smaller steps. Completing the steps gets you to your milestones, and reaching your milestones gets you to your goal. So naturally, you need to also determine what those steps are.

Here's an example.

Goal: Travel to Brazil

Milestone 1: Secure monies necessary to travel and make the trip happen.

Steps:

- Determine how much the trip will cost.
- Set a budget and a plan to save for the trip.
- Determine how long it will take to generate the funds.
- Plan your trip dates based on your savings plan.

Milestone 2: Have time off from work to travel.

Steps:

- Based on your identified travel time line, coordinate your work schedule with your employer or with your clients/customers if you're self-employed.

Milestone 3: Secure places to stay and plan trip activities.

Steps:

- Research options of places to stay.
- Investigate things to do there.
- Book it.

This process makes everything and anything doable. When you take a giant goal that seems nearly impossible to achieve and you chunk it down into digestible steps, suddenly it's within your reach.

CHAPTER SEVEN

Developing Your Determination Muscle
Doing What It Takes to Get to Your Mountaintop

HAVE YOU EVER TAKEN ON A CHALLENGE SO DAUNTING THAT YOU were tempted to give up? Or had to face a crisis—either emotional, physical, or spiritual—that threatened to knock you down? I'm sure you've heard the saying, "When the going gets tough, the tough get going," but how do you do that? How do you keep moving ahead when every cell in your body is crying out, "I can't"— when you feel unable to overcome the discomfort, exhaustion, or fear that's blocking your path? The answer lies in developing the bounce-back muscle I call your Determination Muscle.

A strong Determination Muscle gives you the ability to stay focused on your ultimate objective and the resolve to continue putting one foot in front of the other until you reach it.

Your Determination Muscle isn't just for surviving catastrophes. Although it's crucial for climbing out of life's valleys, you use it to ascend to your mountaintops as well. The Take-Action Muscle we discussed in chapter 3 gets you started on your journey, but it's the Determination Muscle that keeps you going till the end. It supplies the power you need to accomplish your goals.

A weak Determination Muscle yields a life filled with in-completions and failures. When we repeatedly fall short of our mark, attitudes of hopelessness and victimhood begin to grow in us. We start avoiding challenges, taking the easy way out, and looking for others to blame instead of doing what it takes to strengthen our own endurance.

Many people think being determined means being aggressive and mowing down anyone who gets in the way. That isn't true. Determination doesn't always require your progress to be "fast and furious." When you're truly determined, you're only interested in what will work. Your Determination Muscle enables you to zero in on the most effective approach for getting to your goal—which at times may require patience, caution, or even temporary inaction. It helps you recognize that a slower pace of progress can be the best way to proceed.

Being determined isn't about just gritting your teeth and trudging through the mud. Concentrating on your desired result, which is important for activating your Take-Action Muscle, is doubly important for developing your Determination Muscle. It's the Law of Attraction again: like attracts like. Focus on the difficulties you encounter or on your pain and exhaustion, and you generate more and more of those same feelings or experiences. But keep your sights set firmly on an outcome that inspires and excites you, and that goal will actually begin to pull you in its direction, your feet moving effortlessly and your heart singing with joy. Determination keeps you linked to your highest purpose in life and to achieving your goals.

Though I was born with a fairly developed Determination Muscle, when I unexpectedly found myself in a dangerous situation, I had to engage that muscle "to the max" to survive. There were no simple answers, and for the safety of everyone involved, I had to ignore my normal instincts. It was sink or swim. In each moment, I had to go deep within myself for the strength and courage to stay afloat.

Meeting the Man of My Dreams

Since Jelani had been born, I'd shied away from dating and avoided relationships. As the months turned into years, my loneliness grew deeper and deeper. Every night I prayed to God, "Please send me a man who loves me more than *anything*. A man who adores my essence, nourishes my soul, and is crazy about my body just the way it is, with no modifications necessary."

Then Andrew* came into my life. We met at a conference and fell instantly and completely in love. Andrew was handsome, charming, accomplished, and incredibly romantic—my hero and my soul mate, all rolled into one scrumpdeliumptious package.

Unfortunately, he lived in New York.

In our first breathtaking weeks, we spent entire nights on the phone, sharing our lives, breaking through one another's barriers, and whispering into each other's ears until the sun came up. On several occasions, I found two dozen red roses sitting on my desk when I arrived at work, and at one point, he sent me a brand-new, top-of-the-line phone to replace my beat-up, static-filled one. The note inside the package read, "Your every word is too important to miss. Please plug this in immediately, and then call me!" He truly made my toes curl and my hair straight—and neither are easy tasks to accomplish. When the big purple Barney stuffed animal arrived for three-year-old Jelani along with a card that read, "When you date a woman, you date her entire family. I hope your son enjoys this gift," I knew he was the answer to my prayers.

Yet there were moments when in the pit of my stomach I had a feeling that I wasn't supposed to be in this relationship with An-

---

* Names and locations have been changed to protect privacy.

drew. I couldn't quite put my finger on why not, and since it tasted so sweet to my soul to be with him, I chose to ignore the discomfort that interrupted the happiness I was finally experiencing.

Nearly a year into our long-distance relationship, after many magical phone conversations and blissful weeklong visits together every other month, Andrew looked at me during one of his trips to California and said, "Lisa, I can't live this far from you any longer, baby. I'll quit my job, move away from my mother, my grandmother, and even my daughter, and relocate to California to be with you if you'll have me."

I eagerly agreed.

Two months later, on my final visit to New York before Andrew's move, I had the most perfect evening a woman could ask for. After a wonderful dinner together, Andrew and I climbed onto a white horse-drawn carriage and rode through Central Park. Suddenly the driver stopped the carriage, put his hand into a bag, pulled out a long-stemmed red rose, and handed it to Andrew.

Placing the rose in my hand, Andrew said, "Lisa, this rose is for the joy you've brought into my life." I could feel my heart beating through my coat but managed to remain composed.

We stopped eleven more times for eleven more roses presented with Andrew's loving appreciations of me. By the time he was through, I had a dozen gorgeous, long-stemmed red roses, a face full of tears, and a completely open heart for anything that was possible with this man. When he bent on one knee, I smiled excitedly. As the words "Lisa, will you marry me?" came flowing from his mouth, the dam burst. Babbling like a fool, I stuttered, "Y-y-y-ou want me to be your *wife*?"

"No, I want you to be my sun, my moon, and the air that I breathe."

Even in the midst of my joy, a tiny red flag went up. I had the thought, *Wow! The air that he breathes—that seems intense.*

I'M NOT ALONE

Does your mouth sometimes shout out *yes* while your intuition is urging you to say *no*? Many times we find ourselves in challenging situations and realize in hindsight that there were many alerts we could have heeded. Or we pretend to be deaf, tuning out the clear warning signs coming from our internal radar, and we leap in anyway. Deep down we know we're making a big mistake.

Check one box if you've ever had this experience. Check two boxes if you tend to do this fairly often. Check three boxes if this is a chronic pattern for you.

But I allowed romance to sweep me away. "Yes, *yes*, Andrew!" I belted out in almost complete hysteria (so much for staying composed).

Three months later, Andrew was living in my home. I had decided to allow him to move in with Jelani and me prior to marriage on my father's recommendation. I was surprised, because Daddy had always been very proud that I chose not to have live-in boyfriends in the past, but he gently reminded me that because my entire relationship with Andrew until that point had been conducted over the phone and in weeklong visits, I had not really seen Andrew in his day-to-day life. Though we were engaged, my dad felt I needed to get to know Andrew better before I made the final commitment of marrying him.

Within days of his arrival, though everything on the surface seemed fabulous, I knew in my gut that something wasn't right. My internal radar screamed, *Lisa, girl, back up, slow down, and be careful.* However, I chalked my discomfort up to the fact that I had never lived with a man before. *It will take some time to adjust*, I reassured myself.

Andrew quickly found employment through a reputable placement agency, and as the weeks passed, I found much to admire about his work ethic and dedication to excellence, both at the office and in our home. In spite of his demanding job schedule, he insisted that he cook every meal, clean the house, and wash all the clothes.

At first, feeling protective, I cautiously monitored his interactions with Jelani, but over the next several months, as I observed Andrew helping Jelani learn to tie his shoes, teaching him his ABCs, and becoming his giant playmate, I relaxed my guard and allowed Andrew to step into a space for my son that only his granddad and uncle had been allowed to occupy.

Periodically, negative thoughts came up: *This can't be for real. He's too good to be true.* I hated my recurring doubts. *What is up with my mind?* I asked myself. *Why does something have to be wrong?* I wasn't sure if my thoughts really were just negative self-talk; all I knew was that things were perfect—almost too perfect.

Even so, I'd convinced myself that God really wanted this for me and in fact had sent me signs—when the only sign I'd really received was a big red stop sign inside that I had painted green.

Your Internal Navigation System

Many times we won't listen to that still, small voice inside because it's telling us something we just don't want to hear. Unfortunately, when we don't listen, we're dismissing one of the most powerful and beneficial tools available to us in our lives. For all decisions, large and small—whether picking a partner for a relationship or a business venture, purchasing a home or a car, or even choosing how you want to interact with others moment to moment—it's important to pay attention to your intuition, because that internal navigation system is always operating for your highest good.

Going with your gut, acting on a hunch, following your sixth sense—whatever you call it, each of us has an internal wisdom that knows what's right and knows what to do. When your intuition speaks to you, don't ignore it, make excuses, or rationalize it away. If you do, you'll almost certainly be heading in the wrong direction.

To consistently access your intuition, you first need to learn to distinguish it from your mind's negative chatter. Your intuition speaks softly to you from a place deep inside, a quiet place. It comes as a feeling or a knowing. It guides you to what's better for you or counsels you to back away from what is damaging or potentially dangerous. It keeps you grounded and centered.

Your negative chatter, on the other hand, is anxious and agitated. It's born of your fears and uncertainties, and as you learned in chapter 2, it can talk you out of doing great things. Your chatter often screams, sometimes so loudly that you can't hear your intuition speaking.

When you feel your chatter taking over, be still. Take a few deep breaths and ask yourself, *What should I do in this moment?* Then listen. Your internal navigation system is always there and will unfailingly guide you toward the wiser choice.

Though I heard the whisper, *This relationship is not good; it's not going to serve you,* I ignored it because my chatter was saying, *You'll be alone. You've got to stay with him.* My discomfort came from choosing to disregard the deeper wisdom that was coming from my gut and listening to the voice of my fears and loneliness instead.

Don't let worries about scarcity overpower your instinctive knowledge of what to do. A deprivation mentality will always bring unwanted results and outcomes and can drag you into situations that are damaging. Operating from fear will cause you to drop your integrity bar and tolerate things that compromise your values.

Waking Up

My intuition's message about Andrew, which I refused to acknowledge with my eyes open, began to come through my subconscious mind while I slept. It was right around this time that I first had "the dream." In it, Andrew killed me with his bare hands in our bed, between 2 a.m. and 4 a.m. The level of detail was chilling. Though I'd never believed in getting messages or visions of the future through my dreams, when I had the same nightmare on three separate occasions, it alarmed me deeply. The third time I awoke, gasping and terrified, I could no longer dismiss it as "just a dream."

Was this a warning? I wondered. But the whole thing seemed so over-the-top and ridiculous—this was *Andrew* we were talking about—that I just couldn't take it seriously.

Then about a month later, out of the blue, Andrew began to have spurts of rage and anger for no apparent reason, yelling, making accusations, and attempting to pick a fight with me. Even simple things set him off, like not getting a call back from someone, or not being able to find the remote, or my working too late. Yet as quickly as he seemed to lose his mind, he would mysteriously find it again somewhere in the house. Within minutes, he'd regain his composure and offer an extra dose of love and kindness as a healing balm.

At the time, I shrugged it off, deciding it was just a part of his personality I hadn't seen before. During his flare-ups, I'd wonder if I should rethink the wedding or at least postpone it for a while. But once Andrew was himself again, I immediately became swept along by my own desires and the momentum of my mother and friends—unaware of my concerns—moving full steam ahead on dresses, caterers, invitations, and bridal shower plans.

I'd heard it said that clarity can come either with great joy or with great pain. My night of clarity began like any other night. Andrew and I put Jelani to bed, sitting with him as he recited his nightly prayers.

Then, as we went into our room, Andrew said, "So sweetheart, tell me about your day," his dark, intelligent eyes sparkling with interest.

We laughed and talked, then took a romantic candlelit shower together. When I got out of the shower after him, Andrew stood waiting with a plush towel. He dried my body, guided me to the bed, and oiled me from head to toe, commenting on the parts of my body he loved the most. Then he made beautiful, amazing love to me, the kind that had me seeing fireworks. Afterward, he did what no other man had done before in my life: he cuddled with me, holding me close and gently kissing my neck as we went to sleep. This was bliss. At that moment, I felt sure that we could work through any discomfort I might be feeling in my gut.

Several hours later, I woke up to find hands wrapped around my throat, choking me. It was Andrew, his eyes open but dilated and unfocused, and his grip so tight that I could only get the smallest amount of air. My mind raced hysterically. *Why was he doing this?* I pressed my head to the right and shifted my eyes to see the clock: 3:20 a.m. *Between 2 a.m. and 4 a.m.*

Frantic, I thought, *This can't be happening to me. I can't die like this.* I clawed at his hands, but every time I moved, his grip tightened. Now more than ever I felt the force of his six-foot three-inch, 275-pound athletic frame as I struggled to breathe. As Andrew continued to choke me, I could feel myself fading. My thoughts were wild: *Who will take care of my baby? Where did I put my life insurance policy? Lord, please don't let Jelani find my body.* Then I passed out.

When I opened my eyes, I was alone, and there was light all around me. *I must be dead*, I thought. *There's no way I could have lived through what Andrew did to me.* Assuming that I was in heaven, I looked around. My first impression was that heaven was a lot messier than I'd expected. Then I realized that I was still alive and in my own bedroom. Dazed, I checked the clock and saw it was midmorning. After a brief moment of relief, I panicked. *What the hell happened last night? Where's Jelani? Where's Andrew?*

I ran into Jelani's room. His still body lay on the bed, twisted in such a way that I couldn't tell whether he was just sleeping or dead. I shook him. "Jelani! Jelani! *Pleeeease wake up.*" For a moment, there was no movement. Then his little body stirred and in a sleepy three-year-old's voice, he said, "Good morning, Mommy. Why are you crying?"

Finally daring to breathe, I said, "Mommy's okay, sweetheart. I'm just feeling especially thankful today that God blessed me with you. You go on back to sleep, baby."

Leaving Jelani's room, I quietly made my way down the stairs, confused by the everyday breakfast smells of bacon and biscuits coming from the kitchen. As I entered the room, I braced myself for what was next. Would Andrew attack me again or beg for my forgiveness? *"Good morning, Andrew,"* I said in a sharp voice, fully expecting to surprise him with the fact that I was alive and well.

"Good morning, sweetie," he replied evenly. "Are you ready for breakfast?"

He's so calm, I thought. *This is really weird.* I began to think maybe I'd had another bad dream. Hurrying to the bathroom, I looked into the mirror, searching for evidence of last night's struggle. What I saw made me gasp in horror. Stretched across the base of my throat were angry red welts, the imprint of Andrew's huge fingers. In that moment I knew that this nightmare was very real—and that I had just entered the fight of my life.

I sensed immediately that if I reacted normally—insisting Andrew leave my home, breaking off our engagement, telling my friends and family what had happened—Andrew would snap, severely hurting or perhaps even killing me and Jelani.

And that he would do the same to my dad or my brother if they tried to protect me. I thought of those news stories of women who get restraining orders or go into hiding to escape abusive husbands or lovers—looking over their shoulders for the rest of their lives. I could feel in my spirit that my life truly depended on my ability to creatively navigate myself out of this situation.

I'M NOT ALONE

When you're faced with a crisis, sometimes the easy solution isn't the best one—it can bring unwanted results or even damaging ones. Being forced to look "outside the box" for an alternative answer can be a scary experience: you may feel as though you're crazy and very, very alone.

Check one box if you can relate to this feeling. Check two boxes if you've found yourself in this situation more than once. Check three boxes if this has happened to you a number of times.

Andrew and I didn't speak about the choking incident that day. I wasn't sure what type of mental or physical illness I was dealing with and was afraid of setting him off again. I wracked my brain for reasons to delay or postpone the wedding that would not cause him to become suspicious.

The next day, after Andrew left for work, I decided to find out as much as I could about what I was up against. I picked up the phone and called Chris, one of his cousins I'd met on a visit east.

"Hello, Chris, I need to ask you something and I need you to be honest with me. I love Andrew but I believe that he may have a medical condition that is dangerous for me and for my three-year-old son, Jelani."

He was silent. Suddenly, I was afraid I'd made a big mistake and that Chris would tell Andrew that I had called him, which might put me in serious danger. I spoke with urgency, "Chris, I know he's your cousin, but please, he's already choked me until I passed out. I'm afraid for my life." I began to cry.

When Chris finally spoke, his words were slow and deliberate. He was obviously calculating exactly what to say. "Andrew is bipolar and has been for many years. He battles with extreme rage, sadness, and even suicidal thoughts. He can be dangerous to himself and to those around him when he hasn't taken his medication."

Medication? I thought. This was the first time I'd heard about any medication.

"Lisa, whatever you do, you can't let my cousin know that I was the one who told you."

The fear in his voice seemed even more intense than mine. I gave him my word, thanked him, and hung up.

Next, I called Andrew's mother. I managed to find out that he hadn't brought any of his medication with him to California; he was adamant that he could deal with his condition without it.

A few days later, I cautiously brought up the subject with Andrew. I spoke hypothetically, being careful to not let him know that I was aware of his condition. I was dismayed by his reaction. He told me in no uncertain terms that he would never be willing to take any medication for anything other than a physical illness.

As much as I loved Andrew, if he refused to take his medication, I couldn't see myself taking the chance that Jelani and I could be hurt. The truth was I simply wasn't equipped to take this on. I began devising my plan to get Andrew safely out of my life.

Finding the Dot, Part II

In an emergency, one of the most important things to remember is to stay calm. Though it's tempting to blindly run away in panic, yelling at the top of your lungs, you stand a better chance of getting out in one piece if you use your energy to scope out the area and find the best exit route.

The same principle applies when you find yourself facing *any* difficulty or challenge: you'll usually make better decisions about which course of action to take when you honestly evaluate your position and understand what you're up against.

Just as it takes multiple muscles to lift a heavy object, your Determination Muscle works in conjunction with your other bounce-back muscles to overcome the obstacles you encounter in your life. The first step in building your Determination Muscle is to gain clarity. You do this by calling on your Honesty Muscle.

When things go haywire, begin to restore your balance and peace by "finding the dot." Remember the mall and that sale at Macy's? You can't get where you want to go until you know where you're starting from. If you're in a bad situation, assess how bad it is, what's bad about it, and what you're doing that isn't working. This requires you to be really honest with yourself. This is not the time to worry about why the situation is happening or whose fault it is. Eventually, you may have to face truths you'd rather not address—like how you got into the mess you're in. But to ignite the fire of determination inside you, use your Honesty Muscle to recognize exactly where you are, no matter how painful it is.

In my case, I had to be crystal clear: I was in a relationship that could cost me my life. That wasn't a positive thought, but I needed to acknowledge it. I saw that being explosive, defending myself verbally, or yelling back at him could be fatal. This knowledge guided my behavior. I began to build my Determination Muscle by overriding my automatic reactions and reaching out for more information instead. Even in the midst of my distress, I began to thank God for the clarity that I was receiving. It helped me avoid getting caught up in my emotions.

When you're going through a traumatic experience, it's easy to become frozen with fear, or to get angry, or to curl up in a ball and cry. But we know that where attention goes, energy flows. All those reactions will only create more negative feelings. Be truthful about your position, then ask yourself, *Where do I want to be? What will my life look like when I'm out of this?* Keep yourself focused on what you *want*—not on what you *don't want.*

Even if you aren't in a horrific situation like I was, recognizing when you need to stop what you're doing and change direction is vital. This kind of conscious flexibility helps you to overcome the everyday hiccups, frustrations, and obstacles in life that are bound to happen: being rejected, getting passed over for the promotion you wanted, suffering financial setbacks, or experiencing health problems like illness or injury.

And as we addressed in the last chapter, taking the time to assess your present state and reflect on your next steps can also serve you in attaining your goals: training for a job or degree, changing a habit, exercising, dieting, or saving money for a vacation or other special project. No matter what you face in life, begin your journey by warming up the Determination Muscle with a good dose of finding the dot.

A Bigger Picture

My home, the place that had once been my safe haven, was now the place I dreaded and feared the most. For the next four weeks, I lived on pins and needles, always watching my back, Jelani's back, and Andrew's every move. Doing all this while continuing to give the impression that nothing had changed became more and more difficult to pull off. I began to numb my soul and my spirit in order to stay in character around him. I knew that it was the only way to survive.

| **I'M NOT ALONE** | Sometimes a home or workplace can shift from being a safe and comfortable place to being an environment that fills you with anxiety. You may sense |

something's wrong but not know exactly what—and may find yourself walking on eggshells to avoid making it worse.

Check one box if you've ever felt this way. Check two boxes if this has happened to you a few times. Check three boxes if this is a familiar experience. ☐ ☐ ☐

One day while Andrew was at work and Jelani was off at preschool, I sat in the center of my bed and searched for an answer—for some guidance. "Please, I need to know what my lesson is. What am I supposed to get out of this situation?" I asked out loud. I sat praying for an answer, being more still and more quiet than I had ever been before—and feeling more broken and more shattered, too. For the first time since this nightmare had started, I gave myself permission to cry out loud.

My tears flowed in rivers down my cheeks and onto my chest. I realized how long it had been since I had been calm enough to truly listen.

An inner voice, the voice I call God, began to gently and clearly speak into my heart, "Lisa, you will come through this. Remember this is a moment in your life, not your entire life. When this moment's over, you will be equipped with the tools of resiliency, unwavering faith, perseverance, and humility that you'll be able to use to help others heal—the people who are in dark places like the one you're in today."

I wasn't ready to hear all this yet. Confused and angry, I cried out, "Why am *I* supposed to help heal people? I'm not a superwoman; I'm just an ordinary woman trying to save myself and my son. How can I help anyone when I need help myself?" I stilled myself again, listening for a response in my heart, but I heard nothing. It was clear that the assignment I had just been given was not up for negotiation.

I kept this understanding in my heart as I searched for the path out of this dangerous maze. I was no longer able to go to family functions because of the tremendous temptation to cry out for them to save me. Instead, I sat at home, devising ways to get Andrew to agree to leave long enough for Jelani and me to relocate. I was willing to change everything—my home, my job, and even Jelani's school if I had to.

I laid out a "get-Andrew-out" daily schedule of activities. On Mondays, Wednesdays, and Fridays, I made sure to lovingly suggest—in the course of conversation—that Andrew go home to see his family. I reminded him that they weren't all going to be able to come out for the wedding, and after we were married, since we'd decided to save all our money to put toward buying our own, larger, house, Andrew wouldn't be able to travel much. "Sweetheart, I think a trip home to see your daughter, your mother, and your grandmother would relieve some of the constant stress you're feeling lately. Don't you think it would be a good idea if you went home for a visit now?"

Tuesdays, Thursdays, and Saturdays I arranged for Danielle, Andrew's daughter, to call and speak to him, increasing the already strong longing he had to see his little girl. Sundays, I asked God to strengthen the desire in Andrew's mind and heart to go home.

When I felt myself faltering, I boosted my Determination Muscle by reminding myself of the bigger picture. I held on tight to the vision of Jelani and me, happy and safe in the arms of my family, and reminded myself that God had a purpose for me beyond this hell—and I was going to live to achieve it.

Pick a Target

When you're in the middle of a stressful situation, it's easy to lose sight of where you're headed. Once you know your starting point, the next step in strengthening your Determination Muscle is to pick a specific goal to move toward. Nothing concentrates your energy like having a target in front of you.

But choose that target carefully. The bull's-eye you select has a huge impact on your ability to reach it—the more inspiring your objective, the easier it will be to stay moving.

Your attention is like an arrow. Wherever you aim it is where it's going to land. No matter what the problem is, always aim above the problem to the goal. If you're in a life-or-death situation as I was, your survival depends on it. But it's just as important to pick the right target for everyday breakdowns. When you feel discouraged, unable to lose the weight, end a bad relationship, or get out of debt, aim your arrow high by identifying the ideal: what does the ideal weight look like? The ideal relationship? The ideal bank balance? Keep that front and center.

Don't think of what you're giving up: the cake you're not eating and the remote and recliner you're leaving for your session on the StairMaster, the companionship you'll leave behind, the new "toy" you could buy with that paycheck if you didn't put it in the bank. Instead, picture your healthy body, your perfect mate, financial abundance, or the dream you're saving those dollars to fund. Determination to go toward something is much more powerful than determination to avoid something. When you aim your arrow high, you multiply the strength of your Determination Muscle a hundredfold.

Another way to supercharge the power of your target is ask yourself, *What is the highest good that can come from this situation?* Reach out to your Higher Power for guidance or look inside for wisdom—engage your Understanding Muscle to discover what "gifts wrapped in sandpaper" the challenge or problem in front of you holds. Then envision how these gifts will impact your life and the lives of those around you.

Innately, human beings will do more when it's for something larger than ourselves. Our instinct is to be of service and use to others. When you aim for the highest good for everyone involved, you dig deeper inside yourself to pull out more of your strength. Getting Jelani to true safety and knowing my situation was hands-on training to help other people were bigger inspirations than my own survival. They tapped me into the source of superhuman energy I needed to fuel my determination.

Holding on for Dear Life

As the days went by, Andrew's emotional instability became worse and worse. He began following me into our walk-in closet when I went in to pick out an outfit—and even into the bathroom—and refusing to allow me out, blocking the door with his huge frame and saying absurd things like, "Lisa baby, I just want to spend some alone time with you, with no interruptions. You're always working or talking to someone on the phone; this is the only place I can have you to myself." I'd beg him to let me out, explaining that this wasn't the way to show me he loved me.

Each time this happened, I fought the rage building inside me at his bullying. The rage that made me want to forget my plan to calmly negotiate myself out of this relationship and put it behind me for good and, instead, simply make him pay for tormenting me.

What was amazing was that even in the midst of these storms, I was able to recognize my lessons and blessings. I could feel how dealing with Andrew was forcing me to develop patience and humility, two of the fibers that compose the Determination Muscle. I learned how to keep the peace whenever he was irritated or angry: I lowered my voice so that I did not seem confrontational, I sympathized about whatever made him upset, and I never, ever offered any advice. I learned how to close my mouth, surrendering my need to have the last word.

Most importantly, I didn't let myself brood about the terrible strain I was under. I was determined to do two things: to not let this relationship drag me under and to live a wonderful life again. But I didn't dwell on the first goal; it was my intention, not my focus. Every day I focused on staying balanced and peaceful, no matter what. I let myself see, feel, and imagine the healthy, normal, *safe* life I was aiming for. And like a beacon in the darkness, it lit my way.

The Power of Focus

Focus is the key to determination. Bringing your attention back again and again to your desired goal is the single most important thing you can do to build your resolve, overcome challenges, and achieve success. It is the secret of survivors and champions alike!

Focus has two aspects: what you focus on—your target—and how deeply you focus. As we've already learned, the best target is our higher purpose. With Andrew, it was holding on to the bigger picture that steadied me and kept me strong. In the moments when I wanted to explode on him—and there were many—when I wanted to call in the cavalry, to break down and cry, to pick up something and hit him, I tapped into my inner wisdom and asked, *Why do you need to get through this alive?* And the answer would come to me: you need to walk out alive so your son will have a mother and so that you can teach others how to walk out alive. That larger goal was my lifeline.

How you focus is equally important. The depth and intensity of your focus will determine your success. Let your focus be like a laser, not a floodlight. A floodlight illuminates a lot of ground, but when your focus gets too spread out, you may become overwhelmed by all you have to do or you may try to do too much at once. With a laser focus, you concentrate on one step at a time and complete it before you move to the next step—steadily moving in the direction of your larger goal.

Focus so intently on where you're going that you can feel it in your body. See it. Hear it. Imagine every detail. Make it come alive. Often during that terrible time with Andrew, when I was in the shower, getting dressed, cleaning the house, or cooking dinner, I'd see myself in the front of a room, sharing my story with other people. I pictured men, women, and children coming up to me and saying, "Thank you so much for opening yourself up to us and helping us." Mind you, it was years before any of that ever happened. But I could see it, and I held on to it. I knew the day would come.

This is the point where your Determination Muscle and your I-Know-Like-I-Know Muscle overlap. Seeing something as real before it is takes courage *and* faith.

Desperation: An Awful Perfume to Wear

Then, one morning about eight weeks after the choking incident, I was standing in the kitchen, ready to attend a series of very important business meetings when Andrew turned to me and began speaking in a controlled yet frightening voice: "Lisa, I keep feeling like something is wrong, as though something's changed between us, and you're planning to leave me."

Oh my God, I thought, *he knows*. We were now only three months from our scheduled wedding date, and I had already secretly stopped the seamstress from making our wedding outfits, cancelled the reservation for the yacht that we planned to get married on, and hidden all of the invitations that were supposed to have already been mailed at my girlfriend's house. I was sure that I hadn't left any clues. Frantically, I searched my memory for anything I may have overlooked while I tried to soothe him in the moment. "Sweetheart, I'm not leaving you." As I spoke, I noticed with a lurch in my stomach that his eyes were beginning to take on the same dilated, unfocused appearance they'd had on the night he'd almost killed me.

"Lisa," he said, "I can't imagine you with another man, having him touch you or make love to you."

I looked him square in the eyes and for the first time in months I told him the truth: "Andrew, I can't imagine being touched by another man either." I said this with firm conviction. If I made it through this alive, I was through with men for good.

He continued, "You and I are made for each other, but you don't seem to understand that. Lisa, I think I'd rather see you dead than with someone else."

When I heard that, my heart started beating like one of the jimbay drums in a drumming circle. As I tried to calm him down, I saw that Jelani had come downstairs to find me. I knew that I couldn't let him see what might be coming next.

I quickly bent down, looked into Jelani's beautiful bright eyes, and trying to sound as natural as possible, I asked him to go upstairs and listen to his Barney tape nice and loud. It took everything I had not to just grab my boy and run out the door right then, but I was more afraid we would never be safe if I did. Jelani, sensing my fear, turned around without saying a word and went up the stairs.

Once Jelani was out of sight, I slowly straightened, and still using the calmest voice I could, I said, "Andrew, I do love you, baby. Please don't talk about hurting me."

But as if he hadn't heard me, Andrew glared at me with that scary, blank gaze and said, "If it's not going to be me in your life, then I'm sorry, Lisa, it isn't going to be anyone."

Terrified, I swept my eyes around the kitchen, looking for something to use in my defense. But before I could reach for anything, Andrew came at me. With his huge hands, he picked me up by my throat and held me in the air with my feet suspended at least two feet off the ground. Then, with all of his strength, he threw me clear across the kitchen and into the adjoining family room. As I flew past the kitchen counter, my arm hit the platter with our breakfast on it, flipping it over onto me. My body hit the middle of the entertainment center with so much force that the wind was knocked out of me.

As I lay there, my eyes closed, eggs splashed across the front of my suit, my brain reeled, unable to process this newest horror.

Opening my eyes, I saw Andrew coming toward me, now fully enraged. My mind began to race in two different directions. One part of me was saying, *Find something big, heavy, and sharp and kill this man before he kills you.* The other part of me, knowing I could never kill anyone, urged restraint. *Use honey to quiet him down. End this the right way so he never comes back. Remember, he's sick and unstable.*

As he picked me up off the ground, I took a deep breath and looked straight into his face. In the most composed voice I could muster, I said, "Andrew, look at me. Andrew, look at me, baby." His unfocused eyes settled on mine. Though it was the last thing I wanted to do, I knew that I could bring him back with loving words. "Andrew, you love me, remember? I love you, too, and this is not what you do to people you love. Sweetheart, look at me. You just threw me across the room."

It was working; I could see his facial expression beginning to change. I continued, "Baby, I know you don't want to hurt me, but you just did. You hurt me very badly." As Andrew's eyes began to focus again, he noticed the tears streaming down my face.

"Lisa," he said, his own face crumpling, "do you see how much I love you? I don't want to ever hurt you, baby, but sometimes the thought of you leaving me makes me crazy."

In my head, I was screaming, *Don't blame me for this. I'm not the problem here,* but what came out of my mouth was, "I understand, sweetheart. This really shows that you could use some time at home with your family to reduce your stress level. Please go home. I'll take care of everything while you're gone."

I'M NOT ALONE

Have you ever had to carefully manage your emotions in order to make it through a challenging situation? Do you defuse disagreements by strictly monitoring your tone of voice, facial expression, or comments? This can happen at work with colleagues or at home with your children, spouse, or other family members.

Check one box if you've ever had to do this. Check two boxes if you find yourself in this situation fairly often. Check three boxes if this is a way of life for you.

I left him to think about my offer as I slowly limped upstairs and tiptoed past Jelani's room. I could barely lift my arms to change my clothes. *Still I rise.* The words of Dr. Maya Angelou had never rung so true. As the pain in my body began to grow, matching the pain in my heart and spirit, I reminded myself that no matter how many times I got knocked down, spiritually, emotionally, financially, or even physically, there would always be a chance to get back up. *Still I rise. Still . . . I . . . rise.*

I considered myself a strong, confident, and independent career woman—not the kind of person I associated with victimhood. In fact, when I'd hear women speak of being battered or abused, I'd always wondered, *How could she get herself in a situation like that? Why did she let him abuse her? Didn't she see it coming?* Now I asked myself those very same questions.

I'd once heard a friend say that desperation is a stinky perfume to wear. I stunk. This stunk. And I suddenly knew that was exactly how this horrible situation had all started—with my desperation. For years, I'd believed that somehow I would be more of a woman—more successful, more appealing—if only I were in a long-term relationship. He, whoever "he" was, would complete me, and until he showed up in my life, there would be a void in me—a gaping, painful emptiness inside I couldn't fill myself.

The irony was that Andrew was exactly what I had asked for when I'd prayed for God to "send me a man who loved me more than anything." Andrew *did* love me more than anything else; he was willing to give his life, take my life, and most likely serve life because of that "love." It was one more example of how my thoughts had created my reality. From now on, I would be much clearer in my requests and my prayers—I recognized I was placing orders that could actually be filled.

The kitchen incident finally convinced Andrew that he needed a break from the prewedding pressure I assured him was at the root of his violent outburst. He agreed to go back to the East Coast for a month to see his family.

The day of his departure finally arrived. *Hallelujah!* I drove him to the airport to catch his flight, and when we pulled up to the curb outside the terminal, Andrew turned to me and asked, "Aren't you going to miss me, baby? You seem so content, even joyful, that I'm going." I could see the wheels turning in his mind.

Okay, I told myself, *this is the final act. Pull this off, Lisa, and you're free.* I leaned close to him and whispered, "Sweetheart, I am doing everything I can to hold myself together and not start crying right here." Looking into his face, my eyes actually began to fill with tears. A part of me recognized that I was truly saying good-bye to the man I'd fallen in love with and the dream of living happily ever after I'd once had. His face softened as we gazed into each other's eyes.

We kissed, and as I watched Andrew walk away, I realized I was holding my breath. *Was it really over?* I let the air out of my lungs in one big whoosh. Jelani and I were safe at last.

Leaving the airport, I drove straight to the beach and watched the most beautiful sunset I'd ever seen. I was free. I'd survived. I'd made it across that ocean of fear. I thanked God once again for strengthening my Determination Muscle. Like a lifeboat, it had saved me, carrying me safely over rough waves to dry ground.

Pumping Iron

I'm sure you've had the experience of hitting the wall at one time or another in your life; you've faced a challenge that felt bigger than you could handle. At those times, the only thing to do is to take a deep breath and engage your Determination Muscle to whatever degree you can. You'll be amazed at how much strength you'll find inside, if you've done the processes I've laid out in the chapter so far:

1. Getting honest
2. Picking a target
3. Using the power of focus

To make sure you're as buff as possible, do process 4: give your Determination Muscle proper support and nourishment along the way. You do this by staying firmly connected to your spiritual center and asking the people who love you for assistance.

There may be times when your clarity about your situation is obscured by your emotions. You may be so afraid or so angry or so hurt that you literally can't see straight. Once you realize this is happening, take a moment to regroup. Find that place of peace and knowing inside that we talked about in an earlier chapter—the one about developing your I-Know-Like-I-Know Muscle—and let it keep you anchored to your higher goal.

If necessary, find someone in your Rocket Booster community to help you separate the facts from your emotions. Request that this person not give you advice but simply support you in finding your own solution by listening and perhaps asking questions that help you regain a clear picture of what you want to do.

When you get suggestions from your friends, family, and colleagues, it's good to listen, but always check in with yourself before deciding on a course of action. Stay in touch with your own wisdom and persist with the plan that is based on your personal sense of the bigger picture.

Determination is contagious. To build your Determination Muscle, find a strong, determined person to spend time with—a teacher, family member, or child—someone whose life makes you want to be a better person, and pick role models like Martin Luther King or Mahatma Gandhi, who will inspire you to new heights of staying power, strength, and resolve. Soon you'll become one of those people who moves others to be determined in their own lives.

————————

More than almost any other muscle, you strengthen your Determination Muscle through repeated and sustained use. Whether surviving a crisis, facing a challenge, or going for your dreams, when you have to rise above—or push through—a situation, you create and build this muscle. By consistently engaging the power of determination, what at first seems too heavy gradually becomes doable.

When you emerge from a traumatic, frustrating, or heartbreaking situation, you emerge a greater being. When you learn the lessons attached to that situation, you can't be the same person you were before you went through it.

Having a strong Determination Muscle is the secret to accomplishment. It allows you to take on more and more important and meaningful challenges until you see that there are no limits to what you can achieve.

The action steps that follow are designed to help you build your Determination Muscle to aid you as you go through the valleys and climb toward the mountaintops in your life.

INSPIRED ACTION STEPS

Practicing determination *before* you need it is a good idea. Having to strengthen a weak Determination Muscle at the same time that you're facing a challenge only makes the challenge feel bigger. Doing these action steps will help to keep your powers of perseverance primed and ready to go.

1. **Oh, What a Feeling:** The first step in developing your Determination Muscle is to define how important your goals are. What makes them so vital to you? Determination comes as a result of being laser-focused on something—pushing through anything and everything to get to the goal. Here's one way to home in on your target.

   - Go to a special, quiet place where you feel safe and relaxed. It can be a favorite reading chair in your home, out in nature under a tree, in your place of worship when there's no service going on, or a local park or beach. Just go there and free your mind of whatever stresses may have collected there during your day. This is a time to reflect without any distractions.
   - Pick a goal that you listed in the previous chapter's action step 4—one for which you've already created milestones and related steps. Now visualize not only the goal but also achieving it. See yourself as having already reached this goal, and ask yourself the following questions. Pause after each one, breathing deeply and taking all the time you need to be present with your answer—and the feelings that come with it—before moving on to the next question.

     o Why is this goal important to me? What value does it have in my life?
     o What benefit could achieving this goal bring me?

What joy will I gain? What freedom will I attain that I don't currently have?

○ What makes my goal worth fighting for? Working hard for? Staying up late for? Humbling myself for?

As you do this exercise, you'll likely feel a sense of great empowerment and liberation. Later on, as you work toward your goals and experience difficult or challenging moments, recalling this feeling will enable you to look in the face of fear, frustration, exhaustion, and disappointment and move forward anyway. When you can do this, you'll know you're living inside the reality of determination.

2. **The Thermometer:** Take that same goal you focused on above and create a visual representation of its overall fulfillment. On a blank piece of paper, draw a thermometer like the ones groups use in fund-raising to show how much money has been raised. Write your goal at the top, and divide the thermometer into ten equal parts—10 percent, 20 percent, 30 percent, and so on. Then, using a colored marker, fill in the thermometer to the level you are at today in reaching this specific goal. Place the thermometer where you will see it each day, such as on your refrigerator, bathroom mirror, or office wall, and be sure to update the percentage of your progress toward reaching your goal every Friday. You can do this for as many of your goals as you wish.

3. **Share the Dream:** A goal becomes more real and concrete when you move it from the confines of your own head and inner dialogue and share it with others. Then you can see and feel the power of it *outside* yourself. When you have a goal and no one else knows about it, it's more like a wonderfully inspiring secret. Creating a community that supports your efforts to hit that mark, even if that commu-

nity begins with just one other person, allows you to be truly accountable to yourself and your goal.

• Select a Rocket Booster friend, and share your goals with that person on a regular basis. Each week, spend ten minutes updating him or her on your progress. This process is guaranteed to keep you on track and moving forward and, as an added benefit, will inspire your Rocket Booster friend to establish and meet his or her own goals, too.

CHAPTER EIGHT

Developing Your Forgiveness Muscle
Finding Your Way Back to Love

I'M SORRY. CAN YOU FORGIVE ME?"

When you hear those words, how do you feel? Most of us learn in childhood that "I forgive you" is the proper response to "I'm sorry"—an automatic reply, like saying "You're welcome" when someone says "Thank you." But when you're in a situation that requires your forgiveness, you may find it isn't that easy to do. That's because forgiveness probably isn't what you think it is. If words like *pardon, excuse,* or *let off the hook* enter your mind, then chances are you have it all wrong.

A quick way to test the strength of your Forgiveness Muscle is to ask yourself, *Do any past events in my life drain my spirit when I recall them? Does anything in my personal history still make me instantly angry, hurt, or sad when I remember it?*

If you answer yes to either of these questions, then your Forgiveness Muscle could use a boost. With a weak Forgiveness Muscle, you remain tied to and defined by old circumstances and experiences that no longer serve a purpose. They act like little red stoplights flickering inside. For example, you may have just met the perfect person to have a wonderful relationship with, but you can't seem to commit to it completely because you're still unresolved about an old relationship in which you were hurt. You constantly bring up that achy memory and keep reliving that pain today even though it has passed. Why do you do this? Because you're not done with it, you haven't let it go, and you haven't released it. Put simply, you haven't applied the Forgiveness Muscle yet to spur that healing process.

So many people live holding on to past occurrences that hinder them from reaching their highest good. You really can't move forward and embrace anything new while you have two hands full of old issues, old regrets, old shame, anger, or angst. It's like a closed hand. When you keep a fist full of rage, shaking it at someone and repeating the phrase "I'll never forgive you!" you cut yourself off from opportunities. You think you're punishing the other person, but you're actually hurting yourself and inhibiting *your* life's potential.

I thought I knew what forgiveness was, so I was a bit shocked by what I had to go through once Andrew was gone. Not only did I have to reach deep inside to identify and process my emotions, but I had to redefine the whole concept of forgiveness and come to learn that it really has nothing to do with anyone but me.

Out of the Frying Pan, into the Fire

For the first few weeks after Andrew left, we talked on the phone. As the date approached for him to return, I convinced him to extend his visit for two more weeks. At the end of that time, I was able to tell him what I think he already knew: I wasn't ready to marry him and didn't know when I would be. On our last phone call, though I assured him we would still talk and visit each other, I had already put an order in to the telephone company to change my phone number. My new number would be unlisted.

I never told my family what had really happened. I simply explained that Andrew had some medical challenges that he was not willing to address and that had ended our relationship. I didn't want to relive the terror I'd experienced, or see the horror on their faces, or explain why I'd handled it the way I had. It was over, and I wanted to keep it that way.

Within days of Andrew's departure, I packed our bags, and Jelani and I moved in temporarily with my mother. I couldn't spend another night in the house we had shared.

With Andrew gone, I was sure things would get better, but instead they got worse. For the next few months, I lived under a cloud of fear and anxiety. I kept expecting Andrew to come after me and hunt me down. Anytime I saw a well-dressed black man large enough to be Andrew, I went into an immediate fear-storm. My hands would sweat, my heart would pound, and I'd breathe in shallow gasps as I paced around nervously.

I was unable to be home alone and often burst into tears or started shaking uncontrollably. I had frequent nightmares and would wake up in the middle of the night soaked in sweat, screaming, "Get off of me! I hate you; don't kill me!" and swinging at my phantom attacker with the strength of an angry ox.

Though my weight had seesawed for years after Jelani's birth, my body began to balloon as I let my exercise regimen slide. I couldn't understand what I was feeling or why. I felt like a zombie, going through the motions of life but not really being all there.

Finally, seeing that I wasn't coming out of the dark space I was in, my mother insisted that I go to her doctor to discover what was wrong with me. Though I hadn't come straight out and told her everything, she was able to connect the dots. When she looked at me, her eyes filled with the pain of a mother who could not protect her baby girl from the world. I knew that look; it was the same one I had given Jelani during those weeks and months in which I struggled to find a way out of the dangerous situation I'd placed us in.

As the doctor entered the examination room, I attempted a smile, but with no success. After reading my chart and checking me over thoroughly, she turned to me and said, "Lisa, you're suffering from post-traumatic stress disorder, an emotional condition that can develop following any traumatic or life-threatening experience. Even though a person knows that he or she is safe and away from any threat, post-traumatic stress disorder can show up in the body and mind in many ways, including crying, uncontrollable shaking, trouble sleeping, being afraid to be alone—all symptoms you are experiencing. In addition to that, I'd say you are clinically depressed."

I'M NOT ALONE

Have you ever been so haunted by a past event, recent or not, that it consumes your waking hours and you find it difficult to move on?

Check one box if you've experienced this any time in your life. Check two boxes if it became a major distraction in your life. Check three boxes if your life came to an abrupt stop, as mine did.

☐ ☐ ☐

She wrote out a prescription and handed it to me. I read the words on the prescription once, and then in disbelief, I read them again.

Patient Name: Lisa Nichols
Diagnosis: Severe Depression
Prescription: Prozac

I stared at the words for a long time, speechless at my

diagnosis. Then I looked up at her and said, "Doctor, you mean I'm *sad*?"

"Yes, Lisa, you are extremely sad and you need help. I recommend you begin taking this medication immediately."

Suddenly everything made sense. She was right, I *was* sad. I was sad that I'd been so lonely. I was sad that I hadn't honored my intuition. I was sad that I'd been abused and that my son's life had been in danger because of my choices. I was sad that, yet again, another shot at love had crashed and burned. But now this sadness was costing me too much.

Taking Your Emotional Pulse

It's human to go through periods of unhappiness. Feeling sad can creep up on you—you may not be exactly sure how or even when it started. It can be just a minor blip that quietly passes, or it can bring your life to what seems like a screeching halt. Suddenly, you're forced to call a time-out to reflect because something isn't right. And if you don't give it your attention, you won't get past that bigger challenge so easily.

When you find yourself stuck in a soupy mess of emotions and you're not sure exactly what you're feeling, it's time to take what I call an emotional inventory. This isn't something we normally like to do. In fact, we're more apt to call out *someone else* on his or her emotions, as in "Why are *you* so mad?" than to reflect on our own. But becoming aware of what's going on inside yourself can be incredibly powerful—and revealing. You become fully conscious. When you take your emotional pulse, you begin to put a name on your feelings, which can otherwise be too abstract and intangible. When I heard the word *sad,* it shouted out to me. It felt so real and concrete, like something I could touch. It gave my emotional state a voice, pulling it up from a subconscious level. So many of our emotions hide out in our subconscious; we're not really aware of them or how they are affecting us. But they do, in fact, influence how we think and behave. Once we identify them, we can begin to examine them more closely.

The next time you sense a strong emotion, take some time to put a finger on exactly what you're feeling. Get quiet, turn inward, and just listen. Pretend for a moment that you are your own best friend and ask yourself lovingly, *How are you feeling?* Answer this question out loud by completing the following sentence stem at least six or seven times: "What's up with me *right now* is . . ." Don't be afraid of what comes out. The truth is not only all right, but in this moment, it's absolutely necessary. As you complete the sentence stem, identify the energy your feelings are generating. You may feel it on a physical level—in your muscles, your head, or your stomach. You may notice a change in your breathing or in the tone and pitch of your voice. You may feel like a frightened kitten and want to hide and escape as I did, or you may want to lunge forward like an angry tiger in order to protect yourself. This inventory will peel back the layers and help you understand what emotions you are dealing with.

Your Honesty Muscle also comes into play here. You'll need it so you can be as authentic as possible when you take your emotional pulse. It will help you to recognize whatever is there, whether angst, anger, stress, worry, fear, or as I experienced, a crippling sadness.

Knowing which emotions you're feeling is the first step in using your Forgiveness Muscle. It's like that warm-up stretch before a workout. It both alerts you to the tight spots inside that require your attention and prepares you for the heavier lifting that's ahead.

A Thousand Second Chances

Thanking the doctor for the prescription, I went home and put it in a drawer. I was willing to take the medication, but first I wanted to try another approach. *Lisa*, I told myself, *you make your living teaching others how to climb out of their valleys and to turn their breakdowns into breakthroughs. It's time to take your own advice.*

I knew and taught others that sadness stems from the real or perceived lack of self-worth, love, faith, acknowledgment, or hope. After what I'd been through, I was flat out of most of those. Like a car, my gas tank was empty. I didn't feel that I could go any further; in fact, I was sputtering to a complete stop.

Now, inside my own breakdown, I was about to embark on a test of everything I taught. In that moment, I had to be the possibility that I spoke of to others. I had to be the healing that I professed was attainable. I had to show the resiliency that I asked others to access in themselves. I needed to remind myself who I was as a woman, and more important, who God had created me to be. I needed to fill my own tank.

I began to implement my personal prescription for feeling better by reading inspirational books daily, starting with the Bible and then adding others, including ones by Iyanla Van Zant, Maya Angelou, Marianne Williamson, and Wayne Dyer.

I wrote affirmations specially tailored for my needs on Post-it Notes and placed them all around the house. "My past does *not* equal my future" was posted on the refrigerator. "I get to design the next chapter of my journey" was placed prominently inside the front door. "I am the creator of my own destiny" was on the headboard. The bathroom mirror reminded me "I am beautiful inside and out and I deserve healthy love." I was putting the Law of Attraction to work without even realizing that was what I was doing.

My prescription also included a healthy dose of mirror work. Though this involved regular sessions of looking at myself in the mirror, I didn't use the time to check out my skin, analyze my hair, or evaluate my features. I simply looked into my eyes and was present with myself in the most honest, authentic way possible. And so began my journey of deepening self-love, acknowledgment, celebration, and encouragement.

Gazing into my own eyes, I started by completing the following sentence stems: "Lisa, I'm proud that you . . . ," "Lisa, what I love about you is . . . ," and "Lisa, I'm committed to . . ." with seven different endings for each one. After a few days, I noticed that I was having trouble with the middle stem. When I talked about what I loved about myself, I experienced a dip in my energy. Something inside me wasn't feeling so loving toward Lisa Nichols.

That's when I realized I had feelings of shame and guilt about what had happened with Andrew that still needed to be addressed. I added, "Lisa, I forgive you for . . ." to my set of daily sentence stems.

I'M NOT ALONE	Have you ever attempted to move on but then realized that you couldn't without forgiving yourself first? Your feelings of shame and guilt can keep you stuck in a

painful holding pattern.

Check one box if you've ever had this experience. Check two boxes if you've had these feelings quite a few times in the past. Check three boxes if this has been, or still is, a major issue for you. ☐ ☐ ☐

I repeated the mirror exercise over and over again, day after day, week after week. Every morning before I left for work, I reminded myself of what I had to be proud of, what I loved about myself, what I forgave myself for, and who I was committed to becoming.

My messages to myself were always clear, direct, and heartfelt. I told myself, "Lisa, I'm proud that you are willing to tell yourself the truth, even when it hurts. What I love about you is your willingness to fight for your life. I forgive you for not trusting your gut, your intuition, when it told you something wasn't right. I'm committed to filling up my own tank and not expecting others to do so for me."

I was consciously affirming my present, forgiving my past, and creating my future. I recognized that I was worthy of not only a second chance—but a thousand second chances.

Time to Bounce Back

The foundation for true forgiveness is being present with yourself so you can identify your emotions. But once you've become aware of what they are, it's time to *process* them. This is when you realize you probably have some self-forgiveness to do. You may notice that you carry shame or guilt in the tangled strands of your emotions; you feel bad about the mistakes you've made in the past.

Underneath those negative emotions is the simple need to tune yourself back in to your own self-love. Working in front of the mirror, as I did, is one way to do this, though it can be an extremely intense and challenging experience. You may feel very uncomfortable at first, especially if you've never done it before. But look at it this way: if you aren't willing to do what it takes to accept yourself, you won't be able to resolve these underlying emotions and continue onward to a place of complete forgiveness. So the least you can do is make a commitment to yourself to reconnect with the love you have for just *you*. Don't even think about other people or events that may be adding weight to your emotional baggage. Though I was disappointed with Andrew, I had to deal with the disappointment I felt in myself first. That was enough to handle in the beginning of all my emotional processing.

In workshops, I share a different perspective on the word *intimacy*. When you slow this word down, you get to the most sacred and valuable form of intimacy: into-me-I-see. It turns you inward. Say it slowly out loud without looking at the word on the page, and really hear the words *into, me, I, see*. It's about affirming your faith in yourself by finding out how you feel and getting in touch with what you believe and what you want.

If talking to yourself in front of a mirror isn't for you, there are other ways to explore the experience of intimacy, including reaching out to one of your Rocket Booster friends to enjoy a safe space or attending a workshop or self-development seminar. It may be finding a therapist who can help you sort through all of your conflicting emotions. Just having another voice to remind you that things will be okay can help you to reframe certain events in your mind and pull you up to higher ground, one step at a time.

The goal is to stop blaming yourself for anything that's happened and access your self-love, which has always been there. As you begin to fill your tank back up with unconditional belief in yourself, you begin to make decisions from a more grounded place. You operate with more clarity and move forward with greater assurance, rather than coming from a place of lack or scarcity, which is what happens when your tank runs bone dry. We all crave to be filled up with love, confidence, and possibility, but most people think that *others* should be filling their tanks. It's really our job to do it for ourselves.

Reconnecting with yourself begins the healing process from the inside out. Though it may feel as though you're just scratching the surface of forgiveness, let it be your starting point. And with that life-changing step, the real work begins.

The Total Truth

My self-prescribed filling-my-tank program worked. Within six months, I was over my severe anxiety, sadness, and trauma and could function normally again. As I began to feel more and more like myself, I moved on with my career, continuing to work with teens, teaching them to love themselves as well as to love and forgive others.

But while I talked about forgiveness, I wasn't ready to practice it completely. Though my work in the mirror had helped me to forgive the part I'd played in my nightmare, forgiving Andrew was a different story. I held on steadfastly to my right to hate Andrew forever, to be angry at him, and to never, ever, *ever* forgive him. God would just have to let me slide on this one. How could He expect me to forgive someone who had manhandled me and threatened my life?

Once I was feeling better, I crammed the whole topic of Andrew and what had happened into a room deep inside me and slammed the door shut. I didn't want to talk about it—or even think about it—again.

That door flew open when my good friend Eve and I co-facilitated a workshop for twenty teenagers during a weeklong training. In one of our sessions on forgiveness, Eve explained an exercise called the Total Truth Process that she and I had never done together before. The process had been developed by the authors John Gray and Barbara DeAngelis and was taught to Eve by her mentor, Jack Canfield. She said it was a powerful tool for forgiveness because it helped people release negative emotions like anger, hurt, and resentment.

She began her explanation by saying, "There are many emotions beneath our experience of anger. Once we've uncovered each emotion, ultimately we can get back to love and appreciation. True forgiveness is not about making the other person right or excusing what he or she has done. **Forgiveness is about giving yourself permission to replace anger with love.**"

Even though she was my friend and an amazing teacher, I thought she was full of it. There was no way, with anger like mine, that any love or appreciation for Andrew was possible. I wasn't ready to do that. In my eyes, his abuse justified my anger, nullifying the rules of forgiveness.

Eve went on to describe the eight levels of emotion involved in telling the Total Truth: Anger; Hurt; Fear; Responsibility/ Accountability; Understanding; Wants; Forgiveness, Love, and Appreciation; Agreements.* The goal is to express all your emotions—starting with the negative and moving to the positive—about a person or situation in your life that is causing you pain. She said that on the surface, we may be experiencing anger, but underneath the anger we can always find a feeling of hurt, and underneath the hurt, there's fear. Beneath our fear, there's some form of responsibility that we each can take for what has occurred.

Then she added, "While it may be a stretch, underneath our feelings of responsibility, if we look, we can usually find a level of understanding about what was going on with the other person."

Eve continued, "Underneath the understanding, there is something you want. And, believe it or not, underneath our wants there is love and appreciation."

By this time I was completely uncomfortable, and the chatter in my head was saying, *What are we doing this for? I don't like it.* But, out of respect for her, I kept my mouth shut.

When she was done with her explanation, she asked for a volunteer to demonstrate how this process worked. Though I was skeptical, as her cofacilitator, I decided to volunteer. I figured that if I did, we could quickly and easily get through this exercise and move on to what was next—something more effective.

She instructed me to begin with the sentence stem "I'm angry that . . ." and complete it in my own words. One of the teen participants stood in front of me to represent Andrew. I steeled myself and thought, *This should be easy. I'll go with the flow on the first part about my anger, hurt, and fear, and*

---

* Some people combine these emotions into six levels and put them in a different order. Regardless of how they are sequenced, the effect and outcome are the same. These steps ultimately help you to discover and release your emotions and arrive at the place where true forgiveness begins.

I'll fake the second part on responsibility, understanding,
wants, forgiveness, and love. Then we'll be done!

"I'm angry that you betrayed my trust." As soon as I said
the words, I could feel the fury rising and my tears well up. I
started breathing heavily as I worked to control my mounting
rage. "I'm angry that you violated me. I'm really mad at the fact
that I trusted you. I hate that I loved you."

My hands curled into tight fists at my side, I moved on to the
next level: hurt. "I feel hurt that you emotionally and physically
abused me. I'm hurt that you made me fear for my life and the
life of my son. I'm sad that I ever had to experience that type
of violence." I felt the first tear roll down my cheek and my lips
begin to quiver.

Eve prompted me gently, "I'm afraid that I . . ."

The words poured from my mouth, "I'm afraid that I'll never
let anyone else close to me because of the pain you've caused
me. I'm scared that I may never recoup from this, that I'll never
get over the hurt."

Now my tears were flowing freely. At that moment, I felt
the true power of this exercise. Every thought and emotion
was genuine, and I had to discover each one and deal with it
in front of this group of teens. What had I been thinking when
I volunteered? I looked over at Eve, and she gave me the most
caring and compassionate look, along with a small nod as if to
say, "You're doing well; keep going."

"I'm afraid that my son will remember you." That one hurt
to say. With a sickening jolt, the reality of the extreme danger
that both my son and I had been in hit me once again.

Eve prompted me to move to the next level: "What were
you responsible for?"

This one was hard. I wanted to blame him completely for
everything that had happened. Up until this point, though I
had taken some initial steps to own my part of it, deep down
inside I still clung to my role as a victim. I felt the situation
with Andrew was actually more a matter of being in the wrong

place at the wrong time. Now, facing the total truth, I had to admit not only how overused that poor excuse was but that, in my case, it really wasn't true.

I took a deep breath, and in a voice that was barely audible said, "I take responsibility for not being clear in my request to God. I take responsibility for not seeing the warning signs because I didn't want to see them. I take responsibility for allowing my loneliness to skew my judgment. I take responsibility for endangering my own life."

I'M NOT ALONE	Have you ever used the excuse of being in the wrong place at the wrong time to avoid or minimize the responsibility you know you should take?
Check one box if you've ever used an excuse like this one. Check two boxes if you recognize that you've used it more times than you care to admit. Check three boxes if this phrase could be your middle name.	☐ ☐ ☐

I wanted to quit, to run and hide, but I knew I couldn't stop now. The exercise was uprooting something that I had decided I'd never have to touch, and all of us—the teens, Eve, and I—wanted to see what was on the other side.

Anger Gets an Eviction Notice

People often misunderstand the "responsibility" layer under anger, thinking it's about assigning fault or taking the blame for what's happened. Blame and fault are disempowering because they're only about looking to the past, to a time when nothing can be changed because it's already occurred. Regardless of previous events, you can always take responsibility for how you handle their impact *now*. This empowers you to change the present moment as well as your future.

To evict all those feelings of guilt and shame—and let go of any "mistakes" you've made in the past once and for all—it helps to express, then release the emotions you're feeling, right down to the core. You may find you've been keeping a little pocket of negative emotions off to the side, full of frustrations and hurts you stopped processing during temporary periods of feeling better. The decision to put your feelings aside can happen for any number of reasons: it's too painful or too scary to continue, you don't want to stir up anything that will prevent you from "moving on," or you think you'll have to do something you don't want to do.

My initial forgiveness work—prior to Eve's intervention— had prepared me for this next important step. It had helped to get my emotional processing going and to build the foundation I needed to then deal with these more deeply rooted and raw emotions. But I hadn't addressed my anger, because doing so would have meant opening up the wound again. Now one thing was for sure: I wasn't going to let myself stop processing it until I was done.

People can spend their whole lives skating over the surface of forgiveness while their wounds continue to hurt deep inside. Until we heal, we can't truly live a life of happiness and unlimited possibility. So much energy gets stuck in the pieces of leftover resentment we tuck away after we think we've moved past something. I didn't realize the extent of my anger until Eve literally drew it out of me. And it allowed me to begin to heal more fully—to reach much deeper beneath the surface.

Finding Compassion

Everyone was watching me. It was time to move on to the next stage of the Total Truth Process: understanding. *Wow, what a huge mountain in front of me,* I thought. I took a deep breath and began, "Andrew, I understand that you are not well and that you have a medical condition. I understand that in your own way, you did in fact care for me."

It was strange; I could feel all the anger and sadness begin to drain out of me as I moved into feeling compassion. I had never once, before this moment, tried to understand Andrew. I thought he was out of his mind, and I was angry that he wouldn't take his medicine. I didn't even try to imagine what agonies he may have been suffering. Now, for the first time, I began to understand his personal turmoil.

"I understand that you never had a model to show you what it means to be a man. I understand that you need—and deserve—medical attention. I understand you were doing the best you could with what you had."

Something was happening to me. It was as though my feelings were on automatic pilot. My voice was losing its edge, taking on a softer, more loving tone as I searched for empathy. To my surprise, my anger was being replaced by genuine understanding. Though it was clearly not in my best interest to see him again—nor did I want to—that didn't mean I couldn't have compassion for what he had gone through.

Eve pointed out, "When we open the door to understanding, we are able to find compassion. When we feel compassion, we're more able to forgive. When we forgive, we're able to let go of the self-destructive energy we are carrying around, hidden in our bodies."

"So now, Lisa, what do you want?" Eve asked.

"I want to heal. I want to experience love, healthy love. I want to release this. I want to release him. I want to fully forgive both him and myself. We both made poor choices; we were cocreating the chaos."

I had that feeling again as if something was being released out of me; the tension and hurt were dissipating. Somehow it felt as though the more I spoke these words, the more God smiled and took away from me what wasn't mine to hold on to.

Next it was time to tackle forgiveness. Could I really forgive Andrew? I took the leap. "I forgive you for allowing your mental and emotional condition to impact me and my son. I forgive you for putting your hands on me in a way that was other than loving. I forgive you for not taking your medication."

Opening myself up to forgive Andrew made me see that I had more self-forgiveness work to do. I needed to forgive "me" at a deeper level than I had reached in the mirror. "I forgive you, Lisa, for forgetting your value."

I got it. It hit me like two tons of bricks smack-dab in my heart: forgiving Andrew had nothing, and I mean *nothing*, to do with him—what he had done or who he was or whether he was right or wrong. Forgiveness had everything to do with me and setting that part of my heart free so I could put love in its place.

Anger and love (like faith and doubt) are oil and water; they can't occupy the same place at the same time. I thought with my anger that I'd been teaching him a lesson and making him pay, but instead it was I who had been paying the price. I saw there was no way to love to my full capacity while gripping tightly to my anger. I wanted to let it go.

This desire was put to the test by the very next sentence stem: "I appreciate you for . . ."

Without thinking too much, I again jumped right in. "Andrew, I appreciate you for loving me to the best of your ability. I appreciate you for teaching me the need to set boundaries for myself. I appreciate you for showing me that, just like you, I need to love God and myself, first and foremost, before anyone else. I thank God for you—you've given me a lesson that I'll never forget and one I'll *never* need to repeat again."

Getting to this stage was like standing on the mountaintop after climbing its boulder-strewn face on my hands and knees. My full vision had been restored, and before me lay the world and everything it held for me, spread out in every direction as far as the eye could see. I'd released the poisonous hatred I'd been holding in my heart. All that was left was love and compassion—for Andrew and myself.

When I'd said that I would never have to repeat the lesson I'd learned with Andrew, I knew it was true. It was my declaration of a new beginning. From this day forward, I wouldn't put on the same perfume of desperation. I'd upgrade to a more beautiful one—a fragrant mix of confidence, peace, and unwavering faith. It was up to me.

I was ready for the final level of the Total Truth Process: agreements. What was I willing to do from now on to stand in my greatness? With a full heart, I addressed Eve and the others in the room. "From now on, I will be the example showing others how to love and honor me by loving and honoring myself first. From now on, I will make a clear, specific request to my Higher Power, to the universe, so that I may attract what I really want. From now on, I will look beneath my anger for what it can teach me. From now on, I will recognize the power of forgiveness, the purpose of compassion, and the perfection of love—no matter what."

One by one each teen made his or her way to me and gave me a heartfelt hug. Many of them had tear-streaked faces, evidence that my story had evoked their own experiences. As I looked into their eyes, I saw that although our journeys were different, our breakthroughs were the same. We were no longer students and teacher; they had become my sisters and brothers in healing.

When Andrew had left, I'd thought the nightmare was over. But carrying around my anger and hatred for him kept me trapped in a bottomless pit of misery. Telling the Total Truth had guided my steps from anger to compassion—and finally to forgiveness. Finding my way back to love had truly set me free.

Go to the Deep End of Forgiveness

This is why we need a new definition of forgiveness. If you look up the word *forgive* in a thesaurus, the first synonyms listed are *pardon, excuse, exonerate,* and *absolve.* It's not until you get further down the list that you find the word's deeper meaning: *feel no resentment toward, feel no malice toward,* and *harbor no grudge against.* In our society, we are trained to think forgiving means letting another's behaviors suddenly be okay or excusable, or pretending that whatever hurt us never happened, as in "Forgive and forget." To live with the more complete definition of forgiveness is so much more freeing—and rewarding.

True forgiveness isn't about other people and their actions. True forgiveness is about *you.* In fact, it has absolutely nothing to do with how or why you felt wronged. It's simply a process of releasing any resentment or painful feelings toward yourself or someone else. It's about finding resolution—the ability to rise above a situation—despite how bad or horrible it may be . . . *no matter what.*

I like to use the example of being in a relationship, because it's such a universal experience. In my workshops, when I say, "Your *next* will pay for your *ex*," people always burst out laughing. They immediately know what I'm talking about, and to show this they stand up with their two hands up. Of course, it feels good to rally around our common experience of letting our futures pay for our pasts, but in the end, it serves us much more to recognize that this way of thinking isn't healthy and benefits no one. It leaves us feeling empty and stalled out—incomplete in all areas of our lives, from our romantic pursuits to our professional dreams, health goals, and personal friendships. So how do we choose a different approach? How do we close the door to our past pain forever and expel old thought patterns?

First, you call on your Understanding Muscle to help you to find the lesson or blessing in any experience. Once you've found the gift wrapped in the sandpaper, then flex your Forgiveness Muscle to untie any negative feelings still attached to it. When you do this, you not only extinguish that self-defeating emotion, you usher in compassion, the most rewarding outcome of the forgiveness process. You can find compassion just as I did, when you fully process your feelings and have the courage to go to the deep end of forgiveness.

When you step out of your shoes and into someone else's, it allows you to witness a circumstance or situation from a different perspective. And with that open-mindedness, you will sense a lifting of burdens from deep within. You'll become more flexible and instantly feel better. As rigidity ebbs away from you and empathy flows around you, suddenly the ability to forgive becomes automatic. That empathy then creates the space to accept and acknowledge other people's capacity—for love, for understanding, for forgiveness.

Just think of what it would be like to release any anger you hold toward someone or something that happened in your past—a time you felt you were treated unfairly or betrayed. It could be something that happened ten days ago, last month, or ten years ago. Whether it was related to an intimate relationship, your job or career path, or a family member, it doesn't matter. What does matter is the negative feeling you keep attached to this person or event. You haven't freed up that space in your mind and heart to fill with thrilling new experiences. Time has moved on, but you haven't. You're still held hostage emotionally to those toxic memories. Every time you think about it, you bring back that same feeling to this current moment as if it were real again. It's not!

Now take that experience and remove its power. By doing

so, in this very moment, you choose to terminate its authority over you. You can find your compassion. You can find your empathy. Even the most inexcusable act for which you've never received an apology can become a nonissue because *you* make it that way.

Regrets also lose their control over you when you flex your Forgiveness Muscle for yourself. Think of your biggest regret based on a decision or action that you made—or *didn't* make— and with empathy and compassion for yourself, watch *that* disappear. It can no longer flatten your spirit, incite your emotions, or fog over future opportunities. Anything becomes possible. Your life becomes a demonstration that you're worthy of not only a second chance, but of a thousand second chances. And what's exciting is that when you reach 999, you get to press the Reset button.

I find that virtually everyone has at least one experience from their past that is begging for the attention of the Forgiveness Muscle, even if it's just about forgiving themselves. This muscle ultimately allows you to welcome new things—new love, vibrant health, financial success, and great relationships— into your life. You then can choose to let go of frustrations and disappointments more quickly. You can decide to sever your connection to those parts of your existence that remain tied up and attached to old situations. Imagine heavy cords connecting you to boulders that represent the memories of your painful experiences from your childhood or teen years, a past love, marriage, or whatever. Everywhere you go, you're dragging these boulders of hurt around with you. With a strong Forgiveness Muscle, you can cut all those cords so you're fully present in the now.

To engage the Forgiveness Muscle:

1. Pinpoint your negative feelings revolving around old issues
2. Reconnect with your self-love and begin to forgive yourself
3. Go through the Total Truth Process: honestly process the emotions beneath your anger and hurt and own all of them
4. Find compassion to embrace a deeper level of forgiveness

It helps to start dealing with just those emotions you feel toward yourself, such as disappointment, shame, guilt, and regret. Then take responsibility for what has happened and the fact that *you* have the power to change your response to it. Embrace forgiveness as a process of releasing frustration and pain and unveiling compassion and empathy. This will bring you to a new understanding of forgiveness that grants you an infinite number of second chances in life. You'll find your way back to a place where there is nothing but love.

The following Inspired Action Steps will help you to build this muscle.

INSPIRED ACTION STEPS

I suggest that you do these action steps in order, as they build on one another. Start the process of forgiveness, just as I did, by boosting your self-esteem through affirmations that increase your positive self-talk. On that foundation, work in the mirror to love, appreciate, and if necessary, forgive yourself. Once you've made significant strides in that arena, tackle the Total Truth Process to let go of old hurts and resentments toward others. This will free up your energy for growth and possibility.

1. **Custom Affirmations:** As I shared with you in chapter 2, nothing beats an uplifting affirmation when you feel down, uninspired, angry, betrayed, or guilty. They can help recharge your soul and keep you living a life of No Matter What. Create your own set of personalized forgiveness affirmations tailored to your needs and keep them close by. Write the five that feel particularly appropriate to your present situation on Post-its, and stick them in conspicuous places around your house or personal space. Some ideas are:

     - "Every situation brings a gift to me."
     - "I choose to live in joy, possibility, and understanding."
     - "I have the power to forgive."
     - "My past does *not* equal my future."
     - "I deserve to have a fulfilling, happy life with no regrets."

2. **Mirror, Mirror on the Wall:** Once you have a collection of affirmations going, it's time to do some mirror work. Step into the bathroom or use your bedroom mirror. You'll want to use a mirror in a place where you feel comfortable and have privacy. Fill in your name at the beginning of each of the following sentence stems. Use the following leads to complete the sentences:

- "[Name], I'm proud that you . . ."
- "[Name], what I love about you is . . ."
- "[Name], I'm committed to . . ."

Run through this exercise three times, choosing three different endings for each sentence. As you do this, modify or create new affirmations that reflect what you discover. If feelings of shame or guilt surface, add another sentence to your exercise: "[Name], I forgive you for . . ." The action steps below will help you to further deal with those issues.

3. **Create a Life Time Line:** Identifying old, unresolved issues is crucial for developing your Forgiveness Muscle. But you don't have to identify just the bad memories when you do this. In the following exercise, you'll create a life time line that takes the emotional pulse of any time period in your life to identify those specific experiences—good and bad—that have occurred.

- Take a piece of blank paper, position it in "landscape" position, and draw a line from left to right, horizontally. Divide the line into thirds. Mark the first third "Childhood," the second third "Teen Years," and the last third "Adulthood."
- Recall the three most memorable moments of your childhood. Think of moments when you felt incredibly happy and joyful. Write those down near the part of the line marked "Childhood." Do the same for "Teen Years" and "Adulthood."
- Now think of the three moments, if any, in your childhood, teen years, and adulthood when you were hurt, disappointed, let down, deeply saddened, or had some experience that you would call traumatic or tragic. Record those, if applicable, in their respective time-period slots on the

paper. If you can't come up with three for each, that's okay. Just write what comes to mind. The purpose of this exercise is to identify old issues that are still bothering you.

- Select one of those issues that you haven't resolved yet and that you want to release. Circle that issue on the page. It can be from your childhood, your teen years, or something that happened recently. Once you've identified the issue, you're ready to move on to the next action step.

4. The Total Truth Process: Focusing on the issue you identified in the previous action step, it's time to do the Total Truth Process. This process is done standing up rather than sitting down. Ask a Rocket Booster friend to stand in front of you as a proxy for the person you are addressing as you go through the process outlined below. Starting with Anger, complete the following sentence stems. Some of the stems within the same category are similar. Use them all, however, because you never know which one will trigger the most powerful response.

- Anger
  - I am angry that you . . .
  - I hate it when you . . .
  - I got really mad when . . .
  - I resent that . . .

- Hurt
  - My feelings were hurt when . . .
  - I am really sad because . . .
  - I feel disappointed about . . .

- Fear
  - I am afraid that . . .
  - I am scared because I think . . .
  - I get afraid of you when . . .

- Responsibility and Accountability
    - I'm sorry that I . . .
    - Forgive me for . . .
    - I know that my part was . . .
    - I didn't mean to . . .

- Understanding
    - I understand that you . . .
    - What I know is . . .

- Wants
    - What I really want is . . .
    - I hope that . . .

- Forgiveness, Love, and Appreciation
    - I forgive you for . . .
    - I appreciate you for . . .
    - You're a good friend because . . .
    - What I love about you is . . .

- Agreements
    - I agree to . . .
    - From now on I will . . .

It's important to have your friend there to help you process your emotions and move forward to that place of compassion, love, and forgiveness. You may want to sit down and digest how you feel after doing this exercise. Or you may want to go for a walk with your Rocket Booster friend outside. Give yourself permission to experience your feelings, no matter what they may be.

CHAPTER NINE

Developing Your Highest Choice Muscle
Meeting Your Needs from the Inside Out, and Then Aiming for the Stars

STOP FOR A MOMENT AND THINK ABOUT YOUR LIFE. HOW'S YOUR health? How are your finances? Your relationships? Your sense of spiritual serenity? Your experiences today are a result of your past choices, patterns, and habits. Are you happy with the way you're living, or have you fallen into a less-than-healthy rut that you just can't seem to climb out of?

Nobody's perfect—99.9 percent of us have at least one pattern of behavior that doesn't serve us. We eat or drink or work too much; we choose friendships that don't really honor us; we react instead of responding in challenging moments. Yet in most cases, we still manage to function. Sometimes our negative patterns have small costs—simply slowing down our progress—and at other times, the price we pay for our poor choices is devastating; the choices can ruin our health, relationships, career, or family life.

Your Highest Choice Muscle is the bounce-back muscle that helps you replace toxic behaviors with emotionally and physically nourishing ones, allowing you to truly step into your greatness. If you're overeating to find comfort, drinking too much to relieve stress, or spending too many hours at the office to avoid tension at home, this muscle helps you choose healthier and more direct ways to satisfy those needs.

This chapter builds on chapter 5: Developing Your Honesty Muscle. If we've gotten used to the drama we're creating in our lives, it may be time to wake up and smell the coffee. The message to change direction can come from the outside—by way of a doctor's report or an accident, for example—or from within, with some variation of the thought *This is not who I want to be*. Whatever way the alarm arrives, our Highest Choice Muscle kicks in by first engaging our Honesty Muscle to face the truth of our situation and take responsibility for our part in creating it. But once we've become fully aware of the problem, what do we do?

The key to making lasting, positive change is understanding where our negative patterns of behavior are coming from. There are healthy and unhealthy ways to meet the needs in our lives. Sometimes, feeling desperate, we apply Band-Aids in an effort to feel better fast. These fixes may fulfill the need temporarily but in the long run can do more harm than good. When we make decisions based on unhealthy habits or to fill our needs inappropriately, it moves us away from greater empowerment and happiness.

Having a strong Highest Choice Muscle helps you identify the underlying need you're trying to meet and then choose the best and healthiest course of action you can take to fill that need. It helps you make the choices moment by moment that will move you in the direction of your highest good.

As I've mentioned before, one of the issues I've struggled with in my life has been my weight. For a long time, I alternated dieting and exercising with giving in and buying clothes in the next size up. But as my body got larger and larger, I knew I was damaging my health and my self-esteem. It took a startling question from someone who cared for me to make me finally address the deeper causes of my weight gain.

Why Do I Wear This Jacket?

For the first two years after Andrew left, I stayed in Los Angeles, working and saving money to fund my dream of working full-time with teens. When I was ready to jump in and launch my new company, Motivating the Teen Spirit, I decided to move to San Diego, an area I felt was more conducive to supporting the programs I wanted to create. So one fine summer day, I packed my bags, loaded them into my car along with my son, and drove south on the 405 Freeway—ready for a fresh start.

Though it was hard to leave the shelter of family and friends behind, once I was settled in my new home, I did everything I could to create a new life for myself. During my first year in San Diego, I attended local activities offered by IBI, the coaching organization for entrepreneurs I'd been involved with in Los Angeles, joined networking groups, and made many new friends, including Marc, a fellow entrepreneur I met at church. We weren't involved romantically—after Andrew, I was taking plenty of time off to heal—but we shared a lot of the same interests and enjoyed each other's company. But more than that, we'd made a commitment to support each other's personal growth and had promised to always be honest and authentic with one another.

One afternoon, after going out to lunch, Marc drove me home. We had been talking about our families, our life experiences, our unmarried status, our dreams—the type of meaningful topics that we often discussed. As we pulled into the driveway of my condominium complex, Marc turned to me and asked, "Lisa, why are you wearing that jacket?"

I paused for a moment, confused. *What jacket?* It was a

warm summer day, and I was wearing a sundress. Sensing that we were addressing a deeper issue, I felt a whisper of unease inside. But looking down at my bare arms and shoulders, I simply replied, "I'm not wearing a jacket."

He answered gently, "You *are* wearing a jacket; your weight is your jacket."

Ouch! His words hit me like an arrow between the eyes. I could feel his love, compassion, and genuine concern, and I knew he wasn't trying to hurt me. Still, it was painful and humiliating. I couldn't think of a thing to say.

We sat for a few seconds in silence and then he said, "You actually don't have to tell me why you're wearing the jacket, but at least be honest and tell yourself. And when you find the answer, if you feel you still need to wear it, then wear it. But if you feel you no longer need it, then at least you'll know and you can take it off."

After a subdued good-bye, I walked up the stairs to my townhome, thinking about what Marc had said. Of course, I knew I was overweight. I'd gained eighty pounds since Jelani was born—most of it in the previous three years—but lately, I'd hardly thought about it. It was just one of those high discomfort/low priority problems that I'd put on the back burner as I dealt with all the other pressing demands, responsibilities, and commitments vying for attention in my life.

Over the years, I'd started—and let slide—many, many diets and numerous exercise regimens. Now I realized I'd become resigned to being heavy. Though I wanted to lose the weight, I simply felt powerless around this issue. Marc's blunt but caring words made me wonder if perhaps it was time to ask myself *why* I was carrying around so many extra pounds.

Ignorance Is Not Really Bliss

Do you have a high discomfort/low priority challenge in your life? Or have you become so accustomed to a less-than-ideal situation that you've stopped noticing it? Ignorance can take many forms. We may be oblivious to the patterns in our lives that aren't serving us, or may be ignoring them, or may be bothered by them on some level—like a low-grade infection. We may have become so used to a compromised style of functioning that we just accept it as the way things are. But sooner or later, we're forced to confront reality.

A messenger appears—either in the form of a life crisis, a serious relationship breakdown, an internal call to play bigger, or in my case, the words of a loving friend. This messenger alerts us to the need for change.

Don't make the mistake of "shooting the messenger." If it's a person who supplies us with the wake-up call, we may take offense and react by getting angry or upset, lashing out to protect ourselves or wound the person back. We may try to make it about the other person, focusing on the hurt or anger we feel rather than on what he or she is trying to tell us. If it's an event or circumstance like bankruptcy or divorce or a medical problem that finally opens our eyes to a necessary course correction, we may feel we've been treated unfairly or may curse our bad luck. It doesn't matter how the message comes to us; what's important is that we *don't miss the point!* As we learned in chapters 1 and 3, if we get stuck feeling like a victim, we'll miss the opportunity to improve our lives.

Repeated messages come for a reason. If we keep having difficulties with coworkers, romantic partners, family members, our finances, or our health, what's the common denominator in every situation that's not working? I'm sure you've heard the saying "Wherever you go, there you are." It's possible there's something we may need to look at in ourselves. Instead of complaining about how inconsiderate people are or how unfair our work schedules are or how high our bills are, it's usually more effective to stop and examine what *we're* doing that's contributing to the problem.

Sometimes we don't recognize that we're getting a message. Signals to change our behavior can come from many different quarters, and their meanings may not always be obvious. Individual warning signs we receive may seem insignificant in and of themselves, but taken together, they often make a powerful case for change. Over the years, I've developed a policy: if I get the same message from three different sources, then I know it's an issue I need to deal with in my life. For example, if I feel I have too many balls in the air on one day, get a speeding ticket the next, and my mother tells me that she feels I'm rushing her off the phone the day after that, then I know that there's something I need to pay attention to. In this example, I'm moving too fast, and it's time to get serious about slowing down.

Reflect for a moment. Are you getting the same feedback from a number of different sources? If so, maybe it's time to listen to what the universe is trying to tell you. Like me, you may find it extremely useful.

Peeling Back the Layers

I couldn't get Marc's question out of my head. Once inside the door, I walked straight to my bedroom and stood in front of the mirror. Looking into my own troubled eyes, I asked myself, *Why do I wear this jacket? This isn't who I really am; it's covering up the true me.*

The same old excuses came up in my mind: I hadn't lost my pregnancy weight after Jelani's birth. The pounds I'd put on after Andrew were a result of my depression—a natural reaction to the trauma I'd endured. I'd moved to a new city and was under a lot of stress starting up my new business. But as soon as I finished running down the familiar list, the thought popped up: *That's not the whole truth. Those are contributing factors to your weight problem, but they're not the cause.* Bust-ed!

I'M NOT ALONE

Making excuses is a great way to avoid addressing the real issues in your life for long periods of time. We often start believing the stories we tell to convince ourselves and others that our actions are perfectly reasonable.

Check one box if you've ever had this experience. Check two boxes if you run into this problem a lot. Check three boxes if this describes you to a tee.

For the next few hours, I kept myself busy, channeling my nervous energy into cleaning the kitchen, the bathroom, and my dresser and even organizing my closet. The whole time I kept asking myself, *Why do I wear this jacket?* but nothing more surfaced—except for one odd thing: whenever I walked near my bed and asked that question, I experienced an almost overwhelming feeling of sadness and a painful pressure in my chest. This happened at least three or four times.

Puzzled, I stood for a moment, staring at the bed. Immediately, I felt the dark, stabbing ache in my heart intensify. Ready to know the truth, whatever the cost, I climbed to the center of my California king and asked myself again, *Why do I wear this jacket?*

The answer came in a flood of vivid flashbacks. First, scenes of sensuality: the feel of lingerie on my youthful, slammin'-jammin' body, lit candles around the bed, impressive sexual performances that highlighted my strength and stamina. These were immediately followed by scenes of emotional desolation and pain: memories of lonely mornings and of feeling used, cheap, and ashamed. I began to sob as I reexperienced the agony of losing more and more of myself with each empty act of intimacy.

For the first time, I saw that I'd gained weight so that I'd stop having meaningless sexual relationships. I'd wanted men to love me for who I really was. I'd wanted them to notice my smile, my eyes, my zest for life and bright spirit, not just my "muscular thunder-thighs, my D-cups, and fine rump roast." At the time, I wasn't mature enough to turn down invitations to have sex—as I said earlier, I was afraid I'd be turning down an opportunity to find love. Instead, I made an unconscious decision to protect myself by gaining weight.

But now I realized I'd simply traded one pain for another. By trying to guard my heart in this way, I'd eventually ended up feeling worse about myself (and even lonelier) than before. Becoming so overweight had not only stopped me from having empty intimacies, it had pretty much stopped *all* intimacy. For years, I'd been too ashamed to let anyone into my personal space.

The stark reality of the place this strategy had landed me was shocking and sobering. I cried for three days straight—only taking breaks to care for Jelani. I'd wash my face and put on my happy-mommy smile; I didn't want to upset my son. But as soon as he was in school or playing at a friend's house or asleep, I went back to my bed, continuing to process my feelings and trying to figure out why I'd gone so far down this unhealthy path.

Though the whole process was extremely challenging, I'd finally found the answer to my question: my weight gain had been a misguided attempt to fill a deeper need: the need to feel wanted, loved, and adored; to be approved of, validated, honored, and celebrated. At long last, I was addressing my core feeling of brokenness, the emptiness in me that needed love from the outside to feel full.

Identify the Need

As we know, a strong Honesty Muscle allows us to acknowledge and own our patterns, both negative and positive. When we're ready to start changing the patterns that don't serve us, we engage our Highest Choice Muscle. Once we're aware of *what* we're doing, we can flex our Highest Choice Muscle to discover *why*.

To find the underlying cause of our unhealthy behaviors, we can ask ourselves, *When I drink too much, overeat, automatically put others' needs before my own, work too many hours (or whatever your issue is), what need am I trying to fill?* Excessive drinking, overeating, overworking, and so on, are often unconscious ways of seeking approval, love, power, and so on. In my case, becoming overweight was the unintentional tactic I used to meet my deepest desire—to be loved for my heart, not just my body.

The need at the root of our negative patterns may be multiple layers away from the harmful behavior we want to change. This requires us to go to our core and keep asking ourselves, *Why do I do this? What do I want?* and not stop till we recognize the innermost need we're trying to meet.

It often helps in this process to untangle your emotions. Just as you did for the Forgiveness Muscle, take an emotional inventory. To do this, look at all the feelings you have regarding the situation. For example, if you're a chronic workaholic, working long hours and letting all the other areas of your life collapse, examine the deeper feelings you have about your career. Are you excited and enthusiastic about your goals, or are you terrified of failure? If fear is your dominant emotion, the need to be safe is the one you're probably trying to satisfy.

In my experience working with thousands and thousands of people around the world, the root cause of all problems is one of the following feelings: I'm not good enough; I'm afraid; I need to prove myself. Everything we do is an attempt to address our basic need: to feel okay within ourselves. Some of the things we do are positive and constructive; others are not.

Many times our unhealthy patterns of behavior are like Band-Aids—temporary or partial fixes. They may feel good or work in a limited way, but they don't truly meet our core needs. In fact, they can make things worse in the long run or even create new problems.

These Band-Aids can produce false wins—or Pyrrhic victories, named for Pyrrhus, an ancient Greek general famous for winning an important battle that cost him more than he gained. You achieve a Pyrrhic victory in your life when you achieve your goal but the collateral damage outweighs the benefits. Gaining weight was my Pyrrhic victory—I stopped having empty sex, but at the cost of my self-esteem, my confidence, and my health.

You'll know you're getting close to identifying your root need when you feel uncomfortable and want to quit. Face it, there's a reason you've been doing whatever it takes to avoid feeling this way. Confronting your deepest issues isn't for the faint of heart, but I guarantee you it's the most important work you can do. It's the key to living a life of joy, success, love, and purpose.

Even though we honestly want to improve our lives, if we don't identify what's driving our negative patterns of behavior, we're probably not going to be able to change them. We can read a million diet books, but if we don't tackle what's causing us to eat, it will be harder to lose weight—and keep it off. We can complain about our unreasonable work schedule and vow to cut back on our hours, but if we don't address our deeper fears, we won't be able to make a true commitment to having more balance in our lives.

Without a clear understanding of our motives, we'll keep trying to break our bad habits from the outside in and then beat ourselves up each time we fail. This leaves us feeling even more hopeless, creating a vicious cycle. The bottom line: if you want to achieve *lasting* positive change and become the person you know you can be, use your Highest Choice Muscle to first clearly identify the need you're trying to fill. Then keep that need in clear view, like a target, as you adjust your strategy for meeting it.

Emotional Fitness Therapy

Finally, after crying more tears than I thought was humanly possible, I called BJ, the minister of the church I was attending. Over the last year, we'd developed a close friendship as a result of her spiritual mentoring. I told her I needed her help, and we made an appointment to see each other the next day.

We met at a local coffee shop, and after getting our drinks, we sat down at a table outside. I was nervous, ashamed to talk to a minister about my previous sexual irresponsibility. Looking around to make sure no one else could hear me, I gathered up my courage and told her the whole story.

When I finally finished, we sat for a moment, quiet. The entire time I'd been speaking, BJ's expression had remained open and receptive. Now I saw her shift in her chair as she prepared to respond. *Was she shocked?* I wondered. *Or maybe disappointed in me?*

BJ broke the silence by chuckling. "Honey," she said, giving me a warm smile. "I may be your minister, but I'm a woman, too. Love and sex are sometimes hard to separate. We all make mistakes. God isn't keeping score, so why are you?"

Hearing her words, I gave a huge sigh of relief and felt the weight in my chest ease for the first time in days.

We talked for a long time that morning as I struggled to manage the thoughts and emotions that had taken up residence in my head and heart. After that, I began meeting regularly with BJ, praying, reading scripture, and working to find healthier ways to satisfy my core needs for approval and acceptance.

I'M NOT ALONE

Have you ever confided in another person—especially about behavior or events you're embarrassed or ashamed of— and felt that it released a lot of the charge you were holding inside?

Check one box if you've ever had this experience. Check two boxes if you've experienced this a number of times. Check three boxes if this happens to you a lot.

The dust from the emotional explosion that had shaken my world began to settle, and I could feel my feet planted on solid ground again. With BJ's help, I saw that I had the capacity and the resources to fill up my own tank—to give *myself* the love and validation that I had sought from relationships. This wasn't an "aha moment" but more of an "aha period." No one sprinkled fairy dust or waved a magic wand over my head. It took many months of intention and concentrated focus for me to make the shift and begin to address my deepest needs in a positive and life-supporting way.

BJ also introduced me to Dejinira, a woman in my church who was a personal trainer. When I met her, at first I was a little intimidated. The woman's *muscles* had muscles! During our initial consultation, Dejinira asked me questions and listened carefully to my responses. There was none of the drill-sergeant energy I'd been expecting. Instead, I felt her compassion and her true care for my well-being. Embarrassed about my body, I'd been afraid she would judge me for my obvious lack of fitness. But she extended herself, stepping into my world and taking into account what it felt like to be where I was. I knew then that it was okay to expose everything and not just talk about my workout goals. I even felt comfortable enough to let myself cry in her presence.

I started exercising with her, doing a program I called Emotional Fitness Therapy because it involved both my body and my emotions. Every morning at 6:00, Dejinira supervised as I pounded away on the treadmill, lifted weights, and did endless lunges in the condo exercise room. Luckily, we had the place to ourselves, because in addition to sweating gallons, I laid open my soul.

There were moments when the lunges and crunches were far easier than the emotional cleansing that I'd committed to. During my hour with Dejinira, I spoke of the shame I felt about having gone from being a top athlete and cheerleader to being overweight, and then becoming obese. In between sit-ups, I exposed the excuses I used—my pregnancy, depression, and work schedule—to justify my poor choices. And as I lifted and lowered eight-pound dumbbells, I took responsibility for the unauthorized mergers that had occurred between my butt and my thighs, and my breasts and my belly—and the way I felt about myself because of those mergers. Every day I took one more step toward forgiving myself for my past mistakes and believing that I deserved to be happy, loved, and healthy.

My work with Dejinira also helped me to realize that over the years, I'd become detached from my body—it was just there to hold up my head, and I tried to ignore it as much as possible. I always made a point of dressing in expensive suits and draping myself with eye-catching jewelry in an effort to compensate for my extra girth. Then when people complimented me on my appearance, I'd rationalize that I was okay as I was. Now, as I began to feel my muscle tone and shape returning, I remembered what it was like to nurture my physical health. I reveled in my newfound vitality and energy.

Over the next nine months, I lost thirty-six pounds and gained a new degree of comfort with both my body and my emotions. Building my Highest Choice Muscle empowered me to fill my need to feel loved and cared for in healthy ways—I began to take bubble baths again, scheduled massages, and chose better foods to eat—and it also helped me to keep my higher goals in mind. I began to create the memories I wanted to have. I played more with my son, dancing and singing together at home and taking him to museums and amusement parks. I spent more time outside, breathing in the beauty of the nearby beaches, and I took frequent trips north to see my family.

Today, though I'm still on my journey to optimal health and my ideal weight, there's a clear path ahead. No more Band-Aids or Pyrrhic victories for me. The only solutions I'm interested in are the real ones.

Win-Win Choices

Once you've clearly identified what your needs are, having a strong Highest Choice Muscle helps you choose the healthiest and best ways to fill those requirements.

At this point, you may have to address any feelings of unworthiness you have inside. Sometimes guilt and shame about past mistakes or present chaos in our lives can make us feel we don't deserve to have our needs met. But beating ourselves up stops us from making the highest choices before we even start. If this is your situation, spend some time stretching your Forgiveness Muscle. You can do (or redo) the action steps from the last chapter, paying special attention to the self-forgiveness exercises there.

To forgive yourself completely, you may need to make things right with other people. This may mean making amends for wrongs you've committed, cleaning up unresolved communications, or finishing incomplete agreements with others. This is possible even if the people involved are deceased or no longer a part of your life. Remember, forgiveness is primarily an internal process. By doing this, you create opportunities to make progress in life, unencumbered by the weight of the past.

Using our Highest Choice Muscle also gives us the chance to begin healing the core feelings of brokenness we discovered at the root of our negative patterns. If you found that your deepest need was to get love, approval, or acknowledgment from other people, commit to providing it for yourself. Working with BJ helped me realize that wanting someone else to give me the love I hadn't yet learned to give myself was never going to fill me up anyway. No matter how much love I received, it was like pouring water into a bucket with the bottom rusted through—every drop eventually escaped.

Is your bucket whole? Or does it have holes? Recognizing that some needs have to be filled from inside is the first step toward patching those gaps.

People often ask me, "How will I know that I'm making the highest choice?" I tell them that when you're meeting a need in a healthy way, your actions always lead to more balance in your life. Trying to satisfy a need in an unhealthy way creates the negative patterns of behavior called being an "aholic": a workaholic, an alcoholic, a yes-aholic, and so on. In our urgency to make ourselves feel okay, we often sacrifice the proper functioning of the other areas of our lives.

Another indicator of making higher choices is determining how much harmony your behavior generates. Having a strong Highest Choice Muscle fine-tunes your ability to discern win-win opportunities in every situation. You operate from a place of kindness and fairness—to yourself and to others. You create victories that are authentic from beginning to end.

Begin with the End in Mind

Once you start developing your Highest Choice Muscle, your life takes on a different quality. You're more aware of the long-term effects of your actions. Not only do you make better, more conscious choices every day about your health, your relationships, your finances, and so on, you're more connected to your larger purpose. A strong Highest Choice Muscle helps you to begin every course of action, in the words of author Stephen Covey, "with the end in mind."

I was in my twenties when I first read Covey's book *The 7 Habits of Highly Effective People.* I was on a business trip and remember sitting on my bed in the hotel room reading the chapter titled "Begin with the End in Mind." There's an exercise in that section in which you imagine yourself walking into a funeral parlor for the funeral of a loved one. Covey asks you to smell the flowers and hear the organ music. As you walk down the aisle of this parlor, you see the faces of all the people you know—your family, your friends, and your coworkers—sitting in the chairs. Their faces are sad, and some are crying. When you get to the front of the room, you see a casket. Looking into the casket, you come face-to-face . . . with yourself! You're at your own funeral!

At this, I felt a shock go through my body, but I kept reading. Covey asks you to consider what people will say about you at your funeral. What kind of friend were you? What kind of sister or brother were you? What kind of coworker were you? What kind of neighbor were you?

I put the book down as the true implications of his words flooded my mind and heart. It was the first time I realized that I could write my obituary *now* by the way I lived my life.

It took me many more years to fully step into living with the end in mind. I first had to develop my Highest Choice Muscle, which helped me hold myself to a higher standard. When I returned home from that business trip, I made a few adjustments. I began doing the things that would make me the person I wanted to be: I spent more quality time with my mother and father. I began to volunteer more time working with teens. I gave more attention to my spirituality. And I also stopped doing the things I wasn't proud of, like partying. I didn't want to spend my energy club-hopping or be remembered as a party animal.

As you know, it took me longer to give up trying to enter the room called love through the door called sex, but that was because I hadn't faced my deeper motivations for that unhealthy behavior. The more deeply rooted the challenge, the more time and effort it requires to overcome it. Today, my strong Highest Choice Muscle allows me to make the right choices—the ones that create the story I want told about me when I'm gone.

I'M NOT ALONE   Does thinking about what people will say about you at your funeral have any effect on your behavior now? Contemplating death may be scary, but it's worth it. Letting your legacy shape your life is a powerful way to clarify your current choices.

Check one box if you can relate to this idea. Check two boxes if you're fairly comfortable with it. Check three boxes if it feels exciting to think about shaping your legacy today.   ☐ ☐ ☐

Keeping the end in mind isn't just a onetime event; it takes conscious, continued intention. Our highest goals sometimes lie over the horizon, and we often can't see them in the hustle-bustle of our everyday lives. Using your Highest Choice Muscle is like putting up guide rails or those traffic bumps on the sides of the highway that wake you up when you drift outside your lane—a way to alert yourself if you begin veering away from your highest good. You can get off track for any number of reasons: you can become distracted, discouraged, tired, or frustrated. And leaving the road isn't always a sharp turn; the change can be gradual, a number of small shifts in direction made over time. Those guide rails or traffic bumps help you remember, *Hey, wait a minute, this isn't what I wanted. I'd better get back on the road again.*

One surefire way to develop your Highest Choice Muscle is to ask yourself, *Who's in charge here?* Is it the higher, more aware you? Or the impatient child inside who wants what he or she wants *now*? When making decisions about what to do, the alternative that leads you to your highest good isn't always the easy one. I'm sure you've experienced this yourself. When it's time to leave your warm bed and go to the gym and work out, it's tempting to pull the covers up around your neck and snuggle in for some more sleep instead. When you're trying to stay away from sweets, ordering the fruit plate for dessert can take a great deal of discipline. As we learned in the chapter about the Determination Muscle, the secret is focusing on what you want, not on what you're giving up—and remembering that an even greater satisfaction awaits you as you move closer and closer to your goal. Making higher choices means putting your more "evolved" self in the driver's seat.

If all this sounds like a lot of work, remember, as with any muscle, conditioning your Highest Choice Muscle takes effort—but less and less as you go along. Soon, the experience of living in greater harmony, joy, purpose, and power becomes so attractive, you won't want to waste time with anything less. You stay on target more and aren't sidetracked by little things. You keep the small things small.

When you stay connected to the highest vision you have for yourself, you begin to draw to you people, opportunities, experiences that are at that same level. It feels good to *be* you, and it feels good to be *with* you. You become a magnet for your highest good.

Like your Determination Muscle, your Highest Choice Muscle is vital for both climbing out of your valleys and scaling your mountaintops. It guides you when you're ready to shift the negative patterns you've created in the past by not filling your needs in a healthy way and also keeps you on track to manifest the life you truly want to live.

You engage the Highest Choice Muscle by:

1. Becoming fully aware of the behavior you want to change
2. Identifying the need you are trying to fill through that behavior
3. Finding the best and healthiest way to satisfy that need
4. Aligning your choices with your highest aspirations

Do the Inspired Action Steps that follow to build this gotta-have muscle.

INSPIRED ACTION STEPS

These steps are designed to help you move forward in your life to a place of inspiration and wholeness. To start, I ask you to flex your Highest Choice Muscle with regard to your everyday habits. That means in the first action step, instead of getting caught up in any problems you may have, switch your attention to focusing on solutions. Take the same approach with the rest of the action steps. This is the time to bring your highest and best self to the forefront. Doing this will help lead you more quickly to the life you were born to live.

1. **Discover New Ways to Meet Your Needs:** Think of one current behavior or habit in your life that isn't serving you. Now, *without judgment*, reflect for a minute or two on the need you are trying to fill with that behavior or habit. Ask yourself simply and gently, *Why do I do that? What do I really want?*

   - Once you have an idea of the need you are trying to fill with the unwanted behavior, think of three healthy, life-enhancing ways you could get the result you are seeking. Now, just as an experiment, give at least one of these positive behaviors a try, and see what happens. For example, if you are eating too many snacks after dinner because you're bored, the next time you experience that bored feeling coming over you, you could call a friend, take a walk, or journal about what you want to achieve the following day. Remember, you don't have to *stop* the negative behavior; this is simply about making the highest choice. Once you are getting what you want in a healthy way, the unhealthy behavior will naturally decrease.

2. **Writing Down Your Legacy:** Making your highest choice is really about speaking to your life story. What do

you want your life story to be? One way to answer that is to consider the following questions:

- ○ When people sum up your life at some time in the future, what would you like them to say?
- ○ What will they point out or highlight? What kind of friend were you? Sister? Brother? Mother? Co-worker? Neighbor? Mentor?
- ○ How did you show up in the world? And did you contribute to it while you were here?
- ○ How did you make this a better place to live for all people?

- Now pick two people in your life, such as a family member, a friend, a neighbor, or a coworker. Be sure to choose two people from different circles, such as one from your immediate family and another from your school days or work. Write each of their names at the top of two separate sheets of paper.
- Write one paragraph from each person, recording what they would say about you today—*right now*. Include the highs and the lows; write the unedited, candid truth, even if that means including details that you'd prefer them *not* to remember or say in their descriptions of you. Some things to think about as you do this are your dominant personality traits; your strengths and weaknesses; your chosen career; your spirit; your contributions to society; your talents; your hobbies and passions; your degrees, honors, accolades; and so on.
- Now write a second paragraph for each person recording what you think these two people would say about you *three years from now*. And here's the added wrinkle: assume that you have mastered everything you've ever wanted to master—in mind, in

spirit, in body, in career, in finances—in everything. You've become everything you've wanted to become. You've surpassed all the frustrations and challenges in your life, and you are exactly where you want to be. Now what would those paragraphs reveal about you? How big did you play in the universe? How many lives did you impact? How did your children look at you? What legacy did you leave that was larger than you as an individual?

This is a powerful exercise. It will help you to identify exactly where you need to grow and expand more and which areas in your life deserve the most attention.

3. **Zeroing In on What Matters:** Using a different color ink than the one you used above, circle the characteristics in the first paragraphs that you didn't feel good writing and that you didn't want to write. (If you didn't write them, write them now!) These are the things you don't want to be remembered for and that you've outgrown now that you're aware of them.

   In the second set of paragraphs, circle the accolades, acknowledgments, or words of praise that reflect who you are. These will include the honors you'd like to ensure become a part of your "life's list" of notable accomplishments. Also be sure to circle the ones that you know deep down in your heart are how you want to be remembered. Clearly, this is where you want to focus your efforts, your energy, and your enthusiasm.

4. **Visualize Your Highest Choice Muscle Fully Developed:** The following visualization exercise will help you to see even more clearly into the future and empower you to make the changes and shift in your life today so you move closer to the dream you have of yourself. This exer-

cise works that Highest Choice Muscle extensively, priming it for continual use in the future as it grows stronger and stronger.

- Pretend it's five or six years from now. You've surpassed all expectations you've had for yourself, and now you're receiving a special award because your life story has shown perseverance and resiliency. You demonstrate what it looks like to have all the bounce-back muscles fully developed—your Understanding, Faith-in-Myself, Take-Action, I-Know-Like-I-Know, Honesty, Say-Yes, Determination, Forgiveness, and Highest Choice Muscles, all strong and 100 percent functional. You've become the ultimate example—the poster child—for each of these. In other words, you've become the world's best role model of what it means to live a life of No Matter What.

- Now pretend there are twenty thousand people present in the room where you are to receive this grand award. Millions of others are watching on television. Picture the scene: You look immaculate from head to toe. You're striking, strong, and magnetic. As the host speaks to the audience, describing your life and why you are the best person to receive this award, you realize in that moment that your whole life—everything that's happened to you—has been preparing you for such a time as this.

- You know that after the host finishes acknowledging and introducing you, he's going to hand you a breath-taking symbol of recognition. You approach the podium to accept it and thank the host. As you turn to face the audience, what will you say about the journey that has brought you to this place and about the gratitude you have for each experience you've been blessed with? What will you say about the responsibility you recognize is yours? Write your acceptance speech. Take as many pages in your journal as you like. Or if you prefer, you can speak your acceptance speech into a recording device.

These action steps will help you to recognize the impact you can have on the world and allow you to tap into the limitless possibilities that await you once you've fully developed your Highest Choice Muscle.

CHAPTER TEN

Finding Your Rhythm
Living in Joy and Possibility

IN THE LAST NINE CHAPTERS, YOU'VE BEEN INTRODUCED TO THE NINE major bounce-back muscles—the ones I had to strengthen to overcome the breakdowns, challenges, and fear-storms I faced and to help me to love myself and accept the invitations to live without limitations—*no matter what.*

My life today is a result of constantly stretching the muscles that built my character. I recognize now that the most uncomfortable moments were those when I was pushed beyond my perceived limits. Those were usually the times I thought I was already playing big but was asked to play bigger.

Writing this book is a good example. It was hard. I had to call on *all* of my bounce-back muscles! My faith in myself allowed me to begin this process. After that, the muscles all worked together. I had to say yes; I had to take action; I had to be honest, to remain determined, and to search my soul when I started to waver. I had to understand my life at a deeper level than ever before and relive the forgiveness process—as well as everything that required my forgiveness in the first place. And most of all, I had to keep making choices that led to the highest good for myself and for you, my readers.

There were many occasions when my "yes" became a "maybe" or an "oh, I can't do this"—but my Highest Choice Muscle kept me going. Even with my knees knocking and my teeth chattering, as I wrote down the most personal, revealing, painful, sacred parts of my life (afraid to have strangers read them, but even more afraid that my family would read them), I told myself, "Yes, this is scary, Lisa, but you know you want to serve more, to give more, to inspire more." I felt myself stretching on tippy-toes to reach the spot that would allow me to look back on my life and feel proud and satisfied.

Though our lives are all different, each one of us has those same bounce-back muscles. As you've read through the chapters, I'm sure you've noticed that some of yours are more developed, while others may still need work.

To review, here are the muscles as they appear in the book, along with the four processes you can use to strengthen each one.

To develop your Understanding Muscle
1. Search for the gift in each circumstance.
2. Look outside your immediate situation to the bigger picture.
3. Go into your heart to find compassion.
4. Put yourself in the other person's shoes.

To develop your Faith-in-Myself Muscle
1. Turn off the negative CD playing in your head.
2. Treat yourself with respect and kindness.
3. Borrow faith from others when yours runs low.
4. Surround yourself with your Rocket Booster community: people who love, celebrate, and encourage you.

To develop your Take-Action Muscle

1. Recognize when you're moaning—stuck "lying on the nail."
2. Refocus on your original goal.
3. Be open to other, possibly better, ways to reach it.
4. Keep in view your highest dreams and the ways in which you want to be of service while you're on this earth.

To develop your I-Know-Like-I-Know Muscle

1. Open yourself up to God, Spirit, Nature, the Universe, or whatever you call your Higher Power.
2. Invite that Higher Power into your life now; don't wait to be perfect.
3. Learn to access a larger source of strength at will through meditation, breathing, or prayer.
4. Feel the constant presence of your Higher Power in your heart through gratitude.

To develop your Honesty Muscle

1. Be willing to take an unflinching inventory of what works and doesn't work in your life.
2. Take responsibility for your part in creating your situation.
3. Address the things that don't work with detachment and clarity.
4. Embrace yourself enough to share your truth with others.

To develop your Say-Yes Muscle

1. Hear and acknowledge what life is calling you to do.
2. Test the waters by saying yes in small ways.
3. Commit to playing full out.
4. Formulate practical strategies to live your dreams.

To develop your Determination Muscle

1. Face the truth of your situation.

2. Pick a target to aim for.
3. Use the power of focus.
4. Stay firmly connected to your spiritual center and ask the people you love for assistance.

To develop your Forgiveness Muscle
1. Pinpoint negative feelings revolving around old issues.
2. Reconnect with your self-love and begin to forgive yourself.
3. Go through the Total Truth Process: honestly process the emotions beneath your anger and hurt and own all of them.
4. Find compassion to embrace a deeper level of forgiveness.

To develop your Highest Choice Muscle
1. Become fully aware of the unhealthy behavior you want to change in your life.
2. Identify the need you are trying to fill through that behavior.
3. Find the best and healthiest way to satisfy that need.
4. Align your choices with your highest aspirations.

These were the nine bounce-back muscles that I identified clearly from my own experience. But there are others: there's your Unconditional Love Muscle, your Creativity Muscle, your Integrity Muscle, your Authenticity Muscle (closely related to the Honesty Muscle), and your Letting Go Muscle, to name just a few. As you go through your own life experiences, identify which of the nine muscles in this book you are developing and look for others, too. I believe there are as many bounce-back muscles as there are physical muscles in our body. And like our physical muscles, they are all interlinked and interdependent. Collectively, these muscles move us forward and build our resilience.

It's important not to let the muscles of your character get out of balance or to overwork any one at the expense of the others. When a muscle is weak, we often compensate by putting additional strain on our other muscles. This can cause problems. For example, if your Honesty Muscle is shaky, you may overuse your Take-Action Muscle, staying busy-busy-busy to avoid addressing the things that you really need to look at in your life.

The key is to become aware of your different bounce-back muscles and recognize immediately when you're being called to use them—whether the ones in this book or any others you find you need to develop. When you observe a muscle in you that's strong or that you've made progress in strengthening, celebrate! And when you find yourself reacting negatively to something, notice which muscle is faltering, and tell yourself, *Wow, that muscle isn't developed in me. Now I know about it and can work on it.*

I believe that to strengthen any part of your life, whether it's forgiving yourself or others, believing in your own worth, or taking your health, finances, or relationships to the next level, you first have to be aware of where you are and where you want to go. It's that old finding the dot process again. The goal of this book is to bring your bounce-back muscles to your conscious awareness—to help you understand how these muscles function when they're fully developed and allow you to gauge how far along you are in that process. In some chapters, you might have thought, *I've really got this one down. That muscle is built!* In others, you may have recognized yourself in the "Before" rather than the "After" picture. That's okay. The important thing is what you do next.

Whether you discover that a particular bounce-back muscle is strong or weak, the essential action is the same: keep working that muscle. When you don't use a physical muscle, it begins to atrophy. There was a time when I worked out every day and had six-pack abs. But I can't stop doing sit-ups for fifteen years and think I'm still going to have a six-pack—it's going to turn into a keg.

I believe the muscles of our character do the same thing: if you don't use them, you lose them. If you don't exercise your Forgiveness Muscle for ten years, and then something happens that requires your forgiveness in the eleventh year, it's harder to forgive sooner-quicker-faster. You haven't kept the muscle fibers of compassion and understanding toned, and so you have to build the Forgiveness Muscle up again from scratch. Use this book to make strengthening your bounce-back muscles a daily habit—one as natural as showering or brushing your teeth.

This is best done by taking baby steps—bite-sized, palatable, easily digestible measures—to avoid becoming overwhelmed. And when you walk this path while being kind and loving to yourself, you model how you want others to treat you.

Building the muscles of your character is a cumulative process. Like those sit-ups, the more you do, the more you *can* do! When you stretch your bounce-back muscles to become more loving, forgiving, honest, and so on, your capacity for greatness expands. You go from being a 24-ounce cup to becoming a 32-ounce cup, and then on to being a 64-ounce cup; you're able to hold more of who you really are—and offer more to the world around you.

Where to Go from Here

How you use this book will grow and change as you do. You may find something in one of the chapters that's incredibly applicable today but that six months from now may not be as necessary. At that point, you may discover material in another chapter that's more relevant to your situation. I recommend that you use *No Matter What!* as a go-to resource. This book is not just a onetime experience of reading "Lisa stories" and thought-provoking ideas. It's like a toolbox storing a lot of different tools that you can reach for whenever you need one. If suddenly you're in the middle of something that requires more determination than ever before, take time to review chapter 7 and do those action steps again. When you feel like saying, "I want to live bigger; I want to follow my dreams," then open up the book to chapter 6 and remind yourself how to develop your Say-Yes Muscle.

I hope my story will serve as inspiration—if I could get through my valleys and climb to my mountaintops, so can you—but focus on the how-to sections. You can do the action steps again and again. They'll lead you to make amazing transformations in your own life. Don't think, *Oh, I've already done that.* Your experience of the action steps will change depending on what's going on for you at the moment. I've done the action steps in this book many, many times, and I've had completely different insights and breakthroughs as my understanding of myself and the people around me has evolved and expanded.

I suggest that even after you finish reading this book, you continue to keep the No Matter What journal I asked you to start in the introduction. In the future, when you return to this book's lessons and action steps, don't forget to review your journal, too. It will remind you of the insights you've already gained and give you a yardstick to measure your progress— pieces of information that are extremely helpful to have.

Adopting a No Matter What attitude and way of living is a journey that can be taken with a friend or a small group or a whole community of like-minded people. It's always easier to make changes in your life with support and encouragement.

Find a **No Matter What accountability buddy:** Teaming up with a Rocket Booster friend who's committed to his or her own personal growth *and* yours can help you stay on track. Together, you can reach new heights in toning and strengthening your muscles that neither of you could accomplish alone.

Form a **No Matter What support group:** Joining forces with others committed to building their bounce-back muscles will generate contagious feelings of momentum and drive. The benefits of a support group are endless: it serves as a safe space where each participant can "peel back the layers" to find the truth, identify areas of growth to pursue, set achievable goals, and celebrate wins. (Visit www.Lisa-Nichols .com to join our online support group or to locate a support group in your area.)

Keep your eyes open for mentors in your community—people who have already developed their bounce-back muscles who can serve as role models and be sources of advice and inspiration. (What's really exciting is that with the new global community created by the Internet, your mentors can be from anywhere in the world.)

You can enlist **No Matter What Life Coaches** to assist you in stretching and developing the muscles of your character in the same way you'd hire a personal trainer to help you to meet your physical fitness goals. See the resources section in the back of the book for more information about No Matter What coaching programs and the other resources available to accelerate your progress.

Finding Your Rhythm

Developing your bounce-back muscles won't prevent you from ever finding yourself in unfortunate circumstances or from coming up against challenges; you're likely to have days when you don't feel as great as you'd like to feel, when your faith is tested, when the smaller part of you says, "no, no, no," and you need to really flex that bounce-back muscle to say "yes, yes, yes." Strong bounce-back muscles simply prepare you to move through your challenging times when they occur. You don't get stuck—or, as I put it in the introduction, a speed bump doesn't become a stop sign. Think of it this way: having developed bounce-back muscles won't make your life *perfect*, but those muscles will assist you to *perfectly* manage the life you have.

Once you develop your bounce-back muscles, you're

naturally stronger inside and can share more of yourself with others. You feel capable and ready to cope with whatever life throws your way. Instead of stumbling under the weight of problems, you can dance with them, using your determination, your faith, and your creativity to discover new solutions. I call this finding your rhythm.

For me, finding my rhythm has meant that I am more and more willing to be exactly who I am in every situation. In my work as a motivational speaker, I often share experiences from my own life. As I've developed my bounce-back muscles, I've been able to reveal the deeper truths of my childhood, teen years, and beyond, inspiring others to do the same.

In 2004, my stories found a wider audience when I became the coauthor of *Chicken Soup for the African American Soul*. At the start of that project, I also had to lean heavily on my Faith-in-Myself Muscle to go beyond the self-imposed limitations I had about becoming a writer. For most of my life, writing had been a struggle and an activity I intentionally avoided. By the time I graduated high school, I was convinced that I'd never be able to write much of anything and compensated by concentrating on my speaking skills. But as I began working on the *Chicken Soup* project, I saw that punctuation, grammar rules, and tense agreement were just one part of the writing process. I found myself eager to communicate my thoughts and emotions through the written word. The book took over two and a half years to complete, but somewhere along the way, it transformed into a labor of love and a journey of self-discovery. Then, when I saw that my stories affected adults as well as teens, it was one more enormous step toward celebrating my essence.

Being a *Chicken Soup* coauthor had another, more unexpected, effect on me as well. Once the book was published, it was my job to help promote it. I was scheduled for radio and television interviews and a series of book signings and keynote speeches from coast to coast. I welcomed the opportunity to talk to people all over the country about how to go for their dreams and turn their obstacles into opportunities—and to hear the inspiring and moving stories of their lives, too.

Packing my bags in preparation for going on my book tour, I pulled out all the "machinery" I used to keep my hair styled— hot comb, flatiron, and curlers—plus all the gels and holding spray, and spread it on the bathroom counter. I said to myself, *Do I really want to work this hard to show up for people?* It was a pivotal moment for me. I decided to cut off the treated sections of my hair and let it go natural. Dumping all of my gadgets and goop in a box, I gave it to a friend who I knew would use it. As I entered the most public time of my life, I was finally ready to show the world the "real me."

Or was I?

One day, scheduled to speak at a morning church service in Chicago in front of over five thousand people, I took a red-eye flight that got in about an hour before my appearance. The drive to the church would take about thirty minutes, leaving me just enough time to dress and freshen up before I had to walk out on the stage.

I fly a lot, but I'd never boarded a plane looking like such a bum. I wore faded sweatpants and a workout T-shirt that I had purposely torn three inches down the front so it wouldn't choke me. I wasn't glamorous, but I was comfortable. I needed to be, since the sleep on this flight was all the rest I was going to get before my big presentation and book signing the next day.

As I took my seat, advice given to me long ago popped into my head: always take a spare pair of black pants, black flats, and a blouse onboard a plane, just in case your bags get lost. Why was I thinking about that? I'd been on forty-seven flights during the previous ten months with no problem, so I hadn't brought anything else to wear in my carry-on luggage. *Well,* I told myself, *too late now. I'm sure it will all be okay—it always is.*

I woke five hours later to hear the flight attendant announce, "Please fasten your seat belts for our landing in Chicago, where the local time is 8:54 a.m."

Feeling surprisingly refreshed, I made my way to the baggage claim area. But as the minutes ticked by, I felt my anxiety begin to rise.

9:12 a.m. *Where are my bags?! There are only two people left looking for their luggage, and I'm one of them.*

9:15 a.m. *Now there's only one person looking for luggage: me!*

9:20 a.m. My heart was beating rapidly as I approached the counter in the baggage office. "My bags didn't come out. Can someone please check on them for me?" I could hear the urgency in my own voice as my cell phone began ringing.

"Good morning, Miss Nichols, this is your driver. I'm outside waiting. We have to get going to arrive for the service on time."

I explained that my luggage had not shown up yet. For a moment, there was silence on the other end of the line. Then she spoke in a very calm and reassuring tone, "It will be fine; let me ring the church, and I'll call you back."

I hung up the phone and turned back to the man behind the baggage counter. My stomach sank as I heard those dreaded words: "I'm sorry, ma'am, but your luggage didn't arrive on this flight."

In a frantic voice I replied, "You don't understand. In forty minutes, I'm supposed to be speaking in front of thousands of people. I can't go out there looking like this. *Pleeeease* check again," I begged.

My head was swimming. Anyone who knew me could tell you that fashion and my unique style of dressing were very important to me. I looked down at myself again, trying to see how creative I could be with my outfit. Torn T-shirt, faded sweats, and a pair of well-used tennis shoes—it was no use; even Michelangelo needed *something* to work with.

My phone rang. "Hello, it's your driver again."

I had an idea. "Let's find a store, and I'll pick something up quickly," I told her. But the driver immediately doused this one flicker of hope. She said that it would be impossible to find a clothing store open at 9:30 on a Sunday morning, and besides there just wasn't enough time. The church leaders wanted me to arrive as close to 10:00 as possible. She continued, "Since it's Youth Sunday, the church has requested that you speak in whatever clothes you've arrived in."

Clearly, they had not seen my attire. Feeling sick, I climbed into the limousine parked at the curb. I was really going to have to walk out on the stage in front of thousands of people looking like I'd just stumbled out of bed.

I sat in the back of the limo, unable to control the panic I felt. As we drove, I began wondering why I was *so* freaked out. Of course, it wasn't a good situation, but there was something deeper going on. I closed my eyes and asked for the true source of my concerns and fears to be revealed to me. As I stilled myself, the answer came crashing down on me like a boulder in an avalanche. I had always made a concerted effort to look polished and impeccable. Now I realized that my clothes, my jewelry—my style—had become more than optional; they had become my identity and my protection. In just a few minutes, I was going to appear in front of thousands of people without that polished shield. I felt more vulnerable than I had ever felt before.

Then, in that moment of stillness, I heard a voice inside my heart. *It's time for you to get comfortable with who you are. Your luggage not arriving was no accident. You need to know that you are just fine—even in sweatpants. Wear you today—after all, that's who you should be sharing with the world anyway.*

I was crying freely, feeling a mixture of thankfulness, conviction, surrender and, yes, still some fear. I'd hidden my face behind a folder so the driver wouldn't be alarmed. Now she spoke. "We're here. I'm going to let you out in the front of the church."

As I walked up the steps to the front door, still shaky but more peaceful than I could have believed possible, it swung open, and I saw three women standing silently, each holding something in her hands. As I neared, I could see that one was holding a dress, another a pair of shoes, and the final one a beautiful beaded shawl.

The first woman said, "I'm not sure if this will fit, but it's a dress of mine that's been hanging here for quite some time in case of an emergency." I glanced at her, noticing that she was at least six inches taller and three dress sizes smaller than I was. I forced a polite smile.

I looked at the nice lady carrying the shoes. "I keep these under my desk, in case my feet hurt." Her feet looked to be about a size seven—a lot smaller than my size nines. Again, I smiled politely. They led me to the bathroom to try on their contributions. Out of respect, I thought I should at least try the clothes on, though I was fully ready to mount the stage in sweatpants and a T-shirt if that was God's plan.

To my surprise, it was as if the elegant, cream-colored dress had been tailored just for me. Hesitantly, I tried the shoes, which somehow fit my feet better than Cinderella's glass slipper had fit hers. I shook my head in wonder. *How is this happening?* The final miracle was the beaded shawl, which had been on display in the church bookstore the day before and now completed my outfit perfectly.

I walked onstage, the tears streaming down my face just as the choir sang the last line of a hymn: "God will move mountains for you." Feeling more beautiful than I would have felt in any clothing I could've packed in my bags, I turned to the sea of faces in the audience. Smiling, I said, "God moved some mountains today so that you could meet the real me."

In my heart, I knew that His greater intent was for *me* to

meet the real me and to finally accept my own distinctive rhythm.

When you go back to your core and begin to celebrate yourself and the journey that has brought you to this point, you begin to dance, sing, speak, walk, and talk with a rhythm that is uniquely yours. You begin to experience your own special brand of joy and live a life overflowing with possibility.

Stepping Into Your Greatness

When you're no longer afraid of hurt or failure and have stopped breathing life into your insecurities, then greatness can appear. Your life becomes a series of individual great moments. When you find your rhythm, it becomes contagious and allows others to find their rhythm. Your liberation begins to liberate others. Your life begins to speak louder than you could ever scream or holler. You become such a presence that when you step into a room, your essence, your energy, your being begin to permeate the air around you. People understand who you are without you ever having to explain yourself. They want to be around you, they want to work with you and help you to accomplish your goals. You radiate a greatness that comes back to you a thousandfold. You become the magnet I talked about in the last chapter, drawing to you all that's great.

But remember, this greatness isn't like a light switch that comes on and then stays on forever. You're constantly in choice. And there are going to be times when you have to focus intently in order to make the highest choice. Every day, every minute, you have the opportunity to choose to be powerful, to choose the good, to choose humility, fearlessness, courage, and greatness. It's up to you. And if ever you make the choice to be the smaller you, just know that you always have another opportunity to choose again.

A Life of No Regrets: You Hold the Pen

Based on this new understanding of becoming resilient, I suggest you look at your life differently. Starting today, see how the events in your life, both good and bad, strengthen your character.

Though you can't change the past, you can change *how you look* at the past. Everything that's happened to you either built a bounce-back muscle at the time or can develop a bounce-back muscle now—by applying that muscle to heal the pain you've been carrying around.

Looking ahead in your life, know that events will either show how strong your bounce-back muscles are or make you aware of the specific areas that need improvement.

This is the secret at the heart of living the Law of No Matter What: **No matter what happened in the past, no matter what happens in the present or the future, I can use it for my good!**

You *can* have a life with no regrets. It's possible, and it starts now. The moment you close this book, make a list of every person in your life who's important to you. Then go down that list and tell each one of them, "I love you, I appreciate you, I care for you, I forgive you, I acknowledge you, I owe you an apology"—do whatever's necessary to nurture that relationship or bring it to a place of peace in your heart.

I know I don't want to have one regret—no coulda-woulda-shouldas—when I'm done. On my deathbed, I want to say, "Yes! I did everything I wanted to do—and more." I'm not just talking about things like traveling the world and being successful. I want to have a lifetime in which I celebrated my boy, I appreciated my parents, I spent time with my family, and I treasured my friends.

Just the other morning I took a walk with my grandmother, who told me about her aunt who owned a café back in Arkansas. She shared stories about visiting her aunt when she was a little girl and how the red-hot chili was her favorite dish at that café. I asked my grandmother questions and learned more about what had shaped her life—which in turn had shaped my mother's life and my own. I cherished my grandmother that morning—and I made sure she knew it.

At the end of my life, I want to be able to say I took a risk and I let myself love again. That despite my fears, I answered the call to give more of myself to the world. That I made time to reach out to God. That even though I had breakdown after breakdown, I still gave myself permission to get back up again and again and again.

I believe that a life of happiness, prosperity, and peace is the life we all want to have, and I believe we each have the right to create that life. The story told about you can be the one that you want told. You can write your own obituary now. That's not a morbid thought; that's a powerful thought. You can determine the way you're going to be remembered by the way you choose to live. It's simply a matter of building the muscles of your character each and every day.

———————

The past chapters of your journey are already written—in ink. Don't waste time trying to erase them or avoid them, or feeling blame and shame about them. Allow them just to be. Remember, your past does *not* equal your future.

I leave you with this charge: **The next chapters of your life are blank pages, and only you hold the pen to write your story. Write it with all of the joy, the strength, the forgiveness, the success, and the peace that you want to live. For you—and only you—are the author of your life.**

NO MATTER WHAT RESOURCES

You've started on a wonderful and fulfilling journey with a deeper understanding and a clear set of action steps that will allow you to overcome your obstacles, find peace of mind and joy, and make all of your dreams come true, *no matter what*. To continue and even add momentum to your progress, I've developed the following services and programs. They create a system for growth, offering you both accountability and support along the way.

No Matter What Seminar

Are you ready for a breakthrough in your finances? Health? Relationships? Would you like to go beyond the limits that have always stopped you before and move into a place of endless abundance and boundless opportunities? I have created a two-day seminar that brings to life the best parts of the book, and in addition includes some of my favorite self-development tools and lessons. After these two days, you'll be able to step into your calling, your greatness, and your passion. You'll push past any fear-storm that has you saying no—or timidly whispering yes—so you can boldly and enthusiastically do the things *you* want to do!

No Matter What Teleseminar Coaching Program

Listen to my teleseminars to hear inspiring and informative talks to be a part of a powerful team of people, to apply No Matter What content and lessons on a weekly basis, and to have your progress tracked. I will personally coach you over the phone in the comfort of your home. You will learn how to:

- effectively handle negative self-talk, fear, and doubts—and prosper as a result
- identify and eliminate limiting belief systems to reach and exceed all of your goals
- manage, command, and direct the four key energies that will allow you to create anything

Avoid the travel costs of attending a weekly seminar in person, and allow me to assist you in stepping into the next level of your life.

No Matter What Home Study Course

This comprehensive program, comprised of CDs, workbooks, affirmation cards, transformative lessons, and authentic conversations with some of the masters in the field of human potential will give you practical steps to fully own your authentic power and to create dynamic and fulfilling relationships with your spouse, your children, and other important people in your life . . . including yourself! Through this program, you will begin to communicate with conviction, move and inspire others, lift yourself up when you're down, and increase your sense of well-being.

No Matter What Inspirational Newsletter

Enjoy reading words of encouragement that also serve as powerful reminders and effective anchors of No Matter What attitudes and actions. As you continue moving toward your goals, take pleasure in the testimonials of others within the No Matter What community—people who have had significant wins and have chosen to share their victories to inspire the rest of us. Maybe you'll be moved to share your story of resiliency and faith and inspire others as well.

No Matter What! Paraliminal Audio Session

Based on the breakthrough technologies of Neuro-Linguistic Programming and whole-brain learning, paraliminal audio sessions help you increase your personal power by activating your whole mind with a precise blend of music and words. I cocreated the *No Matter What!* paraliminal audio session with my friend Paul R. Scheele, cofounder of Learning Strategies Corporation, the world leader in this technology. Just put on the stereo headphones, sit back, and listen, and within minutes, you'll begin establishing new attitudes and behaviors at a deep level that will help you achieve your goals in life—*no matter what.*

No Matter What Community and Dialogue Groups

Join online chats with a group of like-minded, upwardly directed individuals who are working toward a common goal of greater success and happiness. Develop accountability buddies who will set and track goals with you. Post your wins, and enjoy being celebrated by the entire No Matter What community.

No Matter What Keynote Presentations

What are your company or personal goals? Perhaps you'd like to increase and up-level your customer service, sales, and company morale. Maybe you want to create healthier, more fulfilling relationships, stabilize your finances and live abundantly, build supreme self-esteem, enjoy optimum health and well-being, or find your passion in life. If you're ready to "break through" and actually attain those goals, I would love to serve your company, organization, or church group with a presentation customized for your specific audience.

For more information on these and other programs, please visit my Web site:

www.Lisa-Nichols.com

ACKNOWLEDGMENTS

I've shared the thrilling journey of getting this book written, published, and into your hands with one of the most dedicated and talented teams I've ever had the pleasure of being a part of. I extend my heartfelt gratitude to the following:

Carol Kline, my writing partner. You are truly a gifted writer who has the ability to step into the story and bring it to life at a whole new level of excellence and brilliance. Your talent and expertise have been invaluable. Thank you for your dedication and commitment to assisting me in producing the best book possible. I believe we did it!

Kristin Loberg. Thank you for being so generous with your limited time and extraordinary writing talent to bring this project to completion. I appreciate the grace, ease, and genuine care that you brought to the development process. You are a gem.

Bonnie Solow, my literary agent. I feel so honored and thankful to have been blessed with such a successful yet caring agent. You had a vision of this book before the first word was ever placed on the page. You've been my advocate, my guiding light of love, and best of all, my friend. Thank you for encouraging me to share my story in my own voice, filled with the "Lisa-isms" that celebrate my unique journey.

To the entire Grand Central Publishing team: Jamie Raab, publisher; Les Pockell, associate publisher; Elizabeth Connor and Anne Twomey in cover art; Kallie Shimek in managing editorial. Special thanks to Diana Baroni, my editor. You've been a pleasure to work with and a joy to learn from. Thank you for helping to make this book as content-strong as it is entertaining. Matthew Ballast and Linda Duggins in publicity. Thank you for playing full out with me and supporting my wide-ranging ideas to reach as many people as possible with this book. I am grateful to all of you for your instant enthusiasm and excitement about this project. I felt it in our first meeting, and it was clear to me that I wanted to play with your team—*no matter what!* And finally, the sales, marketing, and ad/promo groups. Thank you for your expertise and your commitment to this book. I appreciate each and every one of you.

My Motivating the Masses and Motivating the Teen Spirit family-team: Margaret Cox, Lucretia Danner, Paula Graff, Tonya Hedrick, Ahmondra McClendon, James Nichols, Tia Ross, and Denise Thackston. Thank you for your untiring dedication to delivering world-class service and for holding the space for me to have the time to create and deliver this project. I appreciate you intercepting the calls, handling the requests on my behalf, brainstorming with me, transcribing the stories, lovingly nudging me to keep writing, and endlessly praying for me. And for providing the hot tea, candles, smooth jazz, and the shoulders to cry on when the content was emotionally heavy for me. I thank you from the bottom and top of my heart. You are truly the "A-team."

The following people who served as my first business team: Patricia Stevens, Winnie Briney, Selina Heaton, and their families. Thank you for your vision and belief in Motivating the Teen Spirit, before there was any physical evidence that it would be done.

The extended team: Richard Heller, Richard Hofstetter, Marc Geffen, Randy Helfond, Gigi Grose, our newly certified facilitators, and those facilitators in training. I acknowledge and appreciate how each of you has invested your precious resources to truly transform lives. Thank you for your hard work and diligent efforts that have contributed to the success of this project and so many others.

Pete Bissonette at Learning Strategies. You have been the wind beneath my wings and the big brother who watches over my wellness. Thank you for jumping in and playing full out to assist this project to be the best it could possibly be. And to the rest of the amazing Learning Strategies team, for your tireless dedication and commitment to the success of the Lisa Nichols companies. With special thanks to Doreen Johnson, Debra Hughes, and Paul Scheele for your leadership.

The Transformational Leadership Council. How do I say thank you to the community that has been the single most valuable haven I have ever experienced? With you I have been able to grow, learn, share what I know, and spread my wings to soar ever higher. Each of you can take personal pride in the diamonds that are presented in this book because you helped me to uncover them in myself. I love each of you and value your friendship.

Jack Canfield, my friend and my brother. Thank you for being a living example of how the intention to serve people by helping them live their highest good is not only possible but rewarding on all levels. You, my dear friend, make it okay to be on the journey of life both as a teacher and as a student. Thank you, brother.

The Dream Team: Monte Howard, Kelly Carter, and Steve Conte. Just when I thought that the idea of a dream team had gone forever, you three stepped into my life. Your commitment to help me create generational success and prosperity with this project and others warms my heart beyond any words.

The families of the MTS and MTM team. Each of you has continuously supported us by lending your understanding, prayers, and your loved ones to this project and so many others. You are the extended family that makes it all work. Thank you.

My friends at Chicken Soup for the Soul. Thank you for giving me the opportunity to coauthor *Chicken Soup for the African American Soul* and *Chicken Soup for the African American Woman's Soul*. I will forever appreciate that you believed in my ability to produce and represent such an important piece of work. With special thanks to Chicken Soup for the Soul CEO Patty Aubrey for being such a huge cheerleader and a force for possibility, making this book happen. Thank you for insisting that I do it *now*—no matter what.

Health Communications, Inc. Thank you for being my first publisher and helping all of us at Chicken Soup to produce a quality product that changes lives—one story at a time.

Reverend Michael Beckwith. Thank you, my dear friend, for taking time out of your very busy schedule to bless this project on so many levels. I always appreciate when you allow me to share in your sacred place of worship. You continue to help me release the best in me.

CEO Space principals Lynn Hill and Berny Dohrmann. Your commitment to creating a magical yet realistic place for entrepreneurs to meet and share their dreams, and then create clear, concrete plans to achieve them has been invaluable to me. You were the beginning of this awesome and breathtaking journey.

Bill Harris, Alex Mandossian, Barry Spilchuck, Fluke Fluker, and Marci Shimoff. I thank each of you for graciously sharing your time, knowledge, and friendship with me. Your generosity has added value to the content of this book and, beyond that, to my life.

Telepictures. Thank you for recognizing the broad reach of a project that is designed to touch the heart, push a few buttons, and produce change in those who are ready—and even in some who aren't.

The following people who read the manuscript and provided valuable feedback: Tonya Hedrick, Pearlie Daniels, Joe Mathis, Angela Knoll, Monte Howard, Shelau Howard, Adrian Lee, Tia Ross, Reese Ross, Ahmondra McClendon, Anne Jaffe, Tayari Howard, and Katrina Hunt. Thank you for taking time out of your busy schedules to provide your valuable comments. I appreciate each of you.

The participants in the No Matter What community who gathered every week to hear me read the chapters and who offered priceless feedback and comments to help fine-tune this book. Each and every one of you has brought a special element to the community that exists only because you are there. Thank you for the heartfelt moments, the great "shares," and the constant encouragement. You have each touched my heart in a very special way.

All of the participants in my teleseminars, workshops, and training courses. You have shared with me your resiliency, your commitment to succeed, your ability to rise from the ashes, and your dedication to transform this world into one incredible place. You are the fiber that holds the dreams together and the thread that weaves through life, creating a beautiful tapestry of possibility. Your lives are a demonstration for anyone and everyone to create the vision and then live it!

My family. You have been my village of consistent, unconditional love and support, *no matter what*. Thank you for all of your help creating this book. I am grateful that God loved me so much that He placed me in this family. My beautiful king child Jelani, for your friendship and perfect and constant understanding. You inspire me on so many levels. Agnes, my mother, for your tireless stand for me and for being the best grandma Jelani and I could have prayed for. My father, Jimmy, for being my sacred space and the first example of how I should be treated by a man. Jimmy, my brother, for modeling what it means to be the clay and allow God to shape you. My sister, Leslie, for always being my breath of fresh air. My grandmother Blanche for sharing your wisdom and zest. You are nourishment for my soul. My grandmother Haggerty, I am proud to be your granddaughter; thank you for loving me as much as I love you. To the extended Nichols family, you are my foundation of unwavering love. Thank you for reminding me that even with my enormous work in the world I am still responsible for bringing the peach cobbler to family functions.

Dr. D. Levi Harrison. Thank you for being right beside me as I revealed the most intimate parts of my soul in this book and for reminding me that it was necessary to be authentic. And for making me laugh until I cried in order to keep me going. You are joy and love manifested as a man, and I am so grateful for the power of your vision board and its role in bringing us together.

My girls: Denise Thackston, Dejinira Lee, BJ Foster, Alicia Atkins, Margaret Cox, Sherita Herring, Eraina Hysaw, Pamela Loving, Susie Fields, Anne Jaffe, Monica Brown, Sharon "Gayla" McGee, Inga Canfield, Eve Hogan, and Pam Nelson. You have opened up your hearts and poured into me until my tank is overflowing, enabling me to continue serving others from my overflow. You demonstrate how to be strong and powerful women through your humility, grace, and service. You are the angels who have been appointed to my life to bless me with your love. I am so grateful that you accepted the assignment.

And finally, thank you to *all* of the strong women of the world who have been my role models. You've worked hard, rested rarely, loved unconditionally, got up early, and stayed up late. You've shown me how to love when it hurts, forgive repeatedly, and always keep the faith. You have been my examples of strength and perseverance. I've watched you walk to the bus stop or train station with unyielding confidence, facilitate a business meeting with poise and grace, and cook, clean, and entertain with tender care and love. I've noticed the way you move through life lifting up those around you and bringing forth the best in everyone within your community. I've watched you, and you have taught me what it means to be a woman. Thank you for those unforgettable lessons and blessings.

ABOUT THE AUTHOR

LISA NICHOLS is a celebrated motivational speaker, coach, and teacher who has reached millions of people with her inspiring message of empowerment, service, excellence, and gratitude. She is also the coauthor of two books in the bestselling Chicken Soup for the Soul series: *Chicken Soup for the African American Soul* and *Chicken Soup for the African American Woman's Soul*.

Her participation in the self-development phenomenon, the film and book *The Secret*, catapulted Lisa into global popularity. Since then, Lisa has appeared on numerous national radio and television programs.

In addition, Lisa is the founder of Motivating the Masses and CEO of Motivating the Teen Spirit, LLC. Her transformational workshops impact the lives of hundreds of thousands of teens and adults.

Lisa has been honored with many awards in recognition of her empowering work, including South Africa's Humanitarian Award, African Focus International's Ambassador of Goodwill Award, the Whole Life and Wellness International's Emotional Literacy Award, and The Legoland Foundation's Heart of Learning Award. In 2001, the mayor of Henderson, Nevada, proclaimed November 20 "Motivating the Teen Spirit Day" to honor Lisa's triumphs in transforming the lives of the city's teens.

Lisa is considered a leading expert on breakthroughs to success, motivating and inspiring leaders worldwide with her proven formulas for elevating personal and professional achievement. Her programs redesign, refresh, and renew the way we think about business and relationships in today's world.

Lisa is a dynamic speaker with an extraordinary story and a tremendous ability to touch people's hearts and souls. An expert life and business coach, she is a master at accomplishing seemingly impossible goals and teaching others to do the same.

To find out more about Lisa's keynote presentations, workshops, books, and personal appearances, you can contact her at:

Motivating the Teen Spirit
14391 Penasquilitos Dr., Suite C139
San Diego, CA 92129
Phone: 858-376-3700
e-mail: Lisa@Lisa-Nichols.com
www.Lisa-Nichols.com